CONTESTED LIVES

CONTESTED LIVES

The Abortion Debate
in an American Community

FAYE D. GINSBURG

UNIVERSITY OF CALIFORNIA PRESS
BERKELEY   LOS ANGELES   LONDON

University of California Press
Berkeley and Los Angeles, California

University of California Press, Ltd.
London, England

© 1989 by
The Regents of the University of California
First Paperback Printing 1990

Library of Congress Cataloging-in-Publication Data

Ginsburg, Faye D.
  Contested lives: the abortion debate in an American
community /
Faye D. Ginsburg.
    p.   cm.
    Bibliography: p.
    Includes index.
    ISBN 0-520-06492-5 (alk. paper). ISBN 0-520-06493-3
(pbk. : alk. paper)
    1. Abortion—United States—Case studies.
2. Abortion services—United States—Case studies.
3. Pro-life movement—United States—Case
studies.   4. Pro-choice movement—United States—
Case studies.   5. Women social reformers—United
States—Case studies.   I. Title.
HQ767.5.U5G56   1989   88-19887
304.6'6'0978413—dc19   CIP

Printed in the United States of America
2   3   4   5   6   7   8   9

for Benson and Pearl Ginsburg

Contents

Part IV: Reconstructing Gender in America

Preface

This work was influenced, fundamentally, by two people whom I had the good fortune to meet at a formative moment in my own life and intellectual development. These women, Joan Kelly and Barbara Myerhoff, each died recently and prematurely of cancer, Kelly in 1982, Myerhoff in 1985. Though both lived barely half a century, they contributed radically new perspectives in their work and teaching to their respective fields of history and anthropology, and the more specific subjects they each addressed, such as the Renaissance (Kelly 1977) or myth and ritual (Myerhoff 1974). The sense of loss is compounded, knowing that we can only imagine the work they might have done had they lived on into old age. Like other students and colleagues of theirs, I find myself writing to them, for them, as a way of acknowledging that their visions endure in the endeavors of those whom they influenced. This book was written with the hope that it might shed some light on the areas of knowledge that these two illuminated in their work and lives.

The impact of these teachers on my own work is apparent in a number of ways. Certainly, their engagement with feminist scholarship encouraged me to choose as my research topic the enduring conflict over abortion as an issue setting women against each other in contemporary America. My interest in generating life stories in the field and using a narrative approach to interpret them was influenced by Barbara Myerhoff's writing and teaching (1978). Similarly, Joan Kelly's work as a feminist historian (1984) motivated me to analyze my data, in part, through a historical approach to female activism in America.

In addition to these rather direct, scholarly legacies, I learned something about the research process itself from these women. The route to knowledge that Joan Kelly and Barbara Myerhoff each taught and traveled required their students to turn and look at themselves while looking out at "others," even and perhaps especially when studying those whose lives represent a challenge, whose places in the world seem a puzzle. In this pedagogy, understanding comes, in part, from struggling with and grasping the relationship that emerges when the self is part of the process of inquiry. The words sound almost superficial as I write them; however, carrying out research with this intent is both challenging and disturbing. For a scientist, this process goes against the conventions of Western science, built on logical positivism and the privileged role of the observer—conventions that have passed into mainstream anthropology. In the past decade, scholars in the field began to question the virtue of maintaining the illusion of a rigid boundary between the observer and the observed. This seems a logical if late development for anthropology because the mainstay of its method—participant-observation—calls for the systematic violation of that boundary. As Vincent Crapanzano notes in his pioneering study, *Tuhami* (1980b), the recognition of other ways of constituting reality is always threatening and may produce an "epistemological vertigo."

The possible transformative effect of the anthropological encounter is expected when the subject is at some cultural or historical remove. However, when the "other" represents some very close opposition within one's own society, as was the case in my work, taking on the "natives' point of view" is problematic in different ways, especially when research is focused on a social and political conflict. Doing the research for this book often seemed schizophrenic: I was, at any given moment, both curious anthropologist and concerned native. Like internal tectonics, the layers of my own thought and unexamined beliefs began to shift and collide and take new shape in relation to the people I was struggling to understand. The guidance of Joan and Barbara through the fieldwork phase of my work helped me to understand how to use those transformations as a way of gaining insight.

As I became part of the lives of the people I studied and experienced the world from the multiple points of view I encountered in the field, my ideas changed and deepened. My purpose is to offer a perspective that acknowledges the agency, motivation, and intentionality of all those with whom I worked. This perspective is central to this work. With it, I have been able to use anthropology in a way that shows how abortion activists are engaged in a process of reshaping the very conditions that, in some sense, shaped them.

I have made every effort to respect the integrity of both positions in the abortion debate, as I understand them. So, for example, I refer to each group, as would any anthropologist, by the appellation its members prefer. It is not my place or task in this book to take a partisan position. Rather, I hope that readers will suspend for a moment whatever they have always believed to be the "truth" in order to listen to voices other than their own. My intention is to reveal the dynamics of the contemporary dilemma over abortion with appreciation for its complexities, its place in American culture, and the depth of feeling that it arouses for those who have made that cause a central concern in their lives.

Faye Ginsburg
Brooklyn, New York
September 1987

Acknowledgments

It is overwhelming and humbling to summarize the many sources of inspiration and support that sustain long projects such as my own. If I have neglected unwittingly to mention some key person, I offer my apologies in advance.

First, I am grateful to the many people I worked with in Fargo, North Dakota. Their generosity can never be repaid. For all their insight, intelligence, warmth, and good faith I particularly want to thank (listed alphabetically): Dotty Bofferding, Jane Bovard, Betty Coleman, Aloha Eagles, Karen Eisenhardt, Pam Evenson, Curt Frankhauser, Susan Hill, Maura Jones, Ken Kaehler, Bonnie Kern, Cathy Kram, Alice Olsen, Pat Mastel, Sylvia Morgan, David and Judith Perry (deceased), Cindy Phillips, Marilyn Proulx, Susan Richard, Virginia Scheel, Vicky Savageau, Marilyn Sether, Carol Stoudt, Father Wendell Vetter, and Lyn Wilson. I hope they find this book an accurate depiction of their lives and recent history.

Susan Harding and Rayna Rapp have each been invaluable colleagues, providing much-needed encouragement; their work offered me models of the possibilities of politically engaged research. Thanks are due as well to anthropologists Vincent Crapanzano and Jane Schneider who served as my main thesis advisers. Each has been an inspiration through their own research and as teachers who had faith in my abilities from early on. Riv-Ellen Prell, Barbara Kirshenblatt-Gimblett, Pat Sacks, Lyn Tiefenbacher, and Carole Vance have been sources of rich intellectual and emotional support. I am grateful to Jane Atkinson for her thoughtful comments on the first and second drafts, and for suggesting the title of the book; and to my editor, Naomi Schneider, for her enthusiasm.

I also want to thank Greg Pratt, Jan Olsen, and Ben McCoy with whom I carried out the first phase of this project in 1981–82, a documentary, "Prairie Storm," produced for WCCO-TV, Minneapolis, under Executive Producer Mike Sullivan. It was a great pleasure to work with these talented people, and I owe many initial insights to long discussions we had while producing and editing that show.

This work would not have been possible without the financial support I received for my research. For these awards, I am grateful to The Charlotte Newcombe Dissertation Fellowship in Ethics and Values, 1982–83; The American Association of University Women Dissertation Fellowship, 1983–84; Sigma Xi Research Award, 1983; and David Spitz Dissertation Award in the Social Sciences, CUNY, 1983–84.

A much-condensed version of chapters 8–10 appeared as an article entitled "Procreation Stories: Reproduction, Nurturance, and Procreation in Life Narratives of Abortion Activists," published November 1987 in *American Ethnologist* 14, no. 4: 623–36 (copyright 1987, American Anthropological Association). A preliminary version of chapter 7 appeared as an article entitled "The Body Politic: The Defense of Sexual Restriction by Anti-Abortion Activists," in *Pleasure and Danger: Exploring Female Sexuality*, edited by Carole Vance, pp. 173–88 (copyright 1984, Routledge & Kegan Paul).

I owe an immeasurable debt to my parents, Benson and Pearl Ginsburg, who seemed always to take pleasure in my rather unconventional intellectual curiosity; and Debby, Nathan, and Sonya Szajnberg for their much appreciated emotional support. I am grateful to Ted Mooney for his companionship and faith in my creative abilities during the early phases of this work. And finally, I thank Fred Myers for his love, enthusiasm, insight, patience, editorial help, and delicious dinners, all of which helped steer me through the final passage of this voyage.

Chapter One

Introduction

Fargo, North Dakota, is a small metropolitan center and crossroads providing commercial and service industries for the surrounding rural area. Its residents pride themselves on their clean air, regular church attendance, rich topsoil, and their actual and metaphorical distance from places like New York City. The orderly pace of Fargo's daily life was disrupted in the fall of 1981 when the Fargo Women's Health Organization—the first freestanding facility in the state to offer abortions publicly—opened for business. Immediately, it became the focus of a full-scale controversy, which continues to divide and engage many people in this otherwise quiet prairie city. A local pro-life coalition against the clinic formed and, soon after, a pro-choice group emerged to respond to the antiabortion activities. By the end of 1981, each organization had approximately one thousand members and a hard core of ten to twenty activists. Since then, both groups have experienced changes in memberships, philosophies, and strategies.

The battle over the opening of the clinic in Fargo typifies the development of the abortion debate in the 1980s. Though arising from a local event, the controversy has come to represent the construction of abortion and its attendant meanings as they have been debated at the national level in America. For the local pro-life proponents, the availability of abortion in their own community represented the intrusion of secularism, narcissism, and materialism, the reshaping of women into "structural men." Pro-choice activists reacted to right-to-life protesters as the forces of narrow-minded intolerance who would deny women access to a choice that they see as fundamental to women's freedom and ability to overcome sexual discrimination.

Despite the protests that are staged outside the abortion clinic, inside approximately twenty abortions are performed every week. For many women in the region, the clinic was a long-awaited blessing: the Fargo Women's Health Organization has greatly increased their access to reasonably priced, safe abortion services.[1] The administrator makes frequent trips to bring information about the clinic to the surrounding area where information on birth control, let alone abortion, is hard to come by. The small towns where she stops are marked from the expanses of prairie by little more than a grid of eight or nine streets, a railroad stop, a grain elevator, a bar, a coffee shop, and five or six churches. Pamphlets about the clinic sit on shelves in medical waiting rooms next to boxes of Girl Scout cookies and calendars from the local tractor sales outlet. Over half the clinic's patients come from places like this in North Dakota, nearby states, and Canada (Henshaw 1987: table 4). According to the clinic administrator, the average patient is a young, unmarried woman with relatively little sexual experience. In her words,

Pretty typically, our patients come from small towns. They didn't want to plan to have sex. They thought that was bad so they failed to take preventive measures. So they end up getting pregnant because they didn't want to be classified as having premeditated sex. The majority are happy and healthy. If anything is guilt and trauma inducing, it's these people picketing in front of our clinic.

For the individual woman seeking to terminate an unwanted pregnancy, confronting a bomb scare or a phalanx of pickets, or even journeying outside familiar health care settings can serve as condensed reminders of the social stigma still attached to her decision to abort. Despite its legality and frequency, abortion continues to exist in a gray area on the borders of acceptable social and medical terrain (Forrest and Henshaw 1987). The pro-life protests around clinics in Fargo and elsewhere are intended to create conditions for the contemporary experience of abortion that draw attention to its contested status.

In the years since the 1973 *Roe* v. *Wade* decision legalizing abortion, over one thousand freestanding clinics providing first trimester abortions have been established throughout America. In 1985, although they were only 15 percent of all providers, over 83 percent of abortions were performed in such clinics.[2] The introduction of these abortion clinics is rarely easy. The conflict generated by the opening of the Fargo clinic shows at close range how the 1973 Supreme Court ruling is being woven, with difficulty, into the social fabric.

The passions generated in such battles over abortion rights indicate that there is more to the conflict than single-issue politics. It provides a symbolic focus for the assertion of mutually exclusive understandings of a broader range of themes at a time when the society and the place of women in it seem in disarray. The power of this controversy to arouse intense commitment on the part of female activists in particular reveals its potent metaphorical connection to critical sources of cultural and social identity, especially in relation to sexuality and reproduction.

The Setting

I went to Fargo to see this critical "backstage" setting for the national abortion drama,[3] to get a sense of the specific shape and impact it has at the local level, and to understand the abortion controversy from "the actor's point of view" in the context of everyday life. Like Muncie, Indiana, described in the classic *Middletown* studies (Lynd and Lynd 1929, 1937), Fargo, with a population of approximately 62,000, is small enough to provide a coherent social universe; yet its proximity to Moorhead, Minnesota (population 30,000), just across the Red River, makes it sufficiently large to encompass some diversity in class, ethnic, and religious identities.

Fargo has been the marketing and financial center for farmers of the region since the 1880s. White-collar labor—managerial, professional, and technical—makes up more than 40 percent of the local work force; more than 22 percent are blue-collar workers; and the remainder work in service occupations. Education and health industries are major employers in the area. Three universities and five technical schools teach about twenty thousand students. Five hospitals and three clinics make Fargo–Moorhead the largest center for medical care between Minneapolis and Seattle, employing over four thousand people. Retail trade, providing another eight thousand jobs, has flourished since 1972 when a sixteen-acre shop-

ping area was built west of the city on what had been wheat fields
and "prairie chicken" land. A new highway has also encouraged the
growth of numerous motels and fast-food restaurants along its route,
the latest advance in Fargo's hundred-year history as a crossroads
for tourists and traveling salespeople in the region. With a labor
force that is nearly half female and with over one-third of its jobs in
relatively low-paying service work, Fargo's economy is changing in
step with the rest of the United States.[4] The recent discovery of oil
in the area, the use of the state as a nuclear missile base, and the
legalization of gambling for charities have all brought new wealth to
Fargo. Yet, for long-time residents, they also engender a nervousness that undesirable and irreversible social change is being imposed on them from without. While many people in Fargo view
themselves as politically conservative, they also value a tradition of
populism and defense of individual rights.

These values cannot be considered apart from the role of religion in the area. The Fargo–Moorhead area has over ninety
churches serving fifty thousand adult members, over one-third of
whom are Lutheran, and just under one-third are Catholic. The
balance belong to non-Lutheran Protestant denominations, with
Fundamentalist and Evangelical congregations growing faster than
any others in the area. The Chamber of Commerce boasts that the
Fargo–Moorhead area has the highest regular church attendance
of any standard metropolitan area. This fact takes on significance in
light of survey research that shows that regular participation in
church is one of the most significant variables associated with opposition to abortion (Blake and Pinal 1980). That correlation was
demonstrated in the defeat of a referendum vote to liberalize abortion laws in the state in 1972 and again, more than a decade later,
in the reaction of Fargo residents to news that abortion services
were going to be offered in their city.

Fieldwork: The Observer Observed

I have been following the conflict over the Fargo abortion clinic
since it opened in 1981, including twelve months of fieldwork (five
in 1982 and seven in 1983), and a return visit in 1986. During 1982,
I was also working as a producer for a television documentary on
the clinic controversy.[5] For that reason, local people viewed me

initially as a journalist, a position that enabled me to establish rapport quickly with both sides, each of which was seeking publicity. When I returned in 1983, I lived with a family with no direct involvement in the abortion conflict and identified myself as an anthropologist. In addition to following the development of the organizations that formed for and against the clinic and participating in community life in general, I also collected life histories with abortion activists in order to see how their activism and personal and historical experiences were intertwined.

I was concerned, initially, that being a young, unmarried, Jewish, and urban visitor from New York City might pose serious barriers to communication with Fargo residents. Most are married, Christian, and from rural or small-town backgrounds. Much to my surprise, the fact that I was in many ways "culturally strange" to Fargo occasionally served to my advantage. Interviews frequently ended with curious questions regarding Jewish holidays, customs, and ceremonies. Had I been a member of a Christian denomination, I would have had to negotiate my way through the numerous inter- and intra-church conflicts in town and my questions about religion and frequent "church hopping" would have been viewed with some suspicion. As a single woman, my queries and interest in people's feelings about marriage, birth control, motherhood, and the like were treated as natural curiosity; responses were often framed as if I were being counseled for my own future conjugal happiness.

Perhaps the most difficult aspect of my role was my identity as a New Yorker. Stereotypes abound of New York; it is often represented as Fargo's opposite: "Well, they might have *that* [prostitution, "adult" bookstores, abortion] in New York but in Fargo?" New Yorkers are considered rude, snobbish, morally questionable, and unappreciative of middle-American values. As my rapport with people increased, their desire to disengage me from my New York identity became apparent in the sighs of relief and mutterings of "I thought so" that I heard every time I mentioned that I actually grew up in the Midwest, albeit Chicago. My genuine enthusiasm for Fargo life helped mitigate my urban East Coast stigma as well. Over time, my sense of people's lives was enriched as I joined them not only in activities in Fargo but on visits to family farms and hometown reunions as well.

While I went to Fargo to study the contemporary debate over abortion, I focused on people who are, by definition, atypical: female social activists involved at the local level in the 1980s. Implicit in their passion for social change is a particular understanding and critique of the culture at large. I viewed local activists as cultural agents mediating between a social situation they inhabit in the present and a desired alternative future, a world they are envisioning and enacting in their abortion activism. My goal was to understand how this grass-roots conflict shaped and was shaped by activists' experiences of self, gender, family, community, and culture in a specific setting. In a situated contest such as the one in Fargo, one can see more generally how abortion comes to signify conflicting social and personal identifications capable of mobilizing and polarizing people. The close focus of anthropological inquiry helped me delineate how larger cultural processes in contemporary American culture that inform the abortion controversy take on shape and meaning for activists in terms of local knowledge and experience.

The Conflict as a Challenge to Essentialist Views of Women

Although the abortion conflict is a clearly contested domain, the features that distinguish the central actors are not always obvious. Pro-choice and pro-life activists do not divide neatly along ethnic, economic, occupational, or even religious lines. At the local level, where activity is strongest, grass-roots activists on both sides of the abortion issue are primarily white, middle-class, and female (Granberg 1981; Luker 1984).[6] These facts are a reminder that women, even with similar class and cultural backgrounds, rarely experience themselves or act as a homogeneous social group with a universal set of interests. Indeed, the controversy can be seen as a contest in which the very definition of female is "up for grabs." To understand the movements, then, and the different understandings of gender they promote, one must listen to the rhetoric activists use to construct their world, the classic anthropological task of grasping "the natives' point of view."

Women for and against abortion divide most clearly in their view of the causes for and solutions to the unequal effects of sexual activity for men and women in America. Pro-choice activists consider inequalities between the sexes to be rooted in social, legal, and cultural forms of gender discrimination, and they seek to remedy that condition by structural change in the economic and political system. From this point of view, safe and legal abortion is seen as an essential safeguard against the differential effects of pregnancy on men and women. It is a basic condition enabling heterosexually active women to have the power to control whether, when, and with whom they will have children.

Pro-life activists, on the other hand, accept difference, but not necessarily hierarchy, in the social and biological roles of men and women. Their reform efforts are directed toward creating and promoting a social and political context that they feel will protect and enhance one essential condition that, in general, distinguishes men from women: pregnancy and motherhood. In their view, social changes that could be interpreted as casting reproduction and childrearing as a liability are antiwoman. Abortion is thus a condensed symbol for the devaluation of motherhood and the central attribute assigned to it in this culture—the self-sacrificing nurturance of dependents. Abortion represents, in addition, a threat to social guarantees that a woman with children will be supported by the child's father. It is seen as undermining an informal cultural code that links sex with reproduction and male support of families.

In this conflict, then, one sees a struggle taking place over the meaning attached to reproduction and its place in American culture. Regardless of differences, both groups, through a variety of social, legal, and political processes, are working to reform American society according to what they understand to be the best interests of women.[7] Thus, the movements organized around abortion provide arenas for innovation; through them cultural understandings of gender, procreation, sexuality, and dependency are being transformed.

The Right-to-Life Movement and American Culture

This book, though it is concerned with activists on *both* sides of the abortion issue, is engaged more often with analyzing the pro-life position because of the prominent role this movement has played

in the political and cultural shifts of the 1980s. I began to explore
the idea for this research on female grass-roots abortion activists in
1980, the year that Ronald Reagan was elected President, an event
that has come to be associated with what is called the rise of the
New Right.[8] My interest was in trying to understand this rightward
swing in the United States from the viewpoint of those engaged in
conservative social movements at the local level. With a few exceptions (Fitzgerald 1981b; Gordon and Hunter 1977–78; Harding
1981), most who wrote on the topic focused on the political organization and leadership of a few well-known groups and leaders—for
example, Phyllis Schlafly and her campaign to stop the Equal Rights
Amendment (ERA), Jerry Falwell and the Moral Majority, and
Richard Viguerie and the National Conservative Political Action
Committee (NCPAC). Few had gone out and talked to the different
people whom these movement leaders claimed as their supporters,
to find out who they are, how they live, and what motivates them.
Since then, several studies that look at grass-roots activists have
come out, such as Connie Paige's *The Right-to-Lifers* (1983), Kris-
tin Luker's *Abortion and the Politics of Motherhood* (1984a), and
Rebecca Klatch's *Women of the New Right* (1987).

In the 1980s, pro-life activity has been most engaged and effective at the local level and for that reason is particularly appropriate for anthropological research. Right-to-life groups draw their
strength from local social life. Their activity is embedded in the
kind of ongoing face-to-face interaction that is the stock and trade of
the anthropological enterprise, unlike the direct mass-mail organizing of some of the New Right groups such as NCPAC.

The mainstream right-to-life movement has, to some extent, resisted efforts of New Right leaders to claim the abortion issue as
their own both in their rhetoric and by co-opting existing groups.
For the pro-life movement, such alliances are seen as potentially
dangerous to its single-issue organizing style and philosophy. In addition, the political conservatism and laissez-faire capitalism of the
New Right program are often at odds with the mainstream right-to-
life agenda. This movement, like many other single-issue groups,
encompasses a broad range of ideological positions, from radical
pacifism (Pro-Lifers for Survival, an antinuclear group, for example), to liberal Catholics and Protestants, to fundamentalist
Christians. Regardless of differences, most right-to-life activists

not only share the goal of recriminalizing abortion but also see abortion as symptomatic of other social problems. In particular they are concerned that materialism and narcissism are displacing nurturant ties of kin and community. In other words, much of their agenda could be interpreted as a desire to reform the more dehumanizing aspects of contemporary capitalist culture. In this respect, although their solutions differ, the larger concerns of many right-to-life activists resemble, in many ways, those of some of their pro-choice opponents. At the same time, their supposed allies on the New Right who favor a more libertarian conservative philosophy may favor a pro-choice position.[9]

While the pro-life movement is large and diverse, in general, three themes seem to predominate in the metaphorical connections made between abortion and American culture. Broadly outlined, these are:

1. Antagonism to "irresponsible sexual behavior," identified as natural to men and unnatural to women.
2. A concern with the social and cultural devaluation of dependent people. The "unborn child," the elderly, the unwed mother, and the handicapped are central images around which the movement organizes its crusade. They represent the most extreme versions of human dependency in our society—those who because of disability, misfortune, or age cannot function independently or participate in productive activity.
3. A critique of market rationality and instrumentality in human relations, which they see as growing and dangerous trends that must be reversed.

These visions paint a particular portrait of our culture, its central dilemmas, and the remedies that should be instituted. They are tied to two central images of abortion: the destruction of the fetus and the violation of the boundary of the impregnated womb by male figures representing the profit motive. As Bernard Nathanson, the narrator of *The Silent Scream*—a 1984 videotape produced for the right-to-life movement—tells the audience as it watches an abortion take place: "You are seeing the silent scream of a child threatened imminently with its extinction by the presence of an aggressor in its sanctuary."

In right-to-life discourse, these three themes are used to claim

the same ground as other social groups in America, both contemporary and historical. For example, while stereotypes cast right-to-
life advocates as unswervingly hostile to feminism, much of their
rhetoric seeks to engage concerns raised by the women's movement
to justify pro-life arguments.[10] In the book *A Private Choice* by
John Noonan, one of the key philosophers of the movement, abortion is cast as antiwoman, the agenda of upper-class men. Noonan
writes:

When strong and comprehensive anti-abortion statutes were being enacted in nineteenth-century America, the militant feminists had been
outspoken in their scorn and condemnation of abortion. . . . Who wanted
the liberty of abortion in 1970? Only a minority of any section of the population favored it, but the stablest and strongest supporters of the liberty
were white upper-class males. (1979: 48–49)

Noonan goes on to quote from Eugene O'Neill's play, *Abortion,*
written in 1914. In it, the protagonist Jack Townsend, a rich young
college student, impregnates a local town girl for whom he ar-
ranges an abortion, which proves fatal to her and the fetus. Noonan
also provides statistics and legal arguments as evidence for his case
that abortion casts women as the victims of male lust and the uncar-
ing penetration of upper-class privilege into the ranks of the less
fortunate.

Abortion Activism and American
Gender Paradigms

This case poses a counterexample to what some anthropologists
consider to be a general rule of symbolic oppositions between
the sexes[11] in which the assignment of female to nature and "self-
interest" and male to culture and "the social good" is considered to
be the fundamental truth of the symbolic and social organization of
gender worldwide (Ortner and Whitehead 1981: 7). The American
instance I am interpreting subverts this formulation on at least two
counts. First, in the gender model expressed in the rhetoric of
these movements, it is not the natural divisive woman who must be
controlled. Rather the lust of men must be regulated by the "civilizing" influence of women for the benefit of the social good. To
twist a phrase from Lévi-Strauss, it is women in American culture
who are responsible for converting raw masculinity into cooked do-

mesticity, just as they bring into the world the unformed natural matter of infants whom they transform into cultural creatures. As one leader phrased it, in a voice that echoes the cadences of late nineteenth-century feminists,

Who is the New Traditional Woman? She is a mother of the citizens of the twenty-first century. It is she who will more than anyone else transmit civilization and humanity to future generations and by her response to the challenges of life, determine whether America will be a strong, virtuous nation. (Connaught Marshner, quoted in Jepsen 1984: 63–64)

The ideal attributes assigned to gender in a given cultural setting are rooted, at least in part, in what it is that men and women do, or should do in daily life. In their political, economic, and social definitions, American men and women have been set apart as belonging to separate if not mutually hostile spheres of activity, which are, nevertheless, interdependent. Writ small on the human body, the moment of particular risk in the system is expressed in the penetration of the female arena—nurturance, self-sacrifice, child-rearing, and domesticity—by forces identified as oppositional, predatory, and masculine. I am not proposing that one simply rearrange the pieces of a static structuralist gender paradigm. Rather, I am suggesting that in America, gender and sexual practice are continually reinterpreted by female activists through a particular cultural frame: the resistance of women to the imposition of what they see as male cultural forms that corrupt and exploit women if left unchecked.

Female Activists: Historical Precedents and Cultural Patterns

The themes expressed by right-to-life activists in the contemporary abortion controversy—the dangers of male lust, and the protection of the weak against the depredations of self-interest unleashed—are similar to concerns voiced by women activists in America over the past two centuries. They have been most prominent in female-led moral reform movements that have been active periodically since the eighteenth century. These movements emerged with the material and cultural separation of wage and domestic labor that came to be identified as male and female arenas of activity in America. Like activists in the current abortion conflict, prior social re-

formers sought alliances with religious and state authorities so that
law and public policy would conform to and enforce their view of
what would most enhance women's position in this country. (That
their interests may not, in fact, represent the interests of all women
is another matter.)

In this book, I use historical material to provide a broad temporal context for the contemporary controversy over abortion. The
participation of women in past social movements engaged in reformulating the cultural order and the construction of gender in it
demonstrates how these themes are continually reorganized and
given new meaning in relation to socioeconomic change. This
cross-fertilization of historical and anthropological paradigms and
material is particularly helpful on two counts. First, it is a method
for achieving distance in a study of one's own society. Second, a
temporal perspective helps to clarify the historical conditions and
underlying cultural principles through which people struggle to
make sense of problematic experiences in their everyday lives, a
process that results in what Anthony Giddens has called "practical
consciousness" (1979: 24–25).[12] Looking at the abortion controversy as part of "la longue durée" of action on issues pertaining to
women reveals not only how categories of gender and politics are
interwoven, but also how they are "put to empirical risk" in action
(Sahlins 1985) and thus reorganized and reproduced in new form.[13]
However, dependence on the long view can also lead to a determinism in which causality rests in abstract concepts as if they,
rather than people, were the sources of all volition and power in
human action.

Self-Definition through Social Action

Female social reformers, including those in the contemporary abortion battle, are not just acting out cultural constructs or economic
imperatives of which they have no awareness. They are conscious
of the terms of the oppositions that constrain them as they struggle
to transcend constraint, using political activism to challenge in different ways the control of the domestic domain to which they have
been assigned. It is my argument that in so doing, women act continually to adjust the boundaries of those spheres to fit the shape of

new experiences in their lives that seem at odds with the available interpretations of gender.

My focus on activists as agents of transformation reflects recent critiques of theories of action and social movements in which "the characteristics of the actor as a subject remain unexplored or implicit" (Giddens 1979: 55). I have tried in my analysis to attend to the capacity of social actors "to 'explain' why they act as they do" (Giddens 1979: 57). Methodologically, such explanations

only form discrete accounts in the context of queries, whether initiated by others, or as elements of a process of self-examination by the actor. (Giddens 1979: 57)

To understand the "explanations" abortion activists made when consciously connecting their own experience—biographical and historical—to their commitment to the abortion issue, I collected life stories from the activists in Fargo.

My analysis of life stories of these grass-roots abortion activists indicates that the narratives revolve around transitions in the female life cycle that were experienced as stressful and incongruous, generating a "life crisis."[14] Because the narratives were so frequently concerned with transitional reproductive events as well as women's relationship to both biological and social reproduction, I call them "procreation stories." For many of the women I interviewed, a sense of crisis emerged out of the dissonance they felt between the conditions they faced—for example, becoming a mother—and the available cultural resources for structuring that change, cognitively and socially. Specifically, a particular interpretation of abortion becomes part of the explanatory frame through which activists "made sense of" difficult transitions in the female life cycle experienced as discontinuous with the rest of their experience and expectations.

In my view, the shape of these narratives reflects a historical moment when, for a variety of reasons ranging from the increasing labor force participation of women to the new reproductive technologies, there is no clear ideal biography for the female life course. Without a hegemonic ordering for the ever-increasing range of possibilities of a woman's life, the struggles over proposed interpretations are particularly acrimonious.

This is hardly unexpected as increasing numbers of women, especially those with young children, are entering or staying in wage
work, and as what Americans think of as traditional marriage arrangements are increasingly unstable. At least some women reaching adulthood in the midst of such conditions are using their activism on the abortion issue to give orderly if intolerant shape to
such "disorderly" experiences. More generally, what this indicates
is that the relationship of women to procreation and the work of
mothering is the object of tremendous logistical and interpretive
struggle in contemporary America.

Organization of the Book

This book began as an anthropological analysis of a struggle over an
abortion clinic in an American community. While that is my focal
point, I have tried to situate that event in broader contexts. I am
particularly concerned with the temporal dimension of analysis—
for example, in the use of life histories, the following of a social
drama over several years, and the tracing of abortion debates and
moral reform movements over the past two centuries.

The current debate is only the most recent expression of the long
history of changes in the meaning and practice of abortion in America. Chapters 2 and 3 sketch this context, beginning with the first
public controversy over abortion that occurred in the nineteenth
century when abortion served as an issue that consolidated a movement to enhance the status and control of the medical profession in
this country. The result was the enactment of wide-ranging legislation that made abortion virtually illegal throughout the United
States by the end of the nineteenth century, even though the practice of abortion had widespread popular acceptance through the
1860s. The efforts by physicians to criminalize its practice required
that they succeed in reinterpreting its meaning. Through the efforts of the physicians' crusade, abortion and pregnancy became
subject to medical and legal intervention, what Michel Foucault
would call a new sexual discourse in which

the mechanisms of power are addressed to the body, to life, to what
causes it to proliferate, to what reinforces the species, its stamina, its ability to dominate, or its capacity for being used. Through the themes of
health, progeny, race, the future of the species, and the vitality of the so-

cial body, power spoke *of* sexuality and *to* sexuality; the latter was not a mark or a symbol, it was an object and a target . . . an *effect with a meaning value.* (1978: 147–48)

The transformations of "meaning value" in the practice and interpretations of abortion in the twentieth century occurred not only through the efforts of "experts" and state intervention but also via popular agitation. As more and more American women resorted to illegal abortions, particular events and practices—from the early underground abortion referral networks to the thalidomide and rubella scares of the 1960s—helped to catalyze broadly based movements that demanded reform and then repeal of antiabortion laws. The 1973 Supreme Court decision, *Roe* v. *Wade*, was both a product of these and other changes and a catalyst to subsequent developments that Americans have come to identify as the current controversy, particularly the rise of the right-to-life movement.

The tenacity of the conflict over abortion after its legalization indicates how the issue has come to stand for much larger cultural concerns. The activism of the past decade, which has engaged female activists in particular, has taken the shape of an intense, almost populist struggle for contending interpretations of gender, sexuality, and reproduction. Increasingly, the battles are played out over the delivery of abortion services in communities.

In chapters 4 through 7, I describe and analyze the conflict over abortion in Fargo, North Dakota, beginning with its development at the state level. A 1972 statewide referendum on abortion, for example, shows how the social drama over the abortion clinic that occurred a decade later—its themes, players, and performance styles—was first "rehearsed." After the 1973 *Roe* v. *Wade* ruling, as pro-life activism in particular spread to a broad grass-roots base, the signification of abortion as a social issue became generalized and polarized. Although I did not select Fargo for its "typicality," the controversy over the opening of the first abortion clinic in North Dakota is representative of the shape of the conflict in the 1980s.[15] While the social field of the controversy expanded, becoming both more broadly based and ideologically elaborated, the arena of action has been increasingly at the local level.[16] (In 1987, when Chief Justice Warren Burger and Justice Lewis Powell announced their retirements from the Supreme Court, the appointment of their replacements became an additional focus.)[17]

Chapters 5 and 6 describe and analyze the community-based drama and the actors. Both pro-life and pro-choice activists asked for support by presenting themselves as under attack, yet simultaneously claimed to represent the "true" interests of the community. When pro-life forces failed to close the Fargo clinic through local political and legal processes, they changed their strategy. Increasingly, the contest has focused on the women with unplanned pregnancies who are the clinic's actual or potential clientele. In the efforts right-to-life activists make to persuade these women, one can see the metaphors and dramatic themes that give shape, meaning, and visibility to opposing understandings of abortion and its attendant meanings in the local body politic. As chapter 6 demonstrates, this shift has had an impact on players beyond those directly involved in the conflict. In addition to abortion activists, social workers, state agencies, churches, and voluntary groups have become involved in what I am calling a "problem pregnancy industry," as each develops institutional responses to unplanned pregnancy.[18]

Chapter 7 shows how, in a setting like Fargo, where actors are known to each other, moderation is rewarded over radical action. Local norms are respected by actors on both sides and set limits to their behavior. More radical "direct action" right-to-life activists have never really been accepted in Fargo, although their nearly violent behavior is highly visible. This contrast became particularly apparent with the visit of a network television team to Fargo. The show they produced, and community response to it, illustrates the way the conflict is systematically distorted in the national media and the impact such interventions can have on the course of local events.

The knowledge each side has of the other is a prominent feature in the life stories I collected with activists. In them, a particular understanding of both self and other is enacted through abortion activism; this process is the focus of chapters 8, 9, and 10. Chapter 8 lays out the theoretical bases for interpreting activists' narratives. In chapters 9 and 10 I focus on individual narratives to show how abortion provides activists on each side with culture-reconstructing agendas that mesh with their historical and biographical—and especially reproductive—experiences. In both their referential and formal dimensions, activists' stories resemble conversion testimonies, bearing witness to a kind of rebirth. These take a loose generational shape.

Pro-choice stories, analyzed in chapter 9, indicate that the social protests of the 1960s, including the second wave of feminism, were a central experience for almost all of the activists. Most describe their encounter with these movements as an awakening or passage from a world defined by motherhood into one filled with broader possibilities. Right-to-life women (chapter 10) cluster in two cohorts. Those born in the 1920s were most active in pro-life work in the early 1970s. A second cohort, the one currently most active, was born in the 1950s. Many women in this latter group share some feminist sentiments with pro-choice women (e.g., on issues not directly related to sexuality such as comparable worth). Their commitment to the right-to-life movement is described as a kind of conversion, usually tied, in the narrative, to the birth of a child. For younger women in this group, this event often coincides with moving out of the paid work force to stay home and raise children. In their procreation stories, women of each group struggle to come to terms with problematic historical and life-cycle transitions, while simultaneously articulating a particular view of American culture and the place of men and women in it.

In chapter 11, I present evidence to support my argument that the visions and actions of contemporary abortion activists are the most recent expression of enduring cultural themes regarding gender in America, most clearly expressed in female moral reform movements that have been active periodically over the past two centuries. The central gender structure of home and workplace as separate male and female spheres that developed with industrial capitalism in America has endured, even as its expression in the social system has been reformulated self-consciously by female social activists.

Abortion Activism in America and the Issue of Nurturance

Abortion activists in Fargo, like other moral reformers who preceded them in American history, view themselves as directing the transformation of the culture to the betterment of both themselves and the whole society. In this sense, each side offers an embedded cultural critique of the contradictions of a cultural opposition between work and home for women in American culture. Both sides argue against what they see as the sexist elements of the system. The pro-choice activists criticize those structures that confine women to nurturance in the domestic domain and suggest it be expanded to become a more collective responsibility. Pro-life advocates critique a cultural and social system that assigns nurturance to women yet degrades it as a vocation. They promote agendas in which the material and ideological resources of church and state would be assigned to support the status and activities of the domestic domain where nurturance of dependents currently takes place.

What these formulations indicate is how, in a sense, the separation of workplace from home has served as a metaphor for a cultural code in which ideals of individual autonomy and achievement are separated from the fact of human dependency over the life course. In opposition to the market relations of capitalism, nurturance stands for noncontingent and self-sacrificing support and love in "the home." [19] Thus, in American culture, the general social problem of caring for dependents has been "hidden in the household" [20] and nurturance escapes consideration as a larger cultural concern, as it is in other cultures.

At such moments of reformulation of cultural definitions, models from other societies are instructive. New Guinea and Australia provide notable cases in which nurturance and reproduction are broadly defined, and a high valuation is placed on the role of men as well as women in "growing up" the next generation. Writing on the Trobriand Islanders, Annette Weiner points out:

All societies make commitments to the reproduction of their most valued resources, i.e., resources that encompass human reproduction as well as the regeneration of social, material, and cosmological phenomena. In our Western tradition, however, the cyclical process of the regeneration of elements is not of central concern. Even the value of biological reproduction remains a secondary order of events in terms of power and immortality achieved through male domains. Yet in other societies, reproduction, in its most inclusive form, may be a basic principle through which other major societal structures are linked. (1979: 330)

Such cross-cultural comparisons are reminders that our own arrangements are not written into nature. Similarly, the changes brought about in the abortion struggle demonstrate that reproduction, so frequently reified in American categorizations as a biological domain of activity, is always given meaning and value and subject to change within a historically specific set of cultural conditions.

To understand the contrasting views represented by opposing positions on the abortion issue, I needed to see how they took shape in everyday life in a community where the issue was fresh and activists are known to each other. Such concrete placement is essential to any anthropological research, especially in a complex society where the local translation of larger processes often goes unnoticed. In this study, the Fargo conflict acts as a kind of prism that refracts on a human scale the abstractions of each side of the abortion debate. It is my hope that readers will find, as I did, that the facets of this particular place illuminate a larger landscape: the social and symbolic organization of gender, reproduction, and nurturance in the United States.

Part One

Abortion
and the American
Body Politic

Chapter Two

From the Physicians' Campaign
to *Roe* v. *Wade*

Introduction

The contemporary debate over abortion is part of a long history of changes in both its cultural meaning and social practice in America. Reviewing past efforts for or against its legalization calls attention to the changing semantic load that abortion has carried as it has served as the rallying cause for different social groupings. The following overview of abortion as an issue and a symbol in American life demonstrates the interpretive range it has encompassed over the past two centuries.

According to most scholars of the issue,[1] in the nineteenth century the issue of abortion helped consolidate a movement to enhance the status and control of the medical profession in this country. The efforts by physicians to criminalize the practice of abortion required that they succeed in reinterpreting its public meaning during a period when it had widespread popular acceptance. The result was the enactment of wide-ranging legislation that made abortion virtually illegal throughout the United States by 1900.

The physicians' campaign to control abortion as well as their profession was part of the broader centralizing and rationalizing tendencies that characterized America's transition to a regulatory welfare state, beginning in the late nineteenth century. The increase in asylums, schools, charities, prisons, and other such agencies represented a trend in the name of science and social reform, toward state and professional regulation of the care of dependents

(Zaretsky 1982). Similarly, in classifying abortion as both a criminal offense and a health problem, pregnancy and its consequences were increasingly subject to state and medical intervention.

The antiabortion policies achieved by the nineteenth-century physicians' crusade are instructive for the present case. The results of this campaign set the legal doctrine and have framed thought and action on abortion for the last 150 years; from this context, the current activism has emerged.

The Nineteenth-Century Abortion Crusade

Legalization of abortion in the twentieth century was the reversal of years of legal doctrine in which aborting a pregnancy—with provisional exceptions to protect the health of the mother—constituted a criminal act. However, according to historian James Mohr who authored the pioneering study *Abortion in America,* abortion was a relatively common as well as accepted practice during much of the nineteenth century. Until 1821, when Connecticut enacted the first American statute against abortion, America followed English common law in which the destruction of the fetus *after* quickening could be punished by fine and imprisonment (Mohr 1978: 20–21). In nineteenth-century terms, quickening was the transitional point in pregnancy when the woman could feel fetal movement—usually the fourth or fifth month—after which fetal life was considered to have its own integrity (Mohr 1978: chap. 2; Degler 1980: 237).[2]

By 1841, as part of routine revisions of American legal codes, ten out of twenty-six states had enacted statutes making abortion a crime. From the evidence of court cases and physicians' records, abortion was, or at least was considered, a practice resorted to by women who were pregnant out of wedlock and fearful of the social consequences of an illegitimate child. In the eyes of the law, such women were victims, deserving of compassion and protection. Accordingly, legislation was intended to regulate the practice of those performing abortions (Mohr 1978: 43–45).

The push to criminalize abortion anytime after conception began in the latter half of the nineteenth century as part of a concerted effort by "regular" physicians to gain control of the practice of medicine in the United States (Mohr 1978: 147). By the early 1800s, American physicians were competing with midwives, local healers, homeopaths, and, increasingly, abortionists (Mohr 1978: 32–37). The "regulars," trained at established medical schools in traditions of rational research according to an allopathic medical model, were interested in finding ways to restrict and control this virtually open market. The scholarship on this topic and period considers the physicians' antiabortion campaign as central to accomplishing this goal (Mohr 1978: 157; Luker 1984a: 15–18).

The drive of these physicians to professionalize began officially with the founding of the American Medical Association (AMA) in 1847. Ten years later, Horatio B. Storer, a Harvard-trained doctor specializing in obstetrics and gynecology launched a national drive within the AMA to lobby state legislatures to criminalize all induced abortions. In addition, he wrote and encouraged others to publish professional and popular books to persuade the American public that abortion was both dangerous and immoral (Mohr 1978: 147–59). Between 1860 and 1880, the efforts of the crusade bore fruit in the passage of forty antiabortion statutes. These new laws set a legal frame for regulating abortion that differed significantly from the previous statutes based on common law. In the legislation enacted after the Civil War, induced abortion at any point in pregnancy became a crime. In addition, immunities for women were revoked, and the powers of the state were enlisted through antiobscenity laws to restrict the practice of abortion by imposing fines for advertising abortion-related services and materials (Mohr 1978: chap. 8).

In Mohr's view, by playing on fears of the potential dangers of abortion, the "regulars" hoped to gain the support of the state in controlling their competitors. In articles and editorials and in testimonies before legislative bodies, physicians urged that the informally educated practitioners and other "irregulars" be prohibited from practicing not only abortion but medicine in general. At the same time, the campaign provided a means for the regulars to enforce standards of practice and behavior in their own ranks. Antiabortion crusaders would disclaim and testify even against other physicians willing to perform abortions. The campaign also enabled the regulars, who were generally white, well-educated, upper-class, and native-born men, to enhance their status for and control over their own clientele who came, for the most part, from the same social strata (Mohr 1978: 161–70).

Basing the arguments for fetal life on medical research and theories, physicians positioned themselves as an enlightened elite determined to inform an ignorant public. Through their activism, they attempted to demonstrate a position of both scientific and moral superiority.[3] The links these doctors made to abortion and the destruction of American culture foreshadow contemporary right-to-life arguments. According to Mohr,

Lobbying became holy work for those physicians who believed that the United States was damning itself as a society by continuing to commit moral sins on a massive scale without even realizing it. The theme of saving America from itself was a common leitmotif throughout the medical campaign against abortion after 1860. (1978: 166)

Abortion did not, of course, simply appear *ex nihilo* as an appropriate means for the particular ends of American physicians. The nineteenth-century campaign took place in the wake of a dramatic upsurge in the visibility of abortion in America, and in the context of a general shift in the social bases of its practice. Apparently, the increased public awareness of abortion was due, initially, to its commercialization. By 1850, newspapers, magazines, popular health manuals, and even religious publications reaching urban and rural readerships carried advertisements for abortionists as well as abortifacient drugs and home treatments (Mohr 1978: chap. 3). They continued to do so until the 1870s when antiobscenity laws made promotion of abortion illegal.

The boom in business—one woman abortionist reportedly spent $60,000 on advertisements in 1871 alone—is considered both a response to an existing market and a stimulus to its expansion (Mohr 1978: 52). Estimates from a range of sources suggest that during this period, approximately 20 percent of all pregnancies were purposefully terminated.[4] The writings of American physicians are testimony not only to the rise in abortion attempts but to a shift in the social profile and motivations of the population using it.[5] Increasingly, those women who aborted were married, native-born, educated, Protestant women from the middle and upper classes (Mohr 1978: chap. 4).

As the public became more aware of changes in both the frequency and social context of abortion, physicians directed their efforts toward gaining interpretive control over this situation. Whereas in the 1970s evidence of women's widespread use of abortion was used to *justify* efforts to demand its legalization, in the nineteenth century the same trend became a call for criminalizing the practice.

Some scholars argue that the condemnation of women using abortion went beyond the goals of consolidating control over American medicine; it tapped into the conservative and reactionary trends of the postbellum era. The physicians' crusade against abortion, like the nativist and social purity movements that were also prevalent in the late nineteenth century, linked female sexuality to misogynist and eugenic doctrines (Petchesky 1984: 78–79). The writings of Storer and other antiabortion physicians portrayed any practice that interfered with the reproductive functions of white middle-class women in particular as threatening to what they considered to be "female nature." In this construction, women were held responsible for the decline of "the white race"; abortion and birth control came to signify, more broadly, women's "betrayal" of men, marriage, the family, and the very future of society (Gordon 1977: chap. 7).[6]

The Demographic Transition and the Rise of Domesticity

The efficacy of these antiabortion arguments is better understood when placed within the larger context of a general fertility decline in the United States. Between 1800 and 1900, the fertility rate[7] for white American women fell 50 percent, from 7.04—a rate higher than any ever recorded for a European country—to 3.56, a decline Degler calls "the single most important fact about women and the family in American history" (Degler 1980: 181; Coale and Zelnick 1963: 34–35).[8]

The growing practice of fertility limitation and abortion in particular was a topic of increasing public concern in the late nineteenth century. Initially, it was associated in popular writing with city life, despite the fact that birth rates were falling as rapidly in rural as in urban parts of the country, during a period when 80 per-

cent of Americans were still engaged in agricultural production. By
the 1860s, the ubiquity of birth control practice was widely recognized. Abortion in particular was considered common not only in
urban centers but in "every village, hamlet and neighborhood in
the United States" (Mohr 1978: 98–100).[9]

A number of scholars have offered explanations for this "demographic transition,"[10] stressing factors of human intentionality and
consciousness.[11] Some, for example, attribute the fertility decline
to what they call "the rise of the modern family" (Shorter 1977),
influenced and characterized by an attitude of planning and rationality in which children are viewed as investments measured against
current and potential resources—a "new fertility ethic" identified
with capitalism as well as the Enlightenment ideology of individualism (Ariés 1960; Noonan 1966; Flandrin 1976). These cultural
shifts are also seen as contributing to more equality within familial
relations and increasing separation of "pleasure from procreation"
(Stone 1977). Others suggest the fertility decline was part of greater
female independence and control over conditions within their assigned spheres of family and household, a phenomenon historian
Daniel Smith calls "domestic feminism" (Smith 1973).

Such interpretations avoid the pitfalls of assuming that the decline in fertility is the result of "new techniques" or is an unconscious response to socioeconomic conditions. However, this work
has been criticized for universalizing a class-specific marital profile
and demographic trend and for casting women's position in the
nineteenth century in uncritical terms. Although women may have
been gaining more "power" within the domestic sphere, female
lives were also increasingly circumscribed to that arena, and the
work and ideology of maternity and domesticity that defined it
(Petchesky 1984: 44–45; Ryan 1979; Welter 1966).

Strange Bedfellows:
Feminists and Physicians in the
Antiabortion Crusade

Even a cursory reading of the complaints against nineteenth-
century feminism by antiabortion physicians makes clear that they
were less generous than twentieth-century historians in their interpretations of female independence, even though both associated

the increase in abortion with it. Physicians in the antiabortion campaigns attributed the prevalence and spread of abortion to women acting "unnaturally." Abortion was seen as part of a dangerous "female folk culture" handed down from mother to daughter or spread among kin and friends and cast as threatening if for no other reason than the challenge it posed to regular physicians. Birth control and abortion in particular were linked as well to the ideas introduced by the first wave of feminism in the 1850s. In connecting abortion with feminism, physicians shifted the locus of blame from the abortionist to the woman herself who was accused of being "in an abnormal state," taking more interest in selfish and personal ends than in maternity (Mohr 1978: 105). Thus abortion came to signify a disruption of harmonious domestic relations and the social order in general, a construction that resembles much of contemporary right-to-life rhetoric.

Unlike the contemporary case, however, nineteenth-century feminists did not condone abortion. Abortion and birth control were considered immoral in large part out of fear that they would encourage promiscuity on the part of men. Elizabeth Cady Stanton, writing in the first volume of the feminist journal *Revolution* (1868), declared that abortion represented "the degradation of woman." Stanton's colleague Matilda Gage, writing a few months later declared, "this crime of 'child murder,' 'abortion,' 'infanticide,' lies at the door of the male sex" (Gage 1868).[12] In this formulation, opposition to abortion was linked to social goals to advance the position of women more generally through education, the vote, and control over the conditions of motherhood. Broadly put, these feminists interpreted abortion not as evidence of female abdication of motherly responsibilities but as yet one more piece of evidence of the unhappy consequences for women of unbridled male lust (Gordon 1982).

Despite the differences in their broader agendas, nineteenth-century feminists and the physicians who opposed them found themselves in an unlikely circumstantial alliance, particularly in the years after the Civil War (Mohr 1978: 113). What this reveals, in addition to the nature of antiabortion politics and coalitions in the late nineteenth century, is how opposition to abortion encompassed a range of cultural meanings. Feminists and physicians who both fought against abortion held contradictory interpretations of its meaning for the social order. More generally, their respective positions were expressive of a gender antagonism inherent in the sexual division of labor and the cultural separation of male and female spheres at the time. To summarize, each held the opposite sex responsible for what they saw as the decay of the culture and especially, in their view, the pernicious increase in abortion.

Abortion Reinterpreted: From Accepted Practice to the "Evil of the Age"

Despite the stress on gender antagonism in the antiabortion campaign, cases reported in newspapers, medical accounts, and court records indicate that most abortion decisions were in fact made by mutual agreement between the woman and man involved in the pregnancy. As noted, historians cite this as evidence for the rise in "companionate marriages" as well as a growing awareness and expression of sexuality on the part of American women. Some view the evidence of joint decision making on abortion as the outcome of a negotiation between pleasure and upward mobility for middle-class couples (Smith 1973). Others see in the mutuality of the abortion decision a channeling of female sexuality into maternity. In this view, husbands were enlisted to "a cultural mandate that more and more defined motherhood in terms of the care and socialization of children, as opposed to the physical bearing of them" (Petchesky 1984: 74).

Whatever explanation one accepts, it is clear that abortion was not only more visible and widespread but had become part of normal marital patterns among the representatives of the dominant American culture of the time—the white, Protestant middle and upper classes. It seems particularly ironic that the campaign to delegitimize its practice went into full swing at the moment of abortion's greatest acceptance. Recognizing this, the physicians' efforts to persuade both the public and legislators to enact laws that would prohibit abortion relied on their ability to reorganize the framework of meaning in which abortion was understood as legitimate. As in most struggles for political power within a democratic system, their efficacy required that they gain interpretive control.

To succeed in this part of their campaign, the antiabortion physicians undertook a systematic effort to convince the public of abor-

tion's dangers to their health and morals, beginning with the publication of two popular books by Horatio Storer, *Why Not: A Book
for Every Woman* (1866) and *Is It I? A Book for Every Man* (1867).
The physicians' arguments in essence were directed at convincing
American women to abandon the "outdated" doctrine of quickening; their rhetoric assumed that these women were practicing abortion out of ignorance of the nature of fetal life (Luker 1984a: 21).

By the 1870s, this position was making its way into popular
health manuals and the press, most notably in an investigative series "The Evil of the Age" run in the *New York Times* during
1870–71. The pieces portrayed leading abortionists as profiteers,
growing rich through the exploitation of innocent and vulnerable
women. The description of the body of a woman who died from
a botched abortion—"a new victim of man's lust, and the life-
destroying arts of those abortionists, whose practices have lately
been exposed in the TIMES"—is exemplary of their rhetoric (*New
York Times*, August 27, 1871, cited in Mohr 1978: 179). The interpretation of abortion as the fatal product of undomesticated male
sexuality, greed, and materialism apparently provided an appealing story to nineteenth-century journalists and their readers.

Although such understandings recur in twentieth-century right-
to-life arguments, it is important to note distinctions between the
past and the present. The groups that allied in the nineteenth century to endorse criminalizing abortion—physicians, feminists, the
popular media—were the very constituencies most active in advocating its legalization one hundred years later. Likewise, the passive position of clergy on abortion during the nineteenth century is
in marked contrast to the role many religious leaders have taken in
the twentieth century as leaders in right-to-life and pro-choice
efforts.[13]

The Final Victory: The Consolidation
of Antiabortion Policy

The physicians' campaign received an unexpected boost from the
antiobscenity crusade led by Anthony Comstock, head of the New
York Society for the Suppression of Vice.[14] In 1873, Congress passed
"the Comstock laws," which included abortion-related material in
its definition of obscene publications, and appointed Comstock a
special agent to carry out the act. Although the law was directed

primarily at inhibiting traffic in what were considered pornographic and contraceptive products, it nonetheless enabled Comstock to pursue and prosecute abortionists throughout the 1870s. Comstock's zealous enforcement of the new laws coincided with a significant shift in the judicial treatment of abortion legislation in the courts. Although the courts had been tolerant in interpreting abortion cases, beginning in the 1870s they began to take a hard line against abortionists; the burden of evidence and proof shifted to the accused and convictions became more frequent (Mohr 1978: 196–97, 226–36).

In 1878, Comstock succeeded in arresting the country's wealthiest and most well-known abortionist, Madame Restell of New York City. Anticipating her probable conviction, she killed herself twenty-four hours before her trial. The Restell incident served, as have sensational legal cases in the more recent controversy over abortion, as a public drama marking a pivotal shift in the dominant interpretation of abortion. Madame Restell's death dramatized how the physicians' crusade, along with the Comstock campaign, succeeded in persuading the public and judicial bodies in every state that abortion was a criminal act (Mohr 1978: 199).

Although the physicians built their campaign around a rhetoric that claimed the absolute right to life of the fetus, they did not call for the unconditional outlawing of abortion that would seem to follow logically from such a position. Rather, they sought legislation that would permit the physician to determine the need for an abortion in most cases. According to Kristin Luker, this therapeutic abortion exception—allowing abortions if the mother's life is endangered—showed that the aim of the crusade was not to prohibit abortion but to bring its definition and practice entirely under medical control. Physicians, in fact, resisted any legislative efforts to specify what would justify abortions. By leaving the legal language vague, "life of the mother" could encompass a range of possible interpretations, from physical survival to the broadest psychological, socioeconomic conditions affecting a mother's well-being (Luker 1984a: 32–33).

The campaign, then, did not establish the "personhood" of the fetus. Rather it built a broad framework in which abortion was defined as deviant—at best an exceptional medical decision, at worst a crime. This redefining had a number of concrete effects. Advances in antiseptic and surgical techniques at the end of the nineteenth century might have made the procedure even less of a health risk than childbirth (as it is today) (Mohr 1978: 239). However, the new conditions, which meant that it was infrequently or illegally performed, turned the nineteenth-century physicians' insistence on the physical danger of abortion into a self-fulfilling prophecy. A second, predictable effect was an overall increase in disadvantages for the poor and the likelihood that abortion would result in physical and emotional harm to them. Privileged upper-income women had access to the physicians and enjoyed the financial resources that obtaining a legal abortion now required.

What the physicians accomplished in their crusade, then, in addition to consolidating the status and control of medical practice in the United States, was a transformation in the meaning and value of what, until 1850, had been a tolerated if not legitimate act. Their campaign, however, did not succeed in making monolithic the new signification of abortion nor did it eliminate its practice. Assigned to the realm of medical judgment, abortion was removed from public view and debate (Luker 1984a: 34–39). Yet a range of practices and interpretations persisted, all of which emerged again in the 1960s when abortion became once again the focus of a public controversy, a symbol and practice in contention.

The Twentieth Century: Quiet
before the Storm

During the first half of the twentieth century, abortion was not a subject of much public interest. Nonetheless, records indicate that despite the physical danger, illegality, and social stigma involved, American women continued to seek abortions.[15] In the opinion of most participants and observers of the contemporary debate, it was the growing gap between the practice of abortion and the nineteenth-century legal doctrine that catalyzed and defined the first wave of agitation for legislative reform of abortion laws (Luker 1984a: 61; Tatalovich and Daynes 1981: 23–26).

One might well wonder why, until the 1960s, women did not oppose a law that they clearly were inclined to disobey. Linda Gordon suggests that the lack of organized female support for legal abortion in the early part of the century was an outgrowth of sexual and class conservatism, and the belief that "motherhood was a woman's vital source of dignity in a world that all too often denied it to her" (1977: 236). This was manifest in the acceptance, even by feminists, of "race suicide" and "maternal instinct" arguments. Leveled against white middle-class women seeking to control their fertility, these ideas were influential through the 1920s (Gordon 1977: 237–45). The political scientist Rosalind Petchesky maintains that physicians and an increasingly powerful eugenics movement promoting population control absorbed fertility control and abortion into medical and public health frameworks (1984: 83–90). Similarly, Kristin Luker focuses on the medical profession's control of the issue. In her view, other interpretations would gain credibility only when the medical consensus began to disintegrate. The potential for that disintegration was apparent in the wide variation among physicians as to what constituted a danger to maternal health, the primary ground on which abortion was permitted (1984a: chap. 3 and app. 2, 257–59).

In spite of or perhaps because of this situation, many women (and some men) engaged in a practice that resisted and circumvented efforts at legal and medical control of pregnancy. This sort of muted alternative practice engendered a "counter-discourse" (Terdiman 1985: 16) to the dominant interpretation of abortion. Informal networks provided women with the necessary information for procuring abortions outside of hospitals. The circumstantial and direct evidence of community tolerance if not sympathy for the practice testify to the persistence of an oppositional view to the prevailing legal and medical definitions.[16]

By the 1950s, medical advances for treating conditions that had most frequently threatened maternal health—tuberculosis, cardiovascular disease, pernicious vomiting—were such that pregnancies that endangered the survival of the mother became increasingly uncommon (Luker 1984a: 54–55). However, some physicians continued to provide abortions on the basis of other than strictly medical indications. Within the medical profession, the threat of potential conflict between the adherents of strict and broad interpretations of the law (Packer and Gampell 1959) prompted the creation of hospital abortion committees to mediate abortion cases. Whatever their intent,[17] the effect was to restrict further women's access to legal abortion by the 1950s (Luker 1984a: 56). As the decision-making process became more public, however, its legitimacy was increasingly called into question as arbitrary (Schaupp 1964: 353) and sexist (Phelan and Maginnis 1969: 91).

According to Luker, it was this growing breakdown in consensus among physicians performing abortions that generated the first activism for reform of restrictive abortion laws (1984a: 61). In the late 1950s, minor efforts to reform abortion laws to reflect medical practice were initiated, most notably in the well-respected American Law Institute's (ALI) proposal (as part of their draft for a Model Penal Code). The Institute recommended legalizing therapeutic abortions in cases that would "gravely impair the physical or mental health of the mother"; in which the child would be born "with grave physical or mental defects"; or "if the pregnancy resulted from rape or incest" (American Law Institute 1962). However, there was little public interest at the time in pursuing the battles that even minimal reforms would have required.

The Emerging Crisis: Mobilization for Abortion Law Reform

That situation changed in 1962 with the case of Sherri Finkbine, the opening act for what was to become a full-scale social drama. Much as the arrest and suicide of Madame Restell in 1878 marked the denouement of tolerant abortion policies in the late nineteenth century, the Finkbine case revealed the growing breach between existing legal and medical doctrine on abortion and its actual practice. The story quickly achieved the status of a "mythic charter" for the pro-choice movement as one of the central events that first awakened public concern to change restrictive abortion (e.g., Hole and Levine 1971: 283).

Sherri Finkbine was a middle-class mother of four, host of a "Romper Room" television show in Arizona, and married to a history teacher. In 1962, while pregnant for the fifth time, she read a report that the tranquilizer thalidomide, which she had taken in Europe to ease tension caused by her impending pregnancy, was likely to produce extreme birth defects.[18] Finkbine's physician advised and scheduled an abortion, although Arizona law allowed the procedure only to save the life of the mother. Out of concern for other pregnant women who might have been taking the drug, unaware of its potentially harmful effects, Mrs. Finkbine contacted a local medical reporter at the Arizona *Republic*. She asked that a warning be printed and that her name be withheld. On the morning of her scheduled abortion, the *Republic* reported the story on its front page. Fearing prosecution should anyone bring a complaint, the hospital canceled the abortion. The Finkbines' physician requested a court order to perform the operation, claiming it was necessary for preservation of the mother's life. Although the judge dismissed the case and recommended the abortion, the hospital still refused to oblige until the laws were clarified. The Finkbines eventually went to Sweden and received approval for and obtained an abortion there. The fetus was, in fact, grossly deformed (Finkbine 1967: 15–25; interview in Luker 1984a: 62–65; interview in Matthews 1987).

The Finkbines' story became an immediate cause for comment, from small-town papers to leaders of church and state. President Kennedy announced that drug regulations of the Food and Drug Administration (FDA) would be increased and asked Americans to destroy thalidomide tablets. The Vatican issued a statement denouncing the abortion as murder (Tatalovich and Daynes 1981: 45–46).

Mrs. Finkbine was not a radical or activist, nor was she "sexually irresponsible." She had very much wanted her pregnancy and considered abortion justified only in exceptional cases. She judged her choice to be unfortunate but necessary and correct. These qualities made her a persuasive and compelling figure to the American public.[19] The Finkbine case foreshadowed the volatility and polarization of sentiment that came to characterize the national controversy over abortion as it took shape over the next two decades. At the time, it revealed how hospitals were responding more to fear of legal prosecution than to the needs of female patients. This point was central in the mass media's presentation of the issue to the American public. The rhetoric of *Time* magazine in an article entitled "Abortion: Precept and Practice" (July 13, 1962: 52–53) was typical.

Despite strict anti-abortion legislation in the United States and the often exorbitant expense involved in getting to countries with more lenient laws, abortion statistics continue to rise yearly in a striking case of conflict between the mores of a people and their legal code.

The case made clear the growing discrepancy between abortion law and practice. In other words, it revealed the gap between norms and praxis, an inevitable source of change or conflict. The issue was dramatized again in 1964 when a German measles outbreak resulted in the births of over twenty thousand congenitally abnormal babies. In some states, physicians who performed abortions on pregnant women with rubella faced losing their licenses (Tatalovich and Daynes 1981: 47).

These cases helped catalyze a growing movement for abortion reform among workers in the health, social service, and law professions during the early 1960s. This has come to be accepted as "the first stage" of the reemergence of abortion as a social and political issue in the twentieth century. For example, a year after the rubella epidemic, a group of physicians, theologians, and social workers formed the Association for the Study of Abortion to compile and circulate data on abortion in order to garner public support for revising abortion laws (Sarvis and Rodman 1974: 9).

Concomitantly, a second constituency, representing what was to become a more radical force, was beginning to organize by providing public abortion and birth control counseling and referral services.[20] Underground abortion information had been in existence, informally, through networks of women, sympathetic physicians, and social service workers. Although such unofficial referral networks shared with the new "above ground" groups the goal of helping women find qualified and humane abortionists, they remained covert, simultaneously subverting and accepting the law. The new, more militant referral groups operated openly, inviting arrest and conviction in order to challenge the laws (Hole and Levine 1971: 254).

In the late 1960s, abortion rights activists began to gain more credibility and visibility, as well as concrete victories. Between 1967 and 1972, fourteen states passed legislation to permit therapeutic abortions, according to the ALI recommendations, and three states repealed their laws altogether in 1970.[21] The lobbying efforts that helped produce these successes gained strength as a broader range of groups began to affiliate with the expanding abortion rights movement—for example, the National Organization of Women (NOW) (1968); the AMA (1967); the American Civil Liberties Union (ACLU) (1969) (Sarvis and Rodman 1974: 9), and Planned Parenthood World Population (1969).[22] Controversies erupted within many of these associations over the decision to align with forces for legalized abortion. These struggles indicate the range of meanings abortion carried and how, within different contexts, it was being reinterpreted, often quite radically.

Only by the 1940s and 1950s did public and private agencies concerned with fertility control begin to reorganize their views and policies around fears of overpopulation (although many of the eugenic assumptions associated with these groups remained) (Petchesky 1984: 118–22). Accordingly, contraception became not only more acceptable but an explicit goal in policy-making circles, made manifest in a number of government measures taken during the 1960s, notably:

—the FDA's approval of the commercial distribution of oral contraceptives ("the pill") in 1960;

—the Supreme Court's 1965 ruling legalizing the sale of contraceptives to married couples on the grounds of rights to privacy (*Griswold* v. *Connecticut*), a critical precedent to the 1973 abortion ruling;

—President Johnson's approval in 1967 of an annual budget of over $20 million for contraceptive programs.

These actions marked the increasing role of the state and private foundations in creating and carrying out population policy at home and abroad (Petchesky 1984: 124–25). In the context of these developments as well as the growing practice and visibility of abortion, those involved professionally with fertility control began to view abortion as necessary to curbing population growth (Mohr 1978: 250–51). Still, the population control professionals joined the abortion reform movement cautiously, fearing its political volatility. Writing in 1967, Planned Parenthood president Alan Guttmacher voiced the nervousness with which his organization approached the issue:

Today, complete abortion license would do great violence to the beliefs and sentiments of most Americans. Therefore I doubt that the United States is as yet ready to legalize abortion on demand, and I therefore am reluctant to advocate it in the face of all the bitter dissension such a proposal would create. (1967a: 12–13)

Similarly, although the issue of abortion rights has been popularly identified with the women's movement, the first official endorsement of that position at NOW's Second Annual Convention in 1967 generated "a very painful confrontation with our own conflicts on abortion" (Friedan 1968). Members were, apparently, in agreement that abortion should be made legal. The conflict was over strategy; many worried that support for legal abortion would alienate many women from supporting NOW's overall agenda (Hole and Levine 1971).

The Shift from Reform to Repeal: The Abortion Rights Movement

The concerns voiced in the women's movement over the abortion issue were part of a growing division between reform and repeal advocates, an interpretive split that took on organizational expression.[23] Those committed to repealing all restrictions on abortion formed groups—some evanescent, some more enduring—devoted to direct action as a political strategy.[24] For example, in January 1969, the New York chapter of NOW founded New Yorkers for Abortion Law Repeal, which promoted repeal on the basis of radical feminist principles, as did the New York City–based Redstockings. These groups used various political tactics, from invading legislative hearings, to holding speak-outs and demonstrations, to lobbying *against* reform campaigns that would still maintain medical restrictions on abortion practice (Willis 1971: 117–18). On August 26, 1970, dramatic demonstrations to repeal antiabortion legislation were held in urban centers across the country (Hole and Levine 1971: 295–99). Radical health activist groups organized referral services, challenging both legal and medical control of abortion.[25] Such action established repeal as a legitimate pro-choice position and created pressure for legislative change.

Although feminists had made clear that their position—access to abortion for all women—differed from the liberal "right to choose" formulation, the two views were conflated as abortion rights activists consolidated around the goal of elective abortion. This new position of the abortion rights movement, which supplanted the medical model, was most clearly expressed in the formation of the first (and eventually the dominant) national group committed to repeal, the National Association for the Repeal of Abortion Laws (NARAL), which became the National Abortion Rights Action League after 1973. NARAL was established at the First National Conference on Abortion Laws, held in Chicago in February 1969 (Lader 1966: 9). It was not just abortion as a medical procedure that was being redefined for activists, but also its position in relation to key symbols in American culture—those of individual liberty and revitalization of democratic process through popular protest.[26] The redefinition of abortion as a democratic right helped bring an expanded constituency into the movement. The list of NARAL's sponsors reflects how the constellation that had emerged by the late 1960s in favor of abortion repeal had grown far beyond the original professional elite to include not only feminists, radical clergy, liberal lawyers and politicians, health professionals, and population control and welfare rights advocates but also more conservative groups such as Church Women United, the Young Women's Christian Association (YWCA), and the Commission on Uniform State Laws.

By 1969, the movement had rejected medical definitions outright and began to attack the very existence of abortion laws by introducing legislation and pushing for the passage of repeal bills into state legislatures, beginning with New York in 1969. Their actions served as a political recognition of the fact that the reasons most women sought abortions were not those indicated by the "therapeutic exceptions" recommended by the ALI—rape, fetal deformity, incest, or maternal health. Rather, they had to do with women's desire to choose if, when, and with whom they would have children, taking into account existing family size, financial considerations, marital status, and work conditions, motives not unlike those of American women born a century earlier.

Through direct action, lobbying, and confrontational politics, the expanding abortion rights coalition succeeded in influencing legislators in New York, Hawaii, Alaska, and the District of Columbia to repeal restrictive abortion laws in 1970.[27] Between 1970 and 1973, however, the failure of a Midwestern NARAL offensive in state after state reflected the growing strength of emerging right-to-life efforts (Tatalovich and Daynes 1981: 63).

As a result, pro-choice forces began to shift their focus from state legislatures to the courts, challenging the very constitutionality of existing abortion legislation. Briefly put, the position they took was that the antiabortion laws that were on the books in most states were constitutionally vague and, more important, were a violation of the civil rights of women, specifically the constitutional guarantees to equal protection and privacy, according to the broad interpretations of the fifth and fourteenth amendments that had been established in the 1965 rulings on contraception in *Griswold* v. *Connecticut* (Lucas 1968). On these grounds, the abortion rights campaign picked up momentum in a new direction. By 1971, seventy criminal and civil cases were pending in over twenty states. Under the pressure of this "judiciary activism" (Tatalovich and Daynes 1981: 65), the Supreme Court agreed to hear two of those cases: *Roe* v. *Wade,* which challenged a nineteenth-century Texas law typical of the antiabortion statutes passed during the physicians' crusade, and *Doe* v. *Bolton,* which questioned the constitutionality of a Georgia law allowing therapeutic exceptions based on the ALI Model Penal Code. On January 22, 1973, the Supreme Court handed down decisions addressing the separate issues raised by each case. The rulings essentially legalized elective abortion in the first trimester with restrictions to protect maternal health in the second, and the potential life of the fetus in the third.[28]

Thus, within the course of 150 years, the interpretation of abortion had come full circle. Almost a century passed between the campaign to criminalize abortion in the late nineteenth century and the push to legalize it in the twentieth. During the 1960s, the pro-choice movement had defined itself out of a diverse set of constituents, as a political and cultural entity, and gained many of its political objectives. With the Supreme Court rulings of 1973, it seemed as if their central goal had been achieved.

Although the decisions were popularly identified as a victory for the feminist demand that a woman have "the right to choose," in fact the ruling grew out of different premises. The doctrine of "the right to privacy" on which the Supreme Court rulings were based was intended to uphold a physician's right to make a medical decision. The court offered no provision or guarantee for making abortion *available,*[29] nor did the health care system respond uniformly to the increasing demand for abortion services. The gradual realization of the uneven availability of abortion in many parts of the country eventually resulted in pro-choice efforts to ensure more widespread, low-cost abortion services (Tatalovich and Daynes

1981: 104). This resurgence of pro-choice activism in response to what was viewed as an abdication of responsibility by the medical community was part of the arena in which the opening of the Fargo clinic in 1981 was staged.

At the time of the rulings, however, the lack of response of the medical community was not anticipated as an issue of concern. Equally unexpected was the strength of the pro-life reaction. The *Roe* v. *Wade* decision still stands as a critical event for the right-to-life movement, marking the transformation of the relatively small pro-life effort that was already in existence into a national, well-organized social movement.

Chapter Three

The Rise
of the Right-to-Life
Movement

Every year on the anniversary of the 1973 ruling legalizing abortion, a "March for Life" is held in Washington, D.C., drawing anywhere from thirty to fifty thousand pro-life supporters from around the country. Leaders of the movement, often at odds during the rest of the year, join together for this event, which usually includes a meeting with the president. Such demonstrations of renewed solidarity and commitment to the struggle are carried out in local communities as well, particularly in areas where there is an abortion clinic.

These annual displays are not only a protest against the legalization of abortion. For many right-to-life activists, the date of the Supreme Court ruling marks a turning point at which they converted to and joined the movement. After 1973, large numbers of "ordinary citizens" and especially women became active, transforming the right-to-life cause into a grass-roots organization that drew its strength from local-level activists (Luker 1984a: 145; Tatalovich and Daynes 1981: 84).

Birth of a Movement:
Single-Issue Politics and Grass-roots
Activism

Although pro-life activism includes a multitude of organizations, the National Right to Life Committee (NRLC) is the largest and

oldest of these, the product of struggles in the late 1960s as ad hoc
groups organized to oppose efforts to repeal antiabortion laws. It
represents the mainstream of the movement, claiming over three
thousand groups around the country. The NRLC organizational
structure reflects its self-image as a "broad-based, voluntary, nondenominational, non-sectarian organization" that draws its strength
from grass-roots support (Leahy 1975: 40). The board has representatives from each state, each of whom has a vote; decisions are
made by majority.

Although much of the movement originated or ultimately developed independently of the Catholic Church, that institution was
and continues to be crucial as a support system. The Church provided an infrastructure, communications network, material backing, ideology, and people—in short, the resources and organizational facility that helped mobilize the movement in its early stages
into a national presence. In 1967, the National Conference of
Catholic Bishops (NCCB) budgeted $50,000 to fight abortion re-
form efforts. The following year, the Family Life Division of the
United States Catholic Conference organized a national network of
the local pro-life leaders who had already begun to consolidate informally (Leahy 1975: chap. 2; Petchesky 1984: 252–62).

By June 1973, local activists were growing more and more un-
comfortable with the Catholic Church's increasing efforts to maintain centralized control. A committee of nationally prominent
pro-life leaders voted, at their annual meeting, to sever formal connections with the Church and established an independent National
Right to Life Committee, electing a Methodist woman as their first
president. While the NRLC has developed along an independent
course from the Catholic Church, the two organizations nonetheless draw support from each other in their efforts to prohibit
abortion. The Family Life Division of the National Conference of
Catholic Bishops (NCCB) outlined a plan to gain support for a constitutional amendment that would recriminalize abortion. Their
method, spelled out in the 1975 "Pastoral Plan for Pro-life Activity"
complemented NRLC's grass-roots organizing efforts. The Catholic
plan called for and eventually established pro-life committees in
the eighteen thousand parishes across the country to monitor and
influence national and local elections.[1]

What distinguishes the NRLC is its commitment to maintaining a diverse constituency from right to left united around the single issue of the "right-to-life." As an editorial in the *National Right to Life News* stated:

It is NRLC's "single-issue" policy which permits it to represent, and to work effectively with, individuals who agree on little *except* the right-to-life issues. (Johnson 1984:6)

For example, contrary to current popular stereotype, the NRLC included a vocal "progressive" component from the outset. Pro-lifers for Survival, an anti-nuclear pacifist group, was founded in 1971 and Feminists for Life organized soon after. Right-to-life "progressives" organized a demonstration in Washington, D.C., in 1972 nicknamed the Woodstock of the right-to-life movement. It incorporated standard symbolic elements of the antiwar movement, from the burning of birth certificates, to the singing of "Give Life a Chance" (Paige 1983: 69, 103). The "progressives" continue to have influence and visibility within the movement.

Although the stated raison d'être of the pro-life movement has been to overturn the Supreme Court ruling through a constitutional amendment,[2] activism has focused increasingly on local-level delivery of abortion services. Pro-life groups adopted, over the 1970s, direct action techniques—creating and imposing local ordinances, harassing local abortion providers, picketing facilities or staging sit-ins at clinics—not unlike those used by the more radical activists in the abortion rights struggle in the late 1960s. In both cases, the intent was, in part, to challenge the law and force judicial clarification on the issue.

For right-to-life advocates, these actions served to test the areas left unclear in the Court's ruling by introducing local, state, and federal legislation to limit the availability of abortion.[3] All of these efforts to create antiabortion regulations were immediately challenged by pro-choice advocates, specifically, the American Civil Liberties Union, the Planned Parenthood Federation, and the Center for Constitutional Rights (Paige 1983: 110). Because rulings on these regulations by local courts were mixed, it was only a matter of time before these questions would be brought before the Supreme Court once again for resolution. However, with two exceptions, the high court declined to rule on any of them until 1983.[4] As a result, these issues endured as expanding and intensifying arenas of local conflict between pro-choice and pro-life forces during the 1970s.

The growing national political strength of the right-to-life movement was dramatically marked in the 1977 Congressional passage of the Hyde amendment, which allowed states to prohibit the use of public funds (Medicaid) to pay for poor women's abortions, except to save the mother's life.[5] Introduction of the Hyde amendment in 1974 resulted in eleven weeks of Congressional debate. Since then, each Congress has accepted a version of the legislation.[6] (The principle on which it is based, that the government is not under obligation to provide support for abortion services, has been expanded in recent years.)[7]

As right-to-life efforts gained ground, pro-choice activists found that feminist arguments were losing ground as a defense of abortion rights. In the arguments over the Hyde amendment, not a single defense of public funding for abortion used the argument that women have a fundamental right to social and reproductive autonomy, a point of view that had been compelling in 1973. Both the arguments over the Hyde amendment and its substance—that the state is not obligated to provide the resources to implement rights it guarantees—indicated the decline of the liberal hegemony of the 1960s.

The New Right and the Abortion Issue

By the late 1970s, the general conservative swing in the country during the earlier part of the decade had consolidated around a coherent political agenda that has come to be known as the New Right. The name is identified with two scenarios: a widespread seachange sweeping the ideological currents of American society to the right; or a coalition of right-wing politicians, religious leaders, and "pro-family" groups, all linked through "hi-tech" mass organizing in an effort to take control of at least the Republican party, if not the country.[8] Whatever the appropriate imagery, in 1977 this constellation of conservatives adopted a strategy to broaden their influence by developing a "pro-family" campaign. In an effort to gain support for their conservative agenda, New Right leaders targeted evangelical and fundamentalist churches as well as single-issue groups concerned with the "traditional" social roles of family, church, and school. Their hope was to fuse them into a "winning coalition" that would bring electoral success to their candidates and programs (Crawford 1980: 36; *Conservative Digest* 1979).[9]

The National Right to Life Committee, well organized at both its top and base, with a dedicated following, was just the sort of single-issue group the New Right was looking for: a popular, cross-class social movement that had not been allied to right-wing causes more generally. For NRLC leadership, to ally with the New Right would have undercut one of the primary benefits of single-issue organizing, which, by tolerating multiple interpretations of opposition to abortion, can sustain a large and diverse membership. The comments of a pro-life writer summarize the right-to-life position on this issue.

[Retaining our independence] underscores the importance of a movement maintaining its perspective and its "soul." If we lose sight of our ultimate purpose, our cause suffers. . . . We are neither the New Right nor the Old Right, nor the official Roman Catholic Church, nor fundamentalist sect; not Republican or Democrat, conservative or liberal, black or white. We are committed to the sacredness of human life and proud of that fact. (*National Right to Life News*, November 24, 1983: 7)

New Right leaders hoped to recast the right-to-life position in its most conservative interpretation, linking it to their vision of the proper role of government, family, and sexuality in American society (*Conservative Digest* 1979). However, important distinctions exist between and even within the two camps in terms of ideologies as well as political strategies. Mainstream pro-life activists, though representing a range of associations from pacifism to millenarian Christianity, generally share a critique of cultural trends representing market rationality, self-promotion, and the prevalence of career convenience over nurturant ties of kin and community. This view is at odds with the militarism and laissez-faire capitalism that are central to much of the New Right program.[10]

Some argue that despite the philosophical incompatibility between the New Right and right-to-life ideologies, in *practice* conservativism for the past three decades has been a complex balancing act between a libertarian celebration of individualism, economic freedom, and capitalism, and a traditionalist emphasis on community, moral order, and the like. The sociologist Jerome Himmelstein, for example, proposes that these themes are sustained in one movement through a division of labor that holds apart the anticapitalist critique embedded in the "female social issues" from the wholly capitalist conservative ideology regarding "male" economic and political issues. Hence, the radical thrust of the former is blunted and reversed by its association with the latter, so that the critique of competitive individualism and materialism is directed at feminism or "secular humanism," not capitalism (Himmelstein 1983; 1986). In other words, the question is not simply what discourse is used, because clearly there are at least two, but on what issues and against what targets it is deployed. In Klatch's view, "it is through the naming of the forces that threaten America [Communism and Big Government] that the two forces converge." (1987: 54).

Such points are well taken; however, my own work leads me to conclude that the philosophical incompatibility between the two positions is indeed problematic for the actors involved. Despite the hopes and plans of the New Right leadership to create what would have been an unprecedented alliance between Catholics, conservative politicians, and Protestant fundamentalists over the abortion issue, such an alliance has been shaky.[11] For example, by 1979 New Right leaders who were frustrated at their inability to win over the mainstream pro-life movement set up their own right-to-life groups that have been in competition with the NRLC.[12] Thus, abortion is a symbol in contention not only between the pro-life and pro-choice movements; the New Right and mainstream right-to-life groups were struggling to gain material and symbolic control over its larger meaning and practice as well.

The antagonism between the factions claiming abortion as their issue finally led to a face-off in Congress in 1981. Although the battle lines were drawn over divergent strategies regarding antiabortion legislation (see n. 2), the fight was not only over political tactics; it dramatized a serious struggle for leadership of the movement and the interpretation of its cause (Bennetts 1981). Division in the ranks was such that ultimately neither proposal made it to the floor for a vote. But although their broader ideological agendas and specific tactics differ, both NRLC and New Right activists were working within the existing political system, hoping to recriminalize abortion and gain legitimacy in the public eye. They have accepted the same "rules of the game" and the shared aim of winning over the American public.

Yet, if votes and elections are any indication of public sentiment, the right-to-life movement was on increasingly shaky ground in the early 1980s, despite ongoing public support of a conservative Republican administration. Newspaper reports following the Congressional fiasco in September 1981 declared the movement to be in serious disarray (e.g., Bennetts 1981).[13] Pro-life efforts in the Congressional elections of 1982 generally failed. According to a *New York Times*–CBS poll, 74 percent of the freshman members of the 98th Congress favored legal abortion, as opposed to 54 percent in the 97th session (*New York Times*, November 4, 1982).

In 1983, the right-to-life cause suffered two serious setbacks. In June, the Supreme Court ruled that various state and local ordinances designed to restrict abortion practice were unconstitutional, underscoring the position it took supporting elective abortion in the 1973 rulings.[14] Soon after, an additional blow was dealt the pro-life cause. A proposed constitutional amendment asserting that a right to an abortion is not secured by the Constitution was rejected by the Senate; the vote was eighteen short of the two-thirds required majority. Together, the events of the summer of 1983 served as an endorsement of the pro-choice status quo.[15]

Right-to-Life Violence: Revival or Last Resort?

Until the summer of 1983, the mainstream right-to-life leadership prevailed over more radical elements of the movement. Confident that victory through legitimate political and educational means was close at hand, local and national leaders argued persuasively against overtly violent direct action that might undercut public sympathy for pro-life efforts. Still, despite the fact that the right-to-life movement was well organized, had gained a large membership, and had become quite sophisticated regarding political action, it had achieved only modest successes in gaining direct political victories through legislative or judicial channels.

The setbacks of 1983 for the right-to-life movement were followed by a dramatic escalation in violence directed against abortion clinics.[16] Figures compiled by the National Abortion Federation, a pro-choice organization, showed 115 violent incidents involving 46 clinics between 1977 and 1982. By contrast, between 1983 and March 1985, there were 319 acts of violence affecting 238 clinics. By the end of 1985, 92 percent of abortion clinics reported harassment, ranging from picketing of clinics to vandalism, an increase of approximately 60 percent from 1984 (Forrest and Henshaw 1987). Apparently, the relatively moderate philosophy and strategy of the NRLC could no longer contain a diverse movement through its efforts to bring about change within the political system. The rise in violent incidents captured widespread media attention and evoked ambivalent reaction from moderate pro-life activists. NRLC president Dr. Jack Willke, for example, condemned the July 4, 1984, firebombing of the National Abortion Federation headquarters in Washington, D.C., by the radical fringe Army of God, acknowledging it can only hurt his own organization's image and future efforts. Nonetheless, he took the opportunity to equate abortion with violence pointing out that "Every second living human being that goes through their [an abortion clinic's] front door is killed."

The histories of those activists apprehended thus far for bombing and arson of clinics since 1983 suggest that the destructive violence at clinics is being carried out by fanatic individuals peripheral to the mainstream, both locally and nationally (Carpenter 1985; Freedman 1987; Mawyer 1985). However, their marginality, both social and in relation to the movement as a whole, hardly renders the actions of such people insignificant. These extremists represent a hyperbolic expression of a more general shift in the style of pro-life protest toward "direct action."

For those who had long scorned the more or less civil tactics that had dominated the movement's political style since 1973, the moment of disarray in 1983 became an opportunity. Splinter groups that advocated "direct action" bordering on violence and terror—harassing patients, holding sit-ins, intimidating abortion providers—emerged with new confidence, convinced that restraint and civility have been ineffective. These activists, whose contempt for the "mainstream style" was openly expressed in epithets such as "wimps for life," focused their efforts on dramatic demonstrations directed at abortion users and providers. Although they distinguish their actions from the bombings and arson that have attracted so much attention, it is not altogether clear where or whether the line between these two kinds of behavior should be drawn.

Proponents claim that "direct action" is rooted in traditions of American civil disobedience, whereas opponents believe their behavior verges on the terroristic in its effects as the threat of greater destruction is now omnipresent at clinics. Tactics have a variety of manifestations which typically include accosting women entering abortion clinics by blocking access, confronting them verbally and bodily, following them or even tracing license plate numbers and calling them at home, entering clinics and disrupting procedures, and pouring glue into front door locks. Actions also extend to those who provide abortion services. Physicians and clinic personnel have had their homes picketed, received threatening letters and phone calls, and been slandered. As vandalism at clinics increases, leases are lost and insurance costs escalate. Security guards, bomb checks, and escorts for patients are now considered essential by many facilities.

For this new style of right-to-life activist, building or maintaining a public image as reasonable citizens is simply beside the point. They are succeeding on their own terms by immediately disrupting abortion services and gaining media attention. Joseph Scheidler, founder (in 1980) of the Chicago based Pro-Life Action League and author of *Closed: 99 Ways to Stop Abortion*, is open in his contempt for letter writers and lobbyists. He espouses the "doctrine of necessity"—a view that violence is permissible as a last resort when it must be used to stop or prevent greater violence (i.e., abortion)—to justify actions such as illegally entering clinic operating rooms and disrupting abortions in progress. As Scheidler puts it:

When the law is so twisted, it is obvious that one has to fight it, and when the law sanctions killing of innocent people, maybe you have to break a law to save lives. (Quoted in Roeser 1983: 15)

While Scheidler claims a philosophy of nonviolence and blames the media for linking his actions with those of violent extremists, he nonetheless makes public his sympathy and identification with those more radical than he.[17]

The zealotry and controversial actions advocated by Scheidler had consigned him to the fringe of the pro-life movement. He was seen as disruptive of efforts to gain the moral and political high ground through prudent action. However, as the pro-life movement attempted to regroup after its 1983 defeats, people like Scheidler gained at least some legitimacy with the mainstream. Scheidler was invited to speak at the NRLC annual convention in 1983. He was among a handful of national pro-life leaders who met with President Reagan in January 1984 during their annual "March for Life" in Washington, D.C. As alternative modes of political discourse appeared closed, more extreme styles of action seemed apparently more appealing, or at least worth the risk. Although Scheidler may be charismatic to some, his extremism undercuts one of the larger objectives of the right-to-life movement: to gain credibility for their position with the American public.[18]

Insofar as public opinion is understood to be shaped by and reflected in the mass media, pro-life activists of all stripes have sought favorable coverage in the print and electronic media, a concern that permeates mainstream pro-life writing. In the words of the 1982 Director of the NRLC Political Action Committee, "Every pro-life group believes it has been victimized by media bias" (Faucher 1983: 63). The title of an article by the editor of the NRLC's newsletter, "Zealots, Zanies, and Assorted Kooks: How the Major Media Interprets the Pro-Life Movement," makes clear how the problem is perceived. He writes that for the "media elite"

Pro-lifers (and even more so pro-family people) are synonymous with repression, political and sexual. The buzz words practically leap off their typewriters: punitive, prudish, Victorian, rigid, repressed, hysterical, etc. (Andrusko 1983: 192).

Consideration of the larger context created by both the media and government response to "direct action" suggests that the extremists have had an advantageous position. The media in general gives disproportionate attention to violence and conflates those who carry out that activity with the movement as a whole. It is not only that violence makes a good story that sells newspapers. The profession of journalism is dominated by liberals who favor a pro-choice position (Lichter and Rothman 1981). Not surprisingly, the more extreme and reprehensible pro-life activities that paint the movement in the worst light receive the most coverage.

At the same time, the Reagan administration offered support to extremists through the opposite approach, claiming that attacks on abortion clinics did not constitute "terrorism" because they were not being carried out by an "organized group" that claims responsibility for them. The FBI's jurisdiction is "true terrorism" that aims to "overthrow the Government." According to one director of an abortion clinic:

This comes dangerously close to official sanction of terrorism. Mr. Webster [the director of the FBI in 1984] almost invites terrorists to go ahead and blow up abortion clinics as long as they don't take credit for it. (Hern 1984)

In an essay *On Violence*, the political philosopher Hannah Arendt wrote:

Violence does not promote causes, neither history nor revolution, neither progress nor reaction; but it can serve to dramatize grievances and bring them to public attention. . . . The danger of violence, even if it moves consciously within a non-extremist framework of short-term goals, will always be that the means overwhelm the end. . . . The practice of violence, like all action, changes the world, but the most probable change is to a more violent world. (1969: 79–80)

In a number of cases, violent right-to-life action has succeeded according to the terms that Arendt spells out. They have achieved the short-term goal of closing or hampering the work of individual abortion clinics. For example, in Everett, Washington, the Feminist Women's Health Center that opened in August 1983 was finally closed after being firebombed three times. Some local moderate pro-life leaders dropped back, disillusioned and disturbed that a movement dedicated to the preservation of life at all costs should resort to violence. At the same time, the bombings carried out by a single individual engendered a support group after the fact. For activists like these, violence is an obvious and rational course of action. In their view, they are purifying a society that they see as having decayed under the influence of secular and material values that diminish the sanctity of life. For more moderate right-to-life advocates, their violence allowed the means to overwhelm the end. In the words of one such local pro-life leader in Everett:

We can still work through the legislature. There are many things we can still do to work toward saving lives without bombing, without terrorizing people. These people will stop at nothing to stop abortion. (Quoted in Mawyer 1985: 59)

It seems paradoxical that those right-to-life extremists who hope to overturn much of the social change of the 1960s consider the civil rights and antiwar movements as models for action. What this reveals is certain consistencies in the style of American social movements, regardless of their position on the ideological spectrum. When the promise of gains through mainstream tactics appears unfulfilled, the appeal of violence grows. Commenting on the conditions under which extremism has emerged in American social history, Thomas Rose writes:

Violence is a political resource when the bargaining process provides no other alternatives, or at least when some groups perceive no other alternatives. Political violence is an intelligible pattern of interaction that exists in America, but we refuse to understand and confront it as integral to our life. (1969: 30)

In other words, the shift to violence is part of a consistent pattern in American history. When a movement is stymied as to an immediately effective strategy, people like Scheidler are both appealing and dangerous. With the pro-life defeats in Congress and the Supreme Court decisions that more or less confirmed *Roe* v. *Wade*,[19] "direct action" offered new life for some activists discouraged at the minimal gains of over a decade of effort. Their dramatic demonstrations gained media attention in whatever form, while internally, radicals and moderates became more competitive for "ownership" of the movement. As available arenas for effective political action were reduced, increasingly, conflicts have centered on the local delivery of abortion services, and court cases brought against pro-life demonstrators.[20]

The Geography of Abortion: From Legal Theory to Medical Practice

Although violent or extreme protests around abortion clinics have captured attention and elicited condemnation from both sides, little attention has been paid to the material, political, and symbolic arrangements that make such action possible. Because most abortions in the United States take place in clinics that are located in small, freestanding buildings, often physically isolated from other health services, they provide an easy target for antiabortion activists. Increasingly, clients must cross through intimidating picket lines to enter these clinics. The question this raises is why abortion, the most frequently performed surgical procedure in the United States, continues to exist on the physical and ideological periphery of the mainstream medical community in America (Jaffe, Lindheim, and Lee 1981: 7). An understanding of this situation is critical to any analysis of the abortion conflict during the late 1970s and early 1980s, and helps clarify the processes through which national policy regarding reproduction is translated into local terms.

In their evaluation of U.S. abortion services, researchers Jaffe, Lindheim, and Lee summed up their findings succinctly:

Implicit in the [Supreme] Court's 1973 decisions is the assumption that doctors and health institutions—except those with religious objections—would respond to women's need for safe termination of pregnancies in a manner that reflects society's delegation to doctors of virtual monopoly control over the delivery of health services (1981: 31).

However, it was not the mainstream medical community that acted to meet this demand. The statistics are compelling. In 1973, out of approximately 6,000 general short-term hospitals in the United States (excluding Catholic hospitals), only 1,064 offered abortions. By 1981, despite the tripling in the number of abortions, only 1,405 hospitals performed them; of these, only 16 percent are public hospitals, which are the main health care resource for poor women (Henshaw, Forrest, and Blaine 1984: 123). A 1980 study of hospital abortion services found that policies were determined either according to the convictions of individual medical personnel or in response to the fears of hospital officials and governing bodies that too high an abortion rate would give their institution the reputation of being an "abortion mill" (Nathanson and Becker 1980). In other words, as was the case in the days before legalization, a hospital's image took priority over the health care needs of women, particularly poor women.[21]

Because of the reluctance of hospitals to provide abortions, and the growing evidence that outpatient abortions could be done with safety (Nathanson 1972: 403), freestanding abortion clinics were established throughout the country. Such facilities, almost nonexistent before 1970 except for a few "underground" operations, numbered 679 in 1982,[22] and accounted for 77 percent of all abortions that year (Henshaw and O'Reilly 1983: table 6) and nearly all the growth in abortion services. Emerging out of the pre-1973 abortion referral network run by feminists, clergy, and health-care activists, these clinics now form a network that operates semiautonomously from the mainstream health institutions—other than through referrals and backup arrangements with hospitals in the event of medical complications.

A recurring theme in right-to-life arguments is that many of the clinics are run "for profit" by physicians, individuals, or corporations. (Some nonprofit organizations are run by women's health collectives, Planned Parenthood affiliates, or voluntary organizations.) Their assertions that abortion is not part of the general health care system but has become an industry unto itself, making millions of dollars from the misfortunes of women, are part of their more general critique of the increasing materialism of American life. The metaphors equating abortion with undesirable commercial establishments are constant: clinics are referred to as "convenience stores," "7-11's," "stop and chops," and the like. Not surprisingly, one of their strategies since 1973 has been to "put abortion out of business" by offering competitive services.

It is ironic that abortion facilities, which were created to fill the breach left by the medical community, are then held suspect because of their lack of affiliation with it. A recent study of nonhospital abortion providers showed virtually no difference between profit and nonprofit facilities in terms of services offered, patient fees, load, and location (Henshaw 1982; Landy and Lewit 1982). According to the Centers for Disease Control (CDC), clinics have a better overall safety record than hospitals and are more accommodating to patients' needs.[23] Although freestanding clinics have successfully filled the vacuum left by the medical establishment, there are still striking differences by region and state in the availability of services. In 1980, there were still no abortion providers in 78 percent of all counties in the country, home to 28 percent of women aged fifteen to forty-four (Henshaw, Forrest, and Blaine 1984: 119). In 1985, that number increased to 85 percent of all U.S. counties (Henshaw, Forrest, and Van Vort 1987: 63). Given the rise in and stabilization of the abortion rate (Henshaw, Forrest, and

Blaine: 1984), one might ask what the effect is of this uneven distribution of abortion services.[24]

Research on factors affecting abortion practice shows that the local availability of abortion services is the single most powerful determinant of variations in abortion rates in the United States (Borders and Cutright 1979: 117–33; Henshaw et al. 1982; Jaffe, Lindheim, and Lee 1981: 34). This is perhaps most evident in the statewide variation in abortion rates (the number of abortions per one thousand women between fifteen and forty-four). While the rate for the United States in 1980 was 29.1, it ranged, by state, from a high of 43.6 in New York and California (with 289 and 535 providers respectively) to a low of 12.0 in Utah (5 providers) and 12.6 in North Dakota and South Dakota, each of which had 2 providers (Henshaw 1982: table 7; Henshaw and O'Reilly 1983: table 9). In assessing such figures, Jaffe, Lindheim, and Lee write:

This extraordinary range [of services] does not occur in the delivery of other health services. One could ask if there are comparably wide differences among women in different communities to account for these extremes. The fact is, however, that there are not large differences among U.S. women in the factors relevant to the abortion decision: rates of unintended pregnancy, contraceptive practice, and desired family size. (1981: 16)

While these authors are correct in emphasizing the ubiquity of the need for abortion services, what they overlook in their evaluation are the social and cultural contexts that resist or encourage the establishment of facilities in one or another locale.[25] When the abortion clinic opened in Fargo in 1981, conflict was almost inevitable. It signified for local pro-life activists the dominance or at least prevalence of a fundamentally different (and unacceptable) interpretation of the world imposed from without. It is through such community level resistance to abortion services in places like Fargo that pro-life forces have been most effective in the 1980s.

Part Two

The Abortion Controversy
in a Grass-roots Setting

Chapter Four

The First Phase
of Conflict

In the preceding chapters, I have scanned a broad context in space and time of the abortion controversy at the national level. In the following four chapters, I shift my focus from the "macroscopic" aspects of the abortion debate to the story of one small city and the people who live there in order to show how consciousness of "big issues" is constituted from and in people's everyday lives. I have altered names and details of lives, in accordance with people's wishes on the matter. Unless otherwise indicated, the quotes used are from interviews or conversations I had while in Fargo.

Introduction

I couldn't believe that an abortion clinic would open up here. In New York maybe, but right here in Fargo? I just couldn't believe it. They've got money behind it and they just railroaded it in. And the laws are on their side. All we can do is pedal on. I'd like it to happen that they stay here and they lose money and they have to shut down because people just don't need abortions in Fargo, North Dakota. (Pro-life activist: Fargo, North Dakota, 1981)

The Fargo Women's Health Organization, a clinic offering abortions and run by a local reproductive rights activist, was the tenth such facility set up in small metropolitan areas by the National Women's Health Organization, a business headquartered in New York City.[1] For the surrounding community, its opening in the fall of 1981 became the focus of a full-scale controversy engaging the attention if not the energies of many of Fargo's citizens.

The first word of plans for the clinic was met with anger and bewilderment. The transformation of a white clapboard house into a "convenience store for abortion," as opponents called it, provided the perfect image of evil imposed on innocence for people unwilling to believe that abortion could be present in their quiet city. The clinic's appearance and location on a commercial strip at the edge of a residential district (so that it is regulated as a business) embodied for some a disturbing image: the world of home and hearth slipping over the boundary of domesticity into the public arena of commercial exchange.

The sentiments of one pro-life activist—nurse, mother of six, widow of a well-known Fargo professional—were typical of many.

It's just a little house, a little paint, a little plumbing and it's a business. I truthfully don't think there are many people in this nice rural community who would start it on their own.

The sense of "we" and "they" was exacerbated by the fact that the clinic is owned by a company in New York City, as if the very need for abortion were being imported from Fargo's structural opposite on the East Coast. In the face of the social change represented by the clinic, the pro-life forces in Fargo rallied, determined to dramatize their resistance.

Social Dramas, Actors, and Changing Scripts

The controversy over the clinic in Fargo seemed to emerge suddenly and dramatically, mobilizing and polarizing people, revealing their passionately held beliefs. The conflict that engaged Fargo activists is the kind of event Victor Turner characterized as a social drama—moments of revelation of social divisions when "people have to take sides, in terms of deeply entrenched moral imperatives and constraints" (Turner 1974: 35).[2] Because anthropological data often are drawn from such occurrences, a major concern in the field has been how to understand the relationship between these events and the more enduring structures of which they are a part. The model of social dramas provides a useful framework for analyzing and understanding fissures in social relations, and the relationship between such events occurring in concrete "arenas" and the larger social structure.

Social dramas are manifest as extended conflicts that typically follow a series of phases: breach of norms, crisis, redressive action, regression to crisis, and eventually either reintegration of the social group or lasting schism between contesting parties.[3] These phases are "not the product of instinct but of models and metaphors carried in the actors' heads" (Turner 1974: 36). In other words, breaches, crises, redressive actions, and schisms are not objective conditions but indicators of values and contested cultural meanings, apparent in different ways to both actors and observers. I will be using these terms to clarify such processes in the playing out of conflicting interests in the Fargo abortion controversy.

I am also expanding the dramatistic metaphor of the social drama to consider the role actors play in constituting the scenario. If one is interested in the transformative potential in social dramas (and social life in general), it is critical to include this generative role of actors. How they incorporate unexpected material and events from beyond the apparent "proscenium" is an important source of innovation in social process. Although the model's analogy to theatrical performance focuses attention on the predetermined nature of certain social scripts, people involved in social dramas also are engaged in altering the very patterns they are enacting. This dialectical process, particularly crucial in the study of complex societies, is an important dimension in the Fargo case. In the organization of daily life, social actors operate not necessarily by a scripted story but are continually improvising, adjusting prior understandings to meet new situations. Recent social theorists have suggested ways of looking at the dynamics through which dramatic lines are constituted, rehearsed, and revised over time, revealing how social actors become involved in establishing or challenging the "writing" or "staging" of particular cultural scripts (e.g., Giddens 1979; Bourdieu 1977; Sahlins 1985). Such ideas are helpful not only in understanding how the abortion conflict represents and constitutes a contested domain in American culture, but also in showing how the actors themselves have been engaged in both enacting and altering its meaning and practice in relation to changing circumstances.

The First Phase of Conflict

To an outside observer such as myself, the highly charged and divisive conflict over the Fargo clinic that erupted with such intensity in 1981 initially seemed to have emerged as the spontaneous response of local citizens to this new situation. After spending time in Fargo and coming to know the key players, I began to see that the clinic drama had been "in rehearsal" for over a decade, and that this background was crucial to understanding the situation in the 1980s. In fact, the abortion controversy first took formal shape in North Dakota between 1967 and 1972, during the introduction of abortion reform initiatives in the state legislature and in a state referendum. These initial conflicts served as a sort of prologue for later events. The controversy in the 1980s, though more a result of local events than the first wave was, came to represent more fully developed divisions regarding the construction of abortion and its attendant meanings as they were taking shape in America. More generally, then, this material reveals how national developments took effect and distinctive shape at the local level.

The Initial Breach

Judging from the lack of public debate regarding abortion during the first half of the twentieth century, the antiabortion statutes and the medical definitions of abortion that were in place throughout the United States were more or less accepted as official policy.[4] In North Dakota, as in many states, the existing law permitted abortions only to save the life of the mother. Though rarely enforced, the law had the expected inhibiting effect on practice.[5] Hospitals in the state rarely performed abortions. A few private physicians were known by word of mouth to be sympathetic in providing abortions for their own patients or referrals to out-of-state physicians for other women.

An older woman who had been part of the early underground referral network described how it operated, and how changes led physicians to start pushing for legal changes.

During the 1930s, a number of doctors who people knew would do abortions practiced here. For example, if a woman in her forties with high blood pressure and four kids got pregnant, they would help her out. In the 1940s and 1950s, it was a common scenario for a teenager to be brought in for a D. and C.[6] The nurses would just deal with it and let it go. But by the end of the 1960s, it was no longer possible for a doctor to do an abortion as they had fifteen years before. They wanted legal protection for what was becoming customary.

This kind of circumstance motivated the head of the state medical association to try and liberalize the law governing the abortions some of the doctors in the state had been performing. The physicians whom he mobilized were the only organized constituency to back the first efforts to legalize abortion.

In Fargo, both the informal provision of abortion practice and the pressure for legislative change developed over time in a pattern similar to that in other parts of the country (Luker 1984a: 92–108). Ronna Hartman, the woman who introduced the initial bill to change the existing abortion law, like others who pioneered abortion reform legislation in the 1960s, had not previously been an abortion advocate. As a freshman representative, Ronna was looking for an issue to represent.[7]

My first session in the legislature was in 1967 and one of the things that struck me was that most specialize in one field. So I thought, "What am I going to be good at?" And here were a whole bunch of men making all these decisions about the lives of women and children and the women themselves know more about it than the men do. So then I thought, "Well maybe that's what I should do." So I started searching around the legislation of other states and the first thing I came across was Colorado's abortion bill, but there was no information about abortion available in Fargo, North Dakota, at that time. I mean you wouldn't even say the word.

I tried to talk to my doctor about it. The impression I got was "Don't rattle any cages. Right now we can do what we have to do, but you start monkeying around and things won't get better. They could get worse." So then I went to the legislative Council Director and I told him I wanted the bill drawn for the legal termination of pregnancy and I thought I was going to lose him right there. He just looked at me horrified and said, "Do you have any idea what will happen to you if you introduce the bill?" And I didn't have any idea.

Her lack of awareness of the issue's potential volatility was due to its relative invisibility at that time. Ronna, like many of the early participants in the abortion reform movement, did not see it as explosive or highly charged, capable of rallying serious opposition (Luker 1984a: 108).

When Ronna proposed reforms in 1967, her interest was in representing women, though she did not yet have feminist backing. As she explained it to me:

There wasn't such a thing [as an organized women's movement] at the time that I knew of. I have always said that I accidentally got into the women's movement. We really didn't hear much about it in North Dakota at that time.

Initially, opposition to reform was minimal; the main support for it was from state medical interests. The proposed bill lacked only five votes to pass. By the next session, in 1969, when Ronna sponsored reform legislation again, antiabortion activists had begun to organize. The Catholic churches, which were beginning to put money and energy into the issue on a national basis, bussed parishioners in from around the state to attend the hearings. The crowd was such that the hearings were moved to the highway department's auditorium. The bill received only fifteen votes and Ronna was deluged with hate mail.

I remember after that bill I actually got sick. I had to leave and go to my hotel room. All this mail, the terrible things they said to me at the time from the floor of the house. It's murder, you're killing babies. . . . They made it seem so awful, things I would never associate with myself.

Her surprise not only at the existence of an opposition, but with the substance of their arguments, indicates how quickly the social construction of the issues altered as abortion became a matter of debate, and, eventually, a symbol for a conflict encompassing and representing two world views. What had been considered a normal legislative procedure in 1967—introducing a bill to change a nineteenth-century law that no longer seemed appropriate—was now defined as a breach of social norms by the newly emerging opposition to abortion reform.

Paradoxically, the first head of North Dakota's Right-to-Life Committee (NDRLC), a Lutheran, a surgeon, and a state representative, had helped draft the first abortion reform bill in 1967. This reflects, in a sense, how similar the activists involved in the first stage of abortion organizing were to each other. Initially, each position was defined and dominated by professionals who came into conflict with the abortion issue through their work (Luker 1984a: 127–28; Leahy 1975: 45–53). Of those who testified on both sides at the state hearings in North Dakota, most were physicians, clergy, and social service workers.

The right-to-life forces in North Dakota in 1969 formed initially on an ad hoc basis in response to efforts to reform and repeal abortion laws in state legislatures. As the chair of the NDRLC recalled:

They [the pro-life leaders] saw where the abortion people were going and that they were working on more and more legislation to liberalize abortion laws. So there was a grass-roots reaction in North Dakota and several other states, you know, not to let this kind of thing that was happening in New York happen here. So some of them got together and said, "We've got to get this going and we need some kind of coalition." So the NDRLC has been grass-roots from the very beginning because it was founded by chapters through the state organizations and then became a national organization, not the other way around.

By 1971, when Ronna introduced abortion reform for a third time, right-to-life activists were well organized though not yet numerous, well known, or popularly based, as Ronna's comments indicate.

This time, before I went out there, I got a telephone call from the Associated Press. "What have you got to say about this new organization?" "What are you talking about?" "Well, that Right-to-Life group." I didn't know anything about it. "Never heard of it. Who's involved?" I asked.

Although the emerging right-to-life forces may have had little public recognition at that time, they were effective nonetheless. Two pro-life leaders from Minnesota gave "devastating testimony," which helped defeat the proposed reforms.[8]

The hearings and votes in North Dakota were in step with the national situation: in state after state, it became clear by the early 1970s that right-to-life forces, though small in number, could successfully block moves to liberalize the existing law on abortion through legislative reform.

Crisis and Redress

Despite the emerging right-to-life opposition in North Dakota, several pro-choice physicians, convinced that popular opinion would be in favor of reforming abortion law, gathered ten thousand signatures for a state referendum on the issue in 1972. They neglected, however, to organize an educational campaign to garner support. When they approached Ronna Hartman for help, she declined; she was nervous of being politically stigmatized in an election year. Two friends, Ethel and Millie, whom she knew from the League of Women Voters,[9] agreed to take over for her. A brief account of the referendum battle in Fargo shows how the issue and the opposing groups were beginning to take shape, creating social and symbolic divisions around abortion that endured, developed, and emerged anew in 1981.

Ethel and Millie, both born in the 1930s, were members of Fargo's professional upper middle class. Each had gone to an elite college, married local professional men, and devoted themselves to raising families and to community activities such as the Parents-Teachers Association (PTA), the YWCA, the American Association of University Women (AAUW), and the liberal Protestant churches to which they belong. Both women saw their interest in abortion rights as an extension of long-standing advocacy of birth control and sex education. Ethel, for example, had worked for nearly a decade as a volunteer at the Family Planning Center that had opened in the 1960s. In recalling her part in that campaign in conversations with me, she linked her overall concern with birth control and abortion to eugenic arguments.

I have always felt that Malthus was right. The population bomb was going to explode, that we are developing an underlying population for which we have no use, a part of society that doesn't fit in. I feel strongly about the government allowing young girls to keep their babies [AFDC programs]. And I think the other great social problem we have is the refusal of the father to take responsibility for the child.

Her social position and attitudes regarding abortion were typical of one segment of the abortion rights constituency at that stage of the movement's development; they tied the issue to class interests, expressed through fear of overpopulation.

Perhaps because of the circles in which they traveled, Ethel and Millie were relatively unprepared for opposition. According to Millie,

The YWCA and the AMA auxiliary and the AAUW came out early with pro-choice statements. They were very modest. They were so rational that we thought there would be no problem getting people to accept it. It was a shock to see what people would do, to find out how angry they were. We thought we were trying to be moderate.

Ethel and Millie may have been protected from knowledge of the explosive potential of the issue due to the social world they inhabited. Yet, as Ethel explained, this world also provided them some measure of protection from the unexpected controversy generated by the campaign.

You really got labeled. You must realize that every hamlet, every little village, everybody had someone to do their advertising, to say how terrible abortion was. And this was a subject you didn't talk about. You didn't know the necessity. It was something you associated with bad girls who needed punishment.

Had my husband been a retail merchant, I would have had to think about doing it. But I had a lot of independence because my husband was head of his own firm and reasonably prominent. I was secure and I didn't care about politics. So I was probably less afraid of all the opposition.

Despite the existence of small and vocal pro-life and pro-choice constituencies, to most residents of North Dakota who voted on the referendum, the very idea of abortion reform was new. In Fargo, many still recall the 1972 campaign as the event that first brought the idea to their attention. Through the referendum process, an issue that might have remained more or less in the confines of the legislature was brought into a more broadly based arena and catalyzed local activists. Thus, the appearance of the abortion issue close to home generated right-to-life support beyond the professional elites who had been involved.

Caroline, a right-to-life activist, provides a sense of how people were recruited during the 1972 referendum.

I didn't have any feeling one way or the other until the referendum came up. Until then, it wasn't an issue I had to think out my feelings on. I was working as an ob-gyn nurse, a labor nurse. I'm sure that accounts for a lot of my feelings about life, working with women who miscarried or had stillborns. The doctor I was working for dragged me to a meeting. Right-to-life was in a formative phase then locally. He was doing a lot of speaking, going out and presenting his views on abortion. He felt it was really important that there be a positive side. We had a slide show. We went around wherever we were invited, to small towns, to church groups, to colleges.

During the period Caroline is describing, around 1972, the issue had not yet come to represent two opposed cultural stances. In fact, most Fargo citizens in favor of abortion, like Ethel and Millie, were surprised at the existence of any opposition to their position. Still, the nature of the controversy as it was defined at that point was much more moderate when compared with the dynamics that took shape a decade later over the clinic. The activists during this first phase, because they shared certain professional interests, were less likely to cast those who took the opposite tack as being wholly unlike themselves.[10] For Caroline, it was not simply that she already had friends who supported abortion rights. She actually developed friendships with her opponents through her activism.

We became friends through speaking together. It's almost humorous. We'd be put opposite each other on TV and then go out for coffee afterwards. At that time, there were so many people who didn't know; today it's pretty commonplace for people to know what abortion is.

To "know what abortion is," as Caroline put it, entails not some particular scientific knowledge of abortion. It refers to an understanding of the significance it took on over time as pro-choice and pro-life activists consolidated both their organizations and a chain of cultural associations that abortion, over the next ten years, would come to represent for each position. The initial stages of that process were taking place in Fargo during the referendum, particularly for right-to-life activists.

Local-National Linkages

Popular pro-life wisdom casts abortion rights advocates as outsiders, imposing their will on "community values." In fact, the right-to-life mobilization, while building on sincere concerns of local people such as Caroline, received more assistance, resources, expertise, and leadership from outside the state than did the North Dakota pro-choice cause, which had virtually no external support at that time. The 1970 abortion repeal victories in four states had stimulated the growth of a national pro-life strategy to combat the growing abortion rights efforts. Meetings and frequent communication supported initially by the Catholic Church reinforced the organizational and personal ties among prominent activists in each state. For example, a right-to-life veteran of the Washington State referendum came to North Dakota to assist them in their battle (Leahy 1975: 38).

By 1971, the NRLC had developed two of their key pieces of literature, the *Handbook on Abortion,* by Jack and Barbara Willke; and the *Life and Death* brochure featuring a greatly enlarged photograph of a fourteen-week-old fetus, which, a decade later, has become both an emblem and a cliché of the right-to-life position. However, in 1972, North Dakota was the "test market" for this new image. Its apparent shock value, coupled with a strategic distribution scheme, proved effective in winning the vote. As Ethel recalled:

They distributed this color brochure with a picture of the fetus door-to-door in Fargo and the rest of the state on Sunday and Monday, so we couldn't respond since the vote was on Tuesday. I remember I went and spoke the night before the election when that darn pamphlet landed on people's doorsteps. I got this absolutely tremulous woman who came to talk to me. You could see that her faith was really shaken. . . . Well the referendum was defeated very badly [78 percent in the state, 64 percent in Fargo], and it was a real setback.

The event dramatized the strength of the opposition sufficiently so that even ten years later, pro-choice activists were chary of publicly advocating abortion rights. At the time of the clinic's opening in 1981, the vote was still cited by right-to-life advocates as proof positive that North Dakotans do not want abortions in their state to receive public approval. At the time, the defeat of the referendum served, temporarily, as a redressive action, an authoritative halt to the spread of a crisis that established previously unvoiced divisions between contesting parties.

During this first local enactment of the abortion controversy, antagonistic groupings were not so much revealed as constituted. The more polarized understandings of the issue that developed over the next decade were just beginning to be formulated in North Dakota. Although overt conflict over abortion was rare in Fargo during the next ten years, the nascent pro-life and pro-choice forces endured and consolidated, evolving in relation to local and national developments. During the 1970s the script was revised, players were recast, and the action was restaged; by the time the controversy erupted for a second time in 1981, the drama had intensified and taken more coherent shape. In a sense, the legislative and referendum battles in North Dakota during the early 1970s served as improvisations for a more fully developed drama on contending cultural themes that abortion was coming to represent.

Revising the Script: The Grass-roots Impact of *Roe* v. *Wade*

In North Dakota, the pro-life forces' sense of success after the defeat of the referendum was short-lived. The January 1973 passage of *Roe* v. *Wade* two months later overrode the vote and spurred many who had joined the North Dakota battle to become more involved in right-to-life work nationally. Ann Webber, an NDRLC officer, recalled:

Well, then in 1973, we were shocked with *Roe* v. *Wade*. We didn't just have an abortion question then. We had a Constitutional question. But it wasn't our idea. It was those seven guys on the Supreme Court that rewrote it. And that surprised the pro-abortionists even more than it surprised us. They were not at all prepared for that kind of success on the basis of one court case.

Ann's assessment of her opposition's response was indeed correct. Ronna Hartman still remembers vividly her own reaction to the ruling.

In 1973, the miracle happened. I was sitting on the education committee and all of a sudden someone slipped a note in front of me that said, "The Supreme Court just legalized abortion." It's very rare you get to see something through to the end like that and it's an incredible feeling.

Although it was a clear pro-choice victory, the Supreme Court ruling had the ironic effect of undercutting the immediate base of the pro-choice campaign. The abortion battle shifted dramatically after the 1973 decisions. The nascent pro-life effort that was already in existence mobilized into a national, well-organized campaign. In direct response to the Supreme Court rulings, the movement was able to recruit and attract a new grass-roots constituency. These constituents transformed the right-to-life cause into a mass movement that drew its strength from local activists (Luker 1984a: 145)

In Fargo, the right-to-life movement picked up momentum in two directions. The experienced pro-life state leadership chose a strictly political route. They began to organize local right-to-life committees throughout the state to push for a "human life amendment" that would declare that all life begins at conception. Such efforts were also backed by the Catholic Church's pro-life network that had a contact person in every parish who, they claimed, could "generate a thousand phone calls in an hour if anti-life or anti-family legislation comes up." The president of the NDRLC who was also a representative to the state legislature promoted the group's agenda primarily by introducing pro-life bills at every legislative session. At the community level, political organizing was more or less inactive.

Reinterpreting "Problem Pregnancy"

A second group of pro-life supporters who first were mobilized in 1972—mostly women in their fifties and sixties—maintained their activism in a different direction. They chose to focus on providing "alternatives to abortion" and founded a chapter of Birthright, an international organization set up to provide emotional and material support for women with unwanted pregnancies, in order to deter them from choosing abortion.[11] The woman who was president of Fargo's Birthright chapter from 1972 until 1982 explained why she chose to channel her interests in that direction. Her sentiments are exemplary of the sort of motivations and understandings that attracted a new constituency to the right-to-life cause in the 1970s. For many, it was an enlargement of the tasks of nurturance that had occupied them, as mothers or health professionals, for much of their lives. The concern of these women, like many other female pro-life activists, was not just for the "unborn child" but for the difficulties that pregnancy can present to women.

I decided to work for Birthright instead of the Right-to-Life Committee because I was a nurse and I wanted to help the girl who was pregnant. It's just placing a hardship on the whole society and I felt I knew the reproductive system. I knew I could talk to them, and I had children. I was a mother, and I love babies. I mean I really like babies. My wedding day I said, "I'll take three girls and three boys." I will always help the girl who was pregnant, no questions asked. If you don't want abortion, then you better help the girl who is pregnant.

The same year that Birthright was founded, one of the two homes for unwed mothers that had been established in Fargo in the 1920s ceased operating because it could not fill its thirty-five beds; the second shifted its services to women with drug or delinquency problems.

Given the visibility and potential availability of abortion, women with unwanted pregnancies—particularly unwed teens—were acquiring a new meaning, not only for activists but for the community in general. In Fargo, this process of reinterpretation of the social meaning of unwanted pregnancies became apparent in confrontations between "professionals" and activists at public community meetings. Social service workers and public school teachers who had been dealing with problem pregnancies expected, as did activists on both sides, that with legalization, abortion services would become available locally. The primary counselor for unwed teens in Fargo, Mary Mintz, recalled her expectations that abortion would be introduced into the area as a matter of course.

I had been doing abortion counseling service since long before the Supreme Court ruling. There were people doing back alley abortions in West Fargo and I would do anything to stop that. For a while I would help patients make calls and then I decided it was dangerous and not right. And then, all of a sudden, girls were hearing about doctors in South Dakota, and I wanted to know if it was safe. So I used to send people to them even though it was three hundred miles away. You could see the handwriting on the wall, that a clinic would open here eventually.

After the Supreme Court ruling, Mary and several other social service workers formed a task force to find someone in the community to provide abortions. After meeting three or four times, the group decided to hold a public meeting on the issue. From Mary Mintz's retrospective account, the response was clearly a shock to her and other social workers.

I'll never forget it. We had placed a very carefully worded ad in the paper just to be sure we would get anyone from the community who was interested. Well, the Catholic churches alerted their people to come to this meeting and make their opinion known. Hate calls started pouring in. Then, at the meeting, . . . I thought I was going to get lynched. Some of the doctors started ranting and raving about abortions, and even one doctor who makes referrals said he would never do it.

One of the pro-life doctors who came to that meeting explained to me what motivated action to obstruct the implementation of local services:

When it becomes legal it becomes right. And if it's available, people will abort much more readily. They'll think it's right. It's just so abnormal. I believe in people's rights but I also believe in maintaining some community standards.

Thus, although right-to-life proponents had only a minimal presence in formal state politics in the mid-1970s, they sought to control through other means the interpretation and practice of abortion at the local level.

Because abortion was legal, pro-life activists shifted the grounds of the conflict to the "gray areas" left unclear in the Court's decision—questions regarding a woman's rights to have *access* to abortion—and aimed at restricting the delivery of abortion services through whatever means possible. In Fargo, "gatekeepers" such as Mary Mintz were targeted and harassed for making abortion referrals. Of the five hospitals and three clinics in the area, none would provide abortions. In a social environment sufficiently hostile to abortion to make powerful hospitals nervous about offering abortion services, it is not surprising that a freestanding independent clinic might be reluctant as well to open for business.

Chapter Five

The Clinic Conflict

Throughout the 1970s, women in the Fargo area who wanted abortions were faced with two unsatisfactory options: driving two hundred fifty miles to have an abortion or locating by word of mouth either of two doctors in the state who offered abortions (one of whom had a poor reputation, according to both pro-choice and pro-life activists as well as medical and social service professionals). Despite the apparent need, the introduction of safe, readily available abortion services to Fargo was slow in coming. It occurred in large measure due to the dedication of one activist, Kay Bellevue. Because of her own negative experiences with health care systems during the birth of her first child, she became involved with the women's movement in the early 1970s. Through that activity Kay made connections to local and national feminist organizations that provided her with critical sources of cultural, social, and material support. Access to these resources was essential to creating the conditions that allowed Kay to fulfill her dream of opening an abortion clinic that would meet the needs of women in the area.

Kay Bellevue moved to Fargo from another Midwestern city in 1972. At the age of twenty-seven, she was married with three children. She had been actively involved for six years with La Leche League, a national organization promoting natural childbirth and breastfeeding, and had developed an interest in feminism. Shortly after moving to Fargo, Kay became aware of and involved with a group that was starting a local chapter of NOW. Her desire and decision to focus on reproductive issues divided her from the others in the group who had lived through the 1972 state referendum defeat of abortion reform.

That was when I really began educating myself on the issues, and I got real frustrated because they [other Fargo feminists] did not want to get involved with abortion. They thought it might be construed as being linked with the ERA and that [passage of the ERA] was of utmost importance to them.

Kay quickly became identified as the spokesperson for the pro-choice position on abortion in the community. She spoke occasionally in public and testified at the state legislature, keeping informed on the issue through contacts at a large abortion clinic in Minneapolis, the nearest large city.

In 1974, a NARAL staff person, looking for an organizer for the Upper Midwest region, got Kay's name from the Minneapolis clinic and contacted her by phone. As Kay recalls:

I remember the phone conversation specifically. She said, "There's going to be an organizing conference in Sioux Falls, South Dakota. I wonder if you would be willing to come down there and attend the conference, see how it's done and make the commitment to do the same thing in North Dakota. You don't have to answer yes or no. I know this is a major decision. I'm sure you want to think about it and talk to your husband about it."

So I went ahead and went to the organizing conference and then I held one in North Dakota. Of course no one was willing to take over the state coordinator's position except me. Although it started out as a larger participatory group, it became in many ways a paper organization, a committee of three to four women.

NARAL's inability to draw support in North Dakota was due not so much to lack of concern, but to the negative stigma abortion still carried in Fargo despite its legalization. Organizing people around pro-choice efforts was difficult in the mid-1970s despite the fact that a local women's movement was gaining momentum. One of the women who worked with Kay on the state NARAL committee in the late 1970s recalled:

We didn't say boo about abortions back then, not around here, anyway, even after legalization. We worked very diligently. We got a brochure together, we had articles of incorporation. We had meetings. But in those days we were pretty quiet.

Setting the Stage: The Emergence of Pro-Choice Activism in Fargo

For most of the women who emerged as pro-choice activists in 1981, the efflorescence of feminism in Fargo between 1974 and 1980 was a central experience. In the following brief sketch of this development, what is striking is how local women claimed authority for feminist action through symbolic actions that identified their efforts with nurturance and domesticity. In Fargo, until the abortion issue was reframed in a way that sustained these associations, the issue of reproductive rights was a difficult agenda for organizing even committed feminists.

Feminism first "went public" in the area in 1974 when a nascent local chapter of NOW marched through the main shopping mall with petitions for the ERA. The next year, a statewide coalition of preexistent women's groups—the YWCA, the AAUW, the Business and Professional Women's Organization, the League of Women Voters—joined with NOW and ran a successful lobbying campaign for passage of the ERA. That same coalition, under the auspices of the three universities in the Fargo area, sponsored a series of public lectures during 1975–76, which Kay took responsibility for organizing. The events covered a range of issues from "morality and others," to "self-determination," to "the family and the law," as well as theater and art events featuring local talent. Entitled "A Declaration of Interdependence," each lecture featured a prominent national feminist figure, such as Betty Friedan or Elizabeth Janeway, along with a local counterpart. In their structure and substance, the events drew connections between national feminist concerns and those of women in the Upper Midwest, as the following statement of intent demonstrates.

The legacy of the Plains begins with the pioneer woman's influence on the land; it is sustained by women's accomplishments in the home and the community, and the impact of women workers on our industries and institutions within our society; it requires the recovery of women as a natural resource. These are the qualities we celebrate in the year of our Bicentennial and Commemoration of International Women's Year.

The series drew ever-increasing crowds; for the organizers, the excitement of the momentum was such that "when the series was over we couldn't let go, and the Baker's Women's Center emerged out of that in the fall of 1976." Statements from the founders of the Baker's Center give a sense of how the women in Fargo were further differentiating their local interpretation of feminism, tied to domestic concerns, from more radical forms.

We are feminists, but we are not rabble-rousing bra burners. We named the group the Baker's Center for Women because we are also feminine and the idea of baking bread is very woman oriented. It also has a spiritual meaning in the sense of breaking bread together, a communion of people with similar needs.

This kind of rhetoric, along with the Center's location at the United Campus Ministry, emphasized the local feminists' insistence on symbolic connections with home, family, and religion. Their selection and accommodation of ideologies to fit their own "practical consciousness" and the social organization of local life allowed them to be effective in achieving at least some of their goals. For example, between 1977 and 1983, a Rape and Abuse Crisis Center grew from a two-person counterculture operation to a well-respected service agency with a staff of ten and an annual budget of $265,000, raised mostly through local philanthropy. As the Center's Executive Director explained:

Our evolution and sensibility fits in with the women's movement here. The Rape Center was identified as feminist to the degree that I would hear a group of businessmen at a restaurant talking about "the amazons who work at the rape center." But there was another blend, which is why the Center made it, of normalcy, of common people strong in their beliefs about feminism but who managed not to turn people off. So community support has really grown. Rape is an easy issue here compared to abortion.

The sketch is intended not only to show the context out of which pro-choice support came; it also indicates that local opposition to abortion was not necessarily seen as antifeminist as it was locally defined. As one feminist activist explained to me:

There is no issue in the women's movement in which I can more readily accept opposition. If someone starts having opposing views on any other issue, I question their support for feminism. The issue of abortion is one where I can tolerate dissension.

Thus, even among ardent feminist activists in Fargo, abortion sometimes drew ambivalent reactions.

In Kay's view, the explanation for the lack of pro-choice support was more simple: even people who felt strongly on the subject were unaware, for the most part, that abortion services were still essentially as unavailable locally in 1980 as they had been prior to legalization. The woman who eventually became the president of the pro-choice group that formed in 1981 described her own misconceptions:

By the time in 1973 when I understood that abortion was legal, I thought you could just go to the Fargo Clinic and get one and I thought great. It's covered by health insurance. It's finally a normal procedure and people understood the need for it.

By the mid-1970s the lack of abortion services and the increasing success of right-to-life efforts to restrict them became more publicly visible. In 1977, the Hyde amendment banning the use of Medicaid funds for abortion passed in Congress. That same year in North Dakota, the state's actions to inhibit even abortion referrals motivated Kay to action. She remembered:

I was out at the state legislature in 1977 testifying against a bill to block federal money from any agency making abortion referrals. I was so pissed off when the bill passed that I went back and listed my home phone number as the Abortion Referral of North Dakota. I did a lot of abortion referrals. And one of the reasons I became so committed to opening something here was people would just call over the phone and say, "Why isn't there something like this available in Fargo?" And the more I got those phone calls, the more I thought something has to be done about this.

Because support from feminists or physicians in Fargo was not forthcoming, Kay's access to expertise and resources outside the local arena was essential to accomplishing her larger goals. Her role as state coordinator for NARAL provided those connections as well as shifting her framework for activism from the political to the medical arena.

Through my involvement with the national organization, it became clear to me that it is a political issue as much as everybody would rather it would not be. And lobbying is not effective unless you have people there who are sympathetic to your point of view. You can talk your head off to the conservatives in the North Dakota state legislature and it doesn't do any good. Anyway, while I was on the NARAL Board, I met Sharon [who had been setting up clinics in small cities throughout the country] and I said, "Gee, if you ever want to come to Fargo let me know." And lo and behold, two years later, in 1979, I got this phone call. "My assistant has done some research and we're really interested in coming to Fargo. Would you be interested in working with us? Without somebody like you, it's not even worth it."

In 1979, Kay began working to set up the clinic. As has been the case for other clinics in small metropolitan areas, one of the most difficult steps was finding a location. Between 1977 and 1979, eight abortion clinics (seven in the Midwest) had been hit by fires. No one in the area wanted to take the risk of doing business with an abortion clinic. Finally, after two years of searching, Kay and Sharon found an old house that they could renovate into a clinic. To keep the owner anonymous, the business was conducted through a blind trust. The local work crews were not informed of the eventual use of the building. Sharon's prior experience in setting up clinics convinced her that as soon as word was out that an abortion clinic was in the works, pro-life people would attempt to bring zoning restrictions against it in order to stop it. Her fears proved to be justified.

The Pro-Life Actors

A veteran of the right-to-life activity around the 1972 referendum recounted to me with some delight how she found out about the clinic through the crisscross of social networks that characterizes Fargo. Her discovery catalyzed the second wave of pro-life activism in Fargo that endures into the present.

John called me up and said, "Corinne, there's an abortion clinic going up in Fargo. My friend who's a doctor at . . . called me up and told me he was approached by an organization wanting to know if they would take care of any girls that needed to be hospitalized." So I said, "Let's start digging. Let's go down to City Hall and see if there are any building permits." I knew they would never list it as an abortion clinic, so I looked at anything that sounded suspicious. I picked the building and I hung around but I couldn't get anything out of the guys remodeling the building. So I asked who was doing the plumbing and the guy was the father of a friend of mine from pro-life. So she got the blueprints and it was obvious then. So we decided, ok, we're gonna form a group. And that's how it all got started.

About a month before the clinic was scheduled to open, a variety of local people opposed to abortion formed a coalition called LIFE— Life Is For Everyone—led by Linda Anderson. Born and raised on a Midwestern farm, Linda is now the wife of a farmer and part-time salesman, a man she met in college in 1973 where they were both involved in the youth division of the NRLC, Save Our Unwanted Lives (SOUL). As a devout Catholic, Linda believes the taking of any innocent human life is wrong, but she sees abortion as a special case linked to broader concerns. Like most of the other pro-life activists in Fargo, she takes the legalization of abortion as a sign of growing narcissism in American society, symbolized by the unwillingness of women to carry an unwanted pregnancy to term.

I think it says an awful lot about our society, an awful lot. You know, when we hear about the "me-ism" concept, this is typical of the abortion issue. Sure it may not be easy to carry a pregnancy through nine months, but here again, are you thinking only of yourself or are you thinking of your unborn child? The decision whether or not to have that child should be made before the woman is pregnant. If she does not want to have a child, then she should take steps so that she does not have a child. If she does get pregnant, then she better be able to accept the responsibility of carrying that child to term and not taking that child's life.

Linda taught home economics and then served as a banquet director at a local hotel until the birth of her first child. By 1983, she had two children and a third on the way. Her time was filled with childcare and running the farm with her husband. As president of LIFE, Linda supervised a board, small office staff, and volunteers and served as public spokesperson for the group.

The mobilization of local pro-life sentiment around the clinic made it clear how much the right-to-life movement had changed since the referendum ten years earlier. While the Catholic Church had played a primary role in 1972, by 1981 the organizing was carried out by leaders of local right-to-life chapters. The NDRLC had been holding state conventions every autumn since 1978 in different cities throughout the state. While these events had little immediate political effect, they served to consolidate networks, provide training for people, and refine the "pro-life position" among members. When the convention was held in Fargo in 1980, the event was organized by Ann and Linda, leaders in the local Right-to-Life chapter and founders of LIFE Coalition. As Ann explained to me,

Linda and I had our baptismal fire at that convention. We went to the national convention that year in Omaha to see the kinds of things they talked about and types of programs we should cover. And then I've gone a few times to the national Board meetings and so I really learned a lot.

The skills they gained and networks they built through organizing the 1980 convention were critical to the successful mobilization of LIFE Coalition in 1981. Rather than the male professionals who had been the core of the early right-to-life opposition, the majority of the members of the group opposing the clinic was female.

The "Backstage" of Local Pro-Life Activism

While at the surface level the LIFE Coalition appeared to have emerged wholly in response to the clinic, it must be understood in the context of the consolidation of the Right-to-Life movement, the rise of a new political conservatism including antifeminism, and the growth and spread of born-again Christianity.

By 1981, the abortion issue had been associated increasingly with a growing conservative antifeminist movement, the emergence of which was clearly marked in 1977 at the International Women's Year (IWY) Conference in Houston, Texas. The Fargo delegation to that event included both pro-choice and pro-life activists. At the conference itself, nearly 25 percent of the delegates were opposed to at least some portion of the proposed feminist agenda and offended by its claims to represent the interests of *all* women.

A similar enactment of these growing divisions among women on the abortion issue occurred at the 1980 White House Conference on Families. The following passage from a Fargo pro-life activist who attended the conference illustrates how in the process of voicing her concerns, she found herself pushed into an antifeminist camp and, as a result, excluded from prior liberal political associations.

In 1980, I was elected to be a delegate to the White House Conference on Families. I was put on a state committee and we just did brain-frying things trying to work out these issues on abortion. And we went back and forth and back and forth. Our committee turned out to be pretty close, fifty-fifty, you know. But I tell you after three days at the state level and going on to the national level, I really drew my opinions on it.

You know, I strongly believe in equal opportunity for women. And I

didn't like being labeled at this White House Conference that I was
against all these rights for women just because I took this stand on abortion.

This anecdote reveals the kind of processes through which the
right-to-life activists came to be indentified as antifeminist, despite
diverging sentiments. All of this was made more complex by the
fact that Fargo's feminists had achieved many of their initial goals.
By 1979, Fargo had an excellent rape and abuse center, a women's
studies curriculum at the university, two daycare centers for low-
income women, several gay and lesbian groups, a women's health
hotline, and, by 1981, an abortion clinic. Although this represented a major accomplishment, for many of the younger women,
the institutions that feminists had struggled to establish over the
past decade were now taken for granted. Feminism was identified,
more often than not, with its reconstruction in the popular media, in
the image of the young, single, upwardly mobile corporate woman.
The conflation of the right-to-life and right-wing positions persists
due to the public distortions of feminism, the difficulty of placing a
right-to-life position within a feminist or liberal program, and the
high public visibility of people like Phyllis Schlafly, although many
pro-life activists do not share her views on other issues. Still, a
small but vocal minority consider their pro-life stance part of a
more general political position philosophically consistent with feminist principles.[1] For example, the following is an excerpt from a col-
umn entitled "True Feminism is Pro-Life" and signed "Feminists
for Life" in the July 1985 LIFE Coalition Newsletter.

Feminism has done much to improve women's lives. Abortion's quick-fix
cure may appear to solve immediate problems, but it leaves worse problems in its wake. We could develop more loving and permanent solutions
through a stronger feminism which avoids placing women in an adversary
relationship with their children, one that celebrates women's ability to
give birth, and one that loves and nurtures every human being, especially
the defenseless.

While support from antifeminist camps was ambivalently received, the success of the right-to-life push in Fargo was aided by
the development of Evangelical Christian activity—what has come
to be known as the New Christian Right—which had taken root
and grown in the area as it had in the rest of the country (Shupe
and Bromley 1984).

In Fargo, this new style of worship was introduced informally as people, and especially women, from mainline congregations began to join and form prayer groups during the late 1970s. These groups were based primarily either at the block or neighborhood level, or through local chapters of national organizations such as Women Aglow.[2] The groups emphasize healing, personal growth, and solving problems such as marital stress, alcoholism, and indebtedness.[3]

Initially the local clerical establishment looked askance at the developing prayer groups. In their membership, they violated what had been strictly maintained boundaries between different denominations, such as Lutherans and Catholics. In their worship style, they promoted practices—such as speaking in tongues and laying on of hands—that were viewed with suspicion, perhaps because of the potential such behavior holds for subverting traditional lines of authority. The popularity of the movement was such, however, that the mainline congregations, nervous that they were losing adherents, began to incorporate charismatic worship style and other related innovations into their own religious practice. By the late 1970s, these groups began to have a more formal presence as memberships in Evangelical and Pentecostal churches began to swell.[4]

The increased visibility of Fundamental and Evangelical Christianity was due not only to increasing membership but to their entry into the political arena as well, on issues such as abortion. In 1980, a number of Fargo right-to-life leaders made an effort to bring one of the influential pastors of the new and growing Assemblies of God congregation into the pro-life ranks. By his own report, the pastor was "converted" to the right-to-life cause after one screening of what has been, until recently, their central film, *Assignment: Life*.[5]

I saw the film *Assignment: Life* and it really shook me up. I didn't even know what right-to-life was about. [Before that] I thought it was a Catholic issue. I showed the film to twenty-two Evangelical ministers here. We reached two thousand people in three showings. When we showed it here, we got a lot of attention. We had pro-choice pickets outside. The media was here. That was great. I like controversy. . . .

As I began to speak out, women would come to me about their problem pregnancies. From doing that, I've grown to hate abortions. And it looks like with the Supreme Court [decisions of 1983] it will become more common. I was fighting it so strongly when the clinic came and there was no way we could stop them. I've learned to accept that it's here and we have to help. We try and build our ministry around needs and that includes the abortion issue.

While his church held no official position on the issue, the fact that this pastor joined the board of LIFE Coalition marked his congregation, unofficially, as a central antiabortion constituency.

Many analyses of the pro-life movement attribute much of its growth and appeal to the urgings of Christian leadership, yet the Fargo case suggests a more complex cause-and-effect relationship. Most of the pro-life activists in Fargo who converted to born-again Christianity did so *after* they had developed a strong commitment to the right-to-life cause. The explanation most often given for the switch in religious affiliation was that these churches took a stronger stand against abortion than their former congregations. This claim was made by former Catholics who became Evangelicals, and in cases where pastors only took a stand on the abortion issue *after* much pressure from right-to-life members who had recently joined the church. One local pro-life woman who left a mainline Lutheran church to join an Evangelical counterpart described this process:

You know, the Pentecostal churches are the fastest growing in the nation—the Evangelicals and the Assemblies of God. And that's true for this area. And it's funny. When LIFE Coalition formed, it was the first time a lot of people from other religions had any contact with Assemblies of God. And some of our good pro-lifers that were Catholic joined the Assemblies at the time that all this was emerging. Like a lot of pro-lifers, I've come to find I'm very conservative with my religion, but I'm very liberal with my political views.

Well, we [she and her husband] joined the Evangelical church and at the same time, the Evangelical community was claiming to be more pro-life. National Christian leaders like Dobson, LaHaye, Schaeffer, and Koop have spoken out enough to say you gotta get involved. In our area alone, in the last couple of years, the biggest amount of our speaking engagements has been for the Evangelicals.

As is the case nationally, this unprecedented alliance around abortion among evangelical Christians, Catholics, and certain mainline Protestant denominations is not particularly solid. On the one hand, "church-hopping" is now frequent and has brought with it an increased tolerance among lay people that was unheard of twenty years ago when Catholic and Lutheran clergy were hesitant even to converse in public together. At the same time, this phenomenon has bred competition for congregants as the Assemblies of God and other born-again congregations draw members away from other churches. In addition, considerable tension persists not only due to competition, but also because of marked differences in political styles and strategies. The pastor of the Assemblies of God clearly understood how these other factors entered into the rather shaky coalition over abortion he maintained with other parts of the community.

I'm a pawn for LIFE Coalition because I'm an Evangelical and they want to expand their base. But we're very aggressive and they perceive us as taking over things. I like the conflict. We're proud of it. LIFE Coalition isn't used to that.

While the pastor of the Assemblies of God views his approach as courageous, the head of the pro-life division of the Catholic diocese sees the Evangelicals as politically naive and potentially undermining in their crusading enthusiasm. In the view of this priest:

We work with First Assemblies. They used to have their own antiabortion group two years ago [1980]. They disbanded it when we formed LIFE Coalition. The alliance is thin. Politically, they are novices. They are so hep on stopping the clinic. We know we are beat from the legal point of view. But we thought we could expose them [the clinic workers] to the public. I feel very good about what we've done. We've had a lot of effect and not come off as condemning or as rabble rousers, but as caring people.

Tensions between the two groups have flared up periodically, particularly since 1983. However, in 1981, in the immediate crisis around the clinic opening, the differences between the "mainstream" right-to-lifers and the Evangelicals were momentarily submerged in the initial press for unity.

From Breach to Crisis: The Clinic Opening

Before the clinic had been opened, the breach between opposing interests escalated to a crisis. LIFE Coalition challenged the clinic's legitimacy by bringing a petition to the City Commission. They requested that the Commission revoke the yet-to-be-opened clinic's building permit on the grounds that abortion had not initially been listed as one of the services it would offer. One of LIFE's Board members described to me how the petition served to generate broad pro-life support in the community, even among those who had not been mobilized previously:

The clinic was the first thing that really brought everybody together. We contacted all the different leaders of the pro-life movement that had their own offices to attend the City Commission meeting. There must have been seven hundred people at that first meeting. We passed out petitions and got signatures there and that was our first mailing list. That's what we call "hallway recruiting." So Linda organized the names, Corinne worked on getting volunteers, and I organized the prayer vigil outside the clinic building. And it was amazing. It had been completely unorganized and then everybody came together. So we opened up about the same time the clinic did. At first, you have the spirit and you don't have the form, and then you have the form and the spirit.

The four-member City Commission voted on the petition in the absence of the mayor, a liberal Democrat who had received substantial support from feminist groups in his election campaign. The vote to revoke the clinic's building permit was two to one, with one abstention. When the mayor returned from out of town the following day, he immediately reinstated the permit. He declared the clinic was fully legal under federal and state law. Discriminatory enforcement of local regulations, he argued, would simply involve the city in a costly, dead-end lawsuit. The members of LIFE Coalition, stymied by the actions of their mayor—a Presbyterian from rural Iowa who is now an economics professor and father of two—predicted his defeat in the mayoral elections six months away.

In the meantime, a second pro-life force emerged. A team of two self-styled Evangelists calling themselves Partners in Vision published a full-page advertisement in a biweekly shopper, denouncing abortion. They asked for contributions for their efforts and a citywide vote on abortion. The Partners then sent letters to fifty-seven hundred business people and professionals, asking them to send money and cast a vote on abortion using a ballot enclosed in the mailing. The last sentence of their letter implied that votes would be made public:

Your failure to respond may be considered as unconcern and a vote in favor of the abortion clinic by the general public.

The editorial run by the Fargo daily newspaper summed up the generally angry response to such tactics.

Our paper has traditionally been opposed to abortion on demand and we continue that policy strongly. But we are opposed to this effort to force a certain segment of our community to express personal views on a moral subject that has nothing to do with their professions or businesses.

All persons have a right to their private views and should not be penalized for exercising that right. This episode has been unfair to those persons who have sincerely objected to the clinic and expressed that displeasure in measured and lawful forms. (Fargo Forum, October 20, 1981)

By dramatizing the mailing as a violation of privacy in the sphere of commerce while applauding "measured and lawful" pro-life protest, the editorial helped to crystallize opposition to Partners in Vision on the part of LIFE Coalition's membership.

More generally, the incident demonstrated how the struggle to gain control over the presentation and interpretation of the abortion issue was occurring as much *within* the local pro-life movement as between it and pro-choice forces. The reaction of LIFE's members to Partners in Vision made clear not only the thinly veiled struggle between the "mainstream" and born-again Christian style and strategy. The pejorative depiction of the Partners as "outsiders" allowed LIFE members to distance themselves from the two. One of the LIFE Coalition leaders explained the situation to me:

They're not part of us. We can't disclaim them too much because it looks like you're disclaiming your own basic principles. We just didn't give them much support or rally to their cause. They might have had their hearts in the right place, but they certainly didn't have their heads in reality. They sincerely believe in the issue, but they're using it to promote themselves. The national media would have taken them and made them the whole story. These two were disassociated people who created a lot of media hype but had no roots. A lot of people who supported them were disappointed that it wasn't going into the mainstream movement. It taught us something though. They could reach a certain element that we hadn't directed ourselves to.

The Partners had only shallow roots in the community and were looked on with some suspicion by the more established residents of Fargo who make up the ranks of LIFE. One Partner, Richard Hilgard, a resident of the area since the late 1970s, was reportedly a salaried special assistant to Jerry Falwell. The other, who had revamped an old tobacco shop into a Christian coffee house he called the Holy Smoke Shop, had only recently settled in town. Because they were relative newcomers to the area, and acted in ways that violated norms of appropriate behavior, Partners in Vision could not command authority as representatives of community sentiment. Thus, they were dangerous to LIFE Coalition insofar as they discredited the latter's efforts to achieve legitimacy through community support and control.

The Pro-Choice Actors

If the activities of Partners in Vision rallied anyone, it was, ironically, their pro-choice opponents. A group calling itself Citizens for a Real Choice (CRC) took out a full-page newspaper advertisement, a statement defending the clinic with over two thousand signatures. Initially, the spokesperson for CRC was Janice Sundstrom, a professional woman active in state and local politics who took a considerable career risk in embracing a public pro-choice stand. Although her current social position and commitment to feminism fit the stereotype that both right-to-life advocates and some social scientists have of pro-choice women, there was little in Janice's early personal biography that would distinguish her from local pro-life women. She grew up in the area, in a family that lost its farm during her childhood. A year after completing Catholic high school, she married her "steady," a man who now works as an accountant. When she became pregnant, Janice dropped out of college to raise her first and then her second daughter. Ten years ago, with her interest in politics growing, she went back to school and eventually earned her law degree. Her abortion activism frames a transformation in self as she came to identify herself with a particular understanding of the collective needs and interests of women, almost a complete reversal of the views she had as a young woman.

I was raised a Catholic and was much opposed to abortion and somehow between 1968 and 1971 . . . I came to realize that women were going to have abortions whether they're legal or not. And unless they're legal, some women will die in the process. My change in attitude, my personal feeling about abortion, grew out of a sensitivity to the place of women in this society.

Although there were no abortion rights groups in place in Fargo in 1981, CRC was able to mobilize almost as rapidly as their LIFE counterparts by tapping into preexisting networks. Formally, these included the numerous feminist groups that had consolidated during the mid 1970s, and the traditionally liberal organizations that had supported the 1972 referendum such as the ACLU, YWCA, and AAUW. Informally, pro-choice activists mobilized friends and kin who had been passive supporters of abortion rights to "go public" in a moment of crisis. The following sentiments, voiced in this recollection by a college librarian who was mobilized to support the clinic, are typical:

When the health clinic controversy came up, it just picked me up and motivated me to get involved. It was a topic of discussion in various groups I attended, like NOW and the Women's Equity Group at the university. And I'd known Kay [Bellevue] through political work. So I got in there very quickly; I was on the original board. But for a while, it was very ad hoc, just a group of concerned people. I was getting signatures for the ad, getting money. There was lots of discussion about what we should do, a big push for going public with our side, letting people who read *The Fargo Forum* [the local daily newspaper] know there are people who are pro-choice. The clinic really needed support then. I guess I first thought of myself as a woman. But the whole born-again movement and this legislating morality, none of that sits too well with me either.

As activists on both sides escalated their campaigns in Fargo, abortion became the topic of countless Sunday sermons and Rotary Club luncheons. Each side dramatically enacted their claims to both religious and secular authority. LIFE Coalition held a rally of four hundred people who marched around City Hall singing patriotic songs, culminating in prayers and a performance by Evangelical musicians. The following Sunday, CRC sponsored an ecumenical prayer service at the university, featuring Gloria Steinem as a speaker. These events served as an assertion not only of a view of abortion, but the relationship of that position to the "community" and who has the authority to define it. In the ongoing claims made by either side, it is not only abortion but Fargo as well that figures constantly as a contested symbolic domain. The following statements made to the press by leaders from each side after the

City Commission vote are illustrative. According to a spokesperson for LIFE Coalition,

Obviously, as far as we're concerned, this is a tragic thing to happen to our fine city. We have been able to avoid it for so long, but it's here now and it really is tragic.

A CRC member claimed:

This represents some real long-term kind of damage to this community. This type of political activity is among the most dangerous, the kind that affects people's relationships with their friends and neighbors for years and even generations to come.

Thus, each group portrays itself as people fighting against trends in American culture being imposed on them, from which their own identity is drawn by contrast. Both sides balance a complicated position of sustaining, simultaneously, an oppositional stance toward a particular vision of American culture and an assumption that their position represented the "true" interests of the local citizenry.

Redressive Acts: Divisions Defined

Despite all the controversy, the clinic opened on October 1, 1981, with only a silent prayer vigil outside, a protest that LIFE members have maintained faithfully ever since, even through the coldest winter on record in North Dakota. Two weeks later, a last effort was made by Partners in Vision to stop the clinic. A petition with eight signatures was presented to the City Commission by an attorney hired by Partners, requesting that the clinic be closed until public hearings could be held to establish local rules for its operation. Just before Thanksgiving, in front of an expectant and divided crowd, the City Commission voted unanimously to deny the petition. Their vote affirmed the position of the mayor and, in a sense, presaged his reelection in April 1982. Pro-life forces were unable to find a candidate to run against the incumbent.

The Commission vote served as a redressive action: it quelled the conflict over the abortion clinic only momentarily. In fact, the leaders of LIFE Coalition were aware that they were likely to lose the battle with the City Commission in terms of its stated goal. However, they saw it, retrospectively at least, as a valuable performance of their position to the community in general. Linda Anderson explained:

Our big problem when the facility opened was that people thought we could stop it. Your most important asset is time in a movement like this because you know the issues. If they see us as strident and antagonistic, the person in the middle will go to the other side. Education is the thing.

The Commission vote was important not only to "educate" people. It also rallied new people to the pro-life cause. During the period of the City Commission hearings, LIFE rapidly built their membership to over one thousand. Organizationally, they formed a board representing various pro-life groups in the community, opened an office, started a newsletter, and began to concentrate on public speaking and gaining a good public image.

The continual regression to crisis that characterized the controversy over the clinic in Fargo is typical of social dramas. However, the contestants are not doomed to repeat endlessly the same dramatic enactment of opposition. As temporal structures, such phased contests are tentative in their resolution and open to new possibilities as long as alternative goals and means of attaining them are possible. With committed activists and a well-organized infrastructure in place, Fargo's right-to-life proponents altered their tactics to meet new conditions, both locally and nationally, in their struggle to stop abortions.

Chapter Six

Interpretive Battlegrounds

Reframing the Clinic: Prayer Vigilantes

During the course of my prayer vigil, I asked God to tell me how he wanted me to pray. After this, the Lord showed me the house—the Abortion Clinic—wrapped in barbed wire. I meditated on the meaning of this, how impossible it would be to enter it if it were bound in this way. Then the wire turned into a crown of thorns, some red with the blood of Jesus. The words came to mind—"My love can close those doors." The prayers of the faithful can bring love to bear. ("Thoughts about Prayer," *LIFE Coalition Newsletter*, December 1981)

These words are the thoughts of a LIFE Coalition member as she prayed in front of the abortion clinic shortly after the City Commission vote. She, like many of Fargo's right-to-life activists who recognized they were unlikely to get rid of the unwanted but legal clinic directly, became determined to gain control over its interpretation. Although the initial battle made the clinic and its opponents into a local cause célèbre and polarized many of Fargo's citizens, the pro-life efforts to close the clinic were unsuccessful. Having tried and failed in the formal political and legal arena, LIFE Coalition members shifted their goals and behavior. Their protest was restaged in the physical environment of the clinic itself.

As with any political controversy in a complex society, the abortion debate changes quickly as both the local and national situation changes. The particular activities discussed here occurred between 1981 and 1983. They were carried out by the key pro-life players at that time, activists who advocated a moderate political approach and were associated with mainstream churches and social institutions. The developments show how the symbolic and material transformations of cultural and social understandings of the pregnant woman in the abortion debate were being reconstituted in the local arena.

The Prayer Vigil

The staple of LIFE Coalition's activities against the clinic in its first year was called the "Prayer Vigil." Pro-life volunteers dedicated at least two hours a week to this action, which entailed walking back and forth along the sidewalk in front of the clinic, praying silently, often with a Bible in hand. Those who participated called themselves "Prayer Vigilantes." They described their actions as "a sacrifice on our part to show the outcry of concern we have over the death chamber in Fargo." Their stated intention, then, was to mark the clinic's presence and offer an alternative interpretation of its activities to passersby. Through the vigil, the pro-life activists launched an effort to reframe the clinic as an arena beyond social boundaries by maintaining an oppositional presence on the edge of the building's property.

Despite its public aspects, the prayer vigil drew little general attention for several reasons. The clinic is on a side street that gets little traffic. Because their presence is so regular and generally low-key, the protesters were considered unremarkable by most Fargo citizens. Rather than become more disruptive in order to attract attention, LIFE Coalition members emphasized their larger goal of developing a reputation for moderation over attracting publicity. This is evident, for example, in the following list of instructions given for the "Peaceful Prayer Walk."

1. This is a 2 person vigil of prayer only, not a demonstration.
2. Pray silently and unobtrusively.
3. Stay on sidewalk—keep moving—do not get in anyone's way.
4. DO NOT: Argue, explain, discuss, answer questions with anyone including press. (If the press comes say only that you'll talk to them at another location when you are finished.)
5. Do nothing demonstrative except walk and pray—no signs or gestures.

6. Do not congregate—2 cars for 2 people.
7. Do not cross the boulevard, grass, etc. Stay on sidewalk.

WE ARE CALLED TO LOVE

The vigil seemed to be effective less as an outward sign to the community, and more as a means of generating internal conviction and support among activists and, in particular, new recruits. One could see this in a number of ways. Almost every issue of LIFE Coalition's monthly newsletter had a short piece on the subjective experience of the vigil in which the prominent themes are critical life choices for women, and women's responsibilities for each others' actions. The following selection is exemplary. In it, the speaker frames the experiences of "the girls" seeking abortions and the counselors who advise them at the clinic in terms of her own sister's difficult life and death.

About 4 weeks to the day before Christmas, I was walking my usual time (from 10 to 11 a.m.) on the Prayer Vigil. I was alone as I usually am on the walk. I had been reading my prayer book and had been reflecting on life as a whole and the importance of each person's life—the hard things we go through, the joys—and all the help we need from each other. My oldest sister had just died on November 7. She had just dropped dead. I was missing her and thinking of her life which included tragedy and much suffering on her part. In spite of her hardships, I thought of her faith in God, her strengths and also her failings and guilt that resulted from these weaknesses.

I then thought about the girls and families where mistakes had been made and these girls were being counselled and having abortions as I was walking there in front of the place where this was going on. I thought about the counsellors. I prayed for all concerned and prayed especially that counsellors were doing just that—a thorough job—and my, what a disservice to the girls if life is treated lightly. Each girl's life is so important that decisions made are of utter importance. She has to live her life the day, or month or year after the counsellor has sat across from a desk and said "whatever." Anyhow, these were my thoughts that morning. ("A Walk in November," *LIFE Coalition Newsletter*, January 1982)

Like Christian conversion testimonies, such narratives serve multiple purposes, simultaneously constituting both the group and the individual's place within it. They provide a vehicle for each participant to infuse the prayer vigil with personal meaning by constructing a narrative that links his or her life to both the goals of the movement and the actual situation encountered in front of the clinic. The testimonies are not only instrumental, providing an activity that sustains interest and activist support; actors consider their prayers to be effective in and of themselves. One woman described her view of the power of prayer in political action:

Prayer is one method of attack and the others—whether legislation, rallies, counseling, personal opinion offered at a crucial time—are all made more effective if prefaced by prayer.

For those who utter and hear the prayers, the very act of praying is transformative. Linda explained its significance to me:

We really believe prayer is one of the most changing things in our society. It's a totally different thing to be in the presence of the abortion facility and the evil performed there. You are battling the evil force and it is draining.

Thus, through the prayer vigil, the area around the clinic was no longer simply a sidewalk, lawn, and entryway but became a highly charged battleground for the interpretation of abortion. Unable to make abortion illegal, LIFE activists were attempting to redefine it, through their words and actions, as "unnatural." The actions of prayer vigilantes were directed at stigmatizing not only the physical site of abortion but also the clinic's clientele who had to encounter protesters in order to have access to abortion. The protests in front of the Fargo clinic became, in a sense, a mise-en-scène ever ready for the potential drama to occur when a woman, influenced by the prayers and actions of pro-life protesters, might change her mind about abortion and, more generally, her understanding of pregnancy in relation to female identity.

Reframing Unwanted Pregnancy

On the first anniversary of the clinic's opening, LIFE Coalition members decided to escalate their activities in response to internal criticisms that they were not being sufficiently active in fighting the clinic, and to external accusations that they showed no compassion for the women seeking abortions. The pro-choice critique pushed LIFE leaders to new actions; they shifted from simply redefining the clinic to addressing the pregnant women choosing abortion.

The Coalition hired a "problem pregnancy counselor" and organized what they call a "sidewalk counseling program." Sidewalk
counselors behave very much like the prayer vigilantes; they walk
quietly, usually in twos, back and forth in front of the clinic. In addition, they approach people entering the clinic, give them literature, and suggest that they think about alternatives to abortion. By
handing out business cards with LIFE Coalition's telephone number, counselors convey that they can offer legitimate sources of
emotional and material support for carrying an unwanted pregnancy to term. If the counselors can engage a woman in conversation, they suggest talking over the decision at a nearby coffee
shop—named, coincidentally, "Mom's." Generally, encounters in
which the woman changes her mind about the abortion are unusual. Indeed, in 1983, when a woman whom the clinic had turned
away because of her ambivalence accepted assistance from a sidewalk counselor, it was a local news item for a week.

Despite the difficulty in achieving their stated goals of reaching
women using the clinic, LIFE puts considerable time and effort
into the counseling endeavor nonetheless. The sidewalk counselor
coordinator described the work involved:

The prayer vigil only requires one or two workshops a year. The counselors have a much more involved process of training. They need workshops, meetings, phone calls, baby-sitting services. The workshops are vital. They provide support, and generate enthusiasm, and we have to
constantly train new people. Mostly they come through other volunteers.
The kind of person who works best is someone who is pro-life but really
feels for the woman. Someone who is super antiabortion can't do it.

Thus, the very form of LIFE's recruitment and activism tends to
generate a more moderate membership. The sidewalk counseling
provides an effective vehicle for bringing in people (usually women)
who are pro-life but are neither vehement in their views nor inclined to more confrontational styles of political activism.

At the training workshops that I attended, at least half of those
present were new volunteers. The meetings usually had about ten
people, two of whom were LIFE staff or board people. Almost all
the trainees were women, usually in their mid to late twenties, and
generally friends of women already engaged in pro-life work who
had urged them to come. Little time was devoted either to coun-

seling technique or political strategy; rather, most of the talk centered on depicting and assigning meaning to the "other," the woman having the abortion. For example, at one meeting, the following typology was offered by LIFE's problem pregnancy counselor:

There are three types you encounter going to get abortions:
1. Women's libber: She needs a lot of education. She's hostile and cold.
2. Ambivalent type: She is conflicted and lets others make up her mind for her.
3. Ignorant: The kind that is really pro-life but doesn't know there is another way.

She then offered a broader interpretation of the meaning of abortion:

With Christianity came the acceptance of the child without it having to bear its father's sins. Abortion is a sign of a decline in the culture. I view it [abortion] as the rape of motherhood, of the gender, of the uterus, of the womb. If you think sex is natural, birth is even more natural. The first love you feel is for your mother. What is the furthest reach of the devil? Not murder, not sex, not rape. It's abortion.

In such discourse—a staple of these frequent, small, face-to-face meetings that maintain and generate pro-life membership—abortion is fused metaphorically with the imagery of decadence and destructive, usually male, sexuality, in this case "a decline in the culture" and "the rape of motherhood." By contrast, abortion is opposed to female experiences of pregnancy, birth, and maternity. The latter are cast as the domain of creation, innocence, pure motive, and nurturance—"the first love you feel is for your mother." In this logic, women who advocate legal abortion are misguided, if not immoral, because they violate boundaries between these domains and in that sense are not appropriately female in their actions.

The activity of sidewalk counseling thus promoted an interpretation of abortion and its meaning in relation to a particular construction of male and female gender that activists themselves felt obliged to uphold. The political performances in front of the clinic were constrained because of the demonstrators' need to display themselves according to this construction of feminine identity in which nurturant love was prominent. One of the pro-life leaders explained the dilemma to me in this way:

In the East, they have sit-ins. I doubt that we'd get women here to do that. The community would turn against us. The women have to deal with

their family and friends. Their husbands have to be supportive. I don't
think we'll ever turn around the situation. The most we can do is meet the
needs on a one-to-one basis. Educating people to know that abortion is
not the way. It's kind of like stirring the pot. We've started with what
we're doing. I don't want to picket out there cause we'll scare them. It's
the most we can do. If we picket we can't reach them. We've worked so
hard to prove we're loving and caring.

For LIFE Coalition members, conforming to their formulated image of moderation, compassion, and nurturance was at least equal
to, if not more important than, the more immediate objective of
stopping women from using the clinic.

The Problem Pregnancy Industry

In spring 1984, LIFE Coalition announced plans to open an "Abortion Action Affiliate (AAA) Problem Pregnancy Center" to back up
its sidewalk counseling campaign. That decision was also part of a
new emphasis in national pro-life strategy to promote "alternatives
to abortion" (*National Right to Life News*, January 12, 1984).[1] It indicated as well the increasing prominence of the "young unwed
mother" as a focus of concern in America since the legalization of
abortion in 1973. In Fargo, she was no longer the guilty social out-
cast to be shunned, but became the catalyst for community efforts
to develop sex education[2] and, most notably, the target of a small
and expanding "problem pregnancy industry." The industry was a
new focus of attention in the Fargo area not only with abortion activists but also among social service, voluntary, and governmental
agencies. Each group has a different understanding of the "problem" and the "solution."

In 1973, the main home for unwed mothers in town was closed
down due to disuse. That same year, a handful of pro-life veterans
of the 1972 referendum established a chapter of Birthright (see
chapter 4, n. 11) to help assist young women with unwanted pregnancies. At that time, Mary Mintz was the only professionally
trained counselor for problem pregnancies in Fargo. Ten years
later, in addition to Mary Mintz, three other professionally trained
"problem pregnancy counselors" were hired at church-related
agencies (Lutheran and Catholic). Two state-sponsored programs
offering nutritional, medical, and social support to pregnant single
women had been organized by the North Dakota State Council on

Problem Pregnancy (formed in 1982). A daycare center for single and poor mothers was for the first time receiving support from the United Way (although it had to redefine its purpose as "preventing juvenile delinquency"). In 1983, several support groups for single mothers sponsored by social service agencies were in place and the local Junior League began a community advocacy group for "school-age parents." A North Dakota chapter of Women Exploited by Abortion (WEBA)—a group "for women who have had an abortion, now realize it was the wrong decision and want to educate other women on the trauma of abortion"—started in 1984. By the end of that year, three pro-life groups—Birthright, LIFE, and a new group called Save-A-Baby—each had their own "problem pregnancy centers." By September 1985, a pro-life home for unwed mothers opened in a former boarding house. In short, over one decade, groups in Fargo dealing with teen-age and unwed mothers, including the abortion clinic, expanded from three to fourteen. During that same period, the number of unwed pregnant adolescents in North Dakota tripled, going from 428 to 1305.

What all this activity indicates is that teenage pregnancy has become, as some have suggested (Joffe 1987; Petchesky 1984), a signifier of sexual disorder, seen as a "social problem" in Fargo and America in general. In the United States, teenagers are approximately one-third of all abortion clients, while women aged twenty to twenty-four and mostly unmarried make up another third. The combination of the rise in teen pregnancy and the legalization of abortion has contributed to the creation of this new category of "problematic women."[3] In an article entitled "Women as a Social Problem," author Nancy Henley discusses how the construction of "problematic women" is an essential part of recent political action on "women's issues":

It is clear that for many of the women's issues to emerge in recent years, the process is one of *redefinition* as much as, or more than, definition. There are assertions of how to name and view a problem, what the "real" problem is, what is wrong with the old definition and so on. . . . Since the definition of a social problem is an important determinant of governmental actions, it is no wonder that inter-group conflict takes place over the definition. (1982: 15–16)

The sense of competition over this new category of "problematic women," defined and redefined, was readily apparent to those concerned with problem pregnancy in Fargo. It emerged in their talk as a kind of systematized social knowledge, what Giddens calls "discursive consciousness" (1979: 5).[4] At the LIFE board meeting when the plan for starting a center was first discussed, for example, the sense of this activity as an "expanding market" was explicit.

It's like a business. If they [the abortion clinic personnel] don't get enough clients, they'll have to close the doors.

The struggle to win both the actual clientele and the power to determine the outcome of unwanted pregnancies is not merely between pro-life and pro-choice activists. One social worker noted:

There really is competition between agencies. They don't admit it. Nobody says we're competing but we are. The bread and butter of this agency is adoption. Sixty-five percent of unwed girls opt to have abortions. And nearly 95 percent of the rest keep their babies who can. Very few release their babies for adoption. I want our agency to be the best and first, so of course I'm competitive.

The increasing competition divided constituents within the pro-life ranks as well. In its initial stages, LIFE had worked together with Birthright, which had been helping pregnant teens find "alternatives to abortion." Birthright had been the project of the first wave of local pro-life female activists, mostly older women, many newly widowed ten years ago. By 1983, most of them were in their mid to late sixties. New LIFE activists, primarily younger women more politically involved in the national right-to-life movement than their predecessors, became increasingly impatient with Birthright. In their view, it was too low-key, unprofessional, and insufficiently public in its local presence. As LIFE focused its efforts more and more on "reaching the woman," which is also Birthright's agenda, the conflict intensified. Under pressure from LIFE, Birthright hired a new director who was instructed to be more aggressive. She began to raise money actively and to advertise in the local paper and on radio stations.

In an attempt to enter the arena of professional social service workers who counseled pregnant teens in Fargo, Birthright also hung posters at some of the agencies in town. The reaction of social service worker Mary Mintz was similar to that of most of her colleagues. As Fargo's primary counselor for unwed mothers since the late 1960s, Mary was not sympathetic to any competition in the field.

I saw this Birthright poster and I tore it down immediately. And two weeks later there was another one. This time, I crumpled it up and put it in my drawer. My boss didn't understand and I had to explain. I said, "Gary, it's like advertising Chevrolets at a Ford dealer. It's another agency."

Despite Birthright's efforts, LIFE decided to go ahead with plans for its own Problem Pregnancy Center, which opened in August 1984. This meant increasing competition for sources of local support for pro-life work. This competition was apparent not only in their conflict with Birthright. A few months later, Richard Hilgard, one of the Evangelical Christian men who had started Partners in Vision, opened yet another pro-life pregnancy support center with his wife, backed by a group called Save-A-Baby; the Board of Directors was made up primarily of congregants from the Assemblies of God. Injury was added to insult when they named their center Life Clinic, a rather obvious attempt to benefit from the carefully cultivated reputation of LIFE Coalition. The LIFE board tried but was unable to stop this new effort, although they did persuade the "clinic" to change its name. The new name they chose for their pregnancy support center, the Women's Help Clinic of Fargo, resulted in a lawsuit filed by the Fargo Women's Health Organization. The abortion clinic claimed that the pro-life group selected a name similar to their own to deceive women into thinking that the Women's Help Clinic offered abortions.

With the other main pro-life counseling group embroiled in legal problems with the clinic, LIFE was determined to try and "control the market" and claims for legitimacy of pro-life alternatives to abortion. LIFE Coalition's Problem Pregnancy Center had few clients in its first year[5]—most were women who had mistaken it for the abortion clinic. Yet the Coalition's investment of time, energy, and money in such an endeavor is an indication that they locate the "problem" that leads to abortion in the ignorance of women with problem pregnancies. Phrased in terms of individual motivation, the woman who seeks an abortion is, to use one counselor's words, considered "confused, kind of weak, and uneducated" about the fetus.

This view that a pro-choice position is due to ignorance of fetal life is the key to the plot line of two of the main pro-life media pieces, the fifty-two-minute film *Assignment Life* and the twenty-eight-minute videotape *The Silent Scream*, released in the summer of 1984. During the time I was in Fargo, *Assignment Life* was shown at least once a month at some pro-life gathering. To judge by audience response, it had a lot of "shock value" for new recruits and solidified conviction among the converted.

Assignment Life is essentially a conversion tale. The main character, a young female journalist, reluctantly takes an assignment from her older male editor to cover the abortion issue. She proceeds on her investigation, conducting interviews with almost all the key leaders in the right-to-life movement, as well as "average women" such as a reformed prostitute, and a child who announces, "If abortion had been legal, I wouldn't be here." The reporter also visits a California gynecologist who allows her to film a suction abortion. At the end, she comes to the conclusion that abortion is murder. The structure of the film is a narrative model for the pro-life conviction that if a woman had proper knowledge of fetal life she would not choose to abort.

The Fetus as Symbol: Conversion, Sacrifice, and Redemption

The idea that knowledge of fetal life, and especially confrontation with the visual image of the fetus, will "convert" a woman to the pro-life position has been a central theme in both local and national right-to-life activism. A popular quip summarizes this position: "If there were a window on a pregnant woman's stomach, there would be no more abortions." This provided the logic underlying the introduction of the fetal image into pro-life political activities in the 1970s; its effectiveness was apparent in campaigns such as the 1972 Fargo referendum (see chapter 4).[6] Over a decade later, updated to the high technology common to the experience of pregnancy in the 1980s, the conversion power of the fetus remains the central element of the recent and very popular work entitled *The Silent Scream*. The tape shows an abortion "from the point of view of the unborn child" via sonogram imagery, a provocative reframing of a technology associated with confirmation of a desired pregnancy and, according to some, the formation of a maternal-fetal bond (Fletcher and Evans 1983).

One of the Biblical verses used in publicity for the 1985 North Dakota Right-to-Life Convention, "Rescue and Restore," underscored this idea that once the fetus is "seen," one has no choice but to become pro-life.

> Rescue those who are being taken to their death; and from those stagger-
> ing toward slaughter will you withhold yourself? If you say, "See we did
> not know this," does not the One who weighs hearts perceive it? And He
> who watches over the soul, does He not know and shall He not repay each
> man for his deeds? (Proverbs 24: 11–12)

As is the case in conversion, the assumption conveyed in the chosen quote is that once a potential convert witnesses a certain "truth" and comes "under conviction," there is only one path to follow (Harding 1987).

More generally, the right-to-life belief that conversion will take place after seeing the "truth" about abortion relies on the way that knowledge of the fetus is constructed. This requires attention to the formal dimensions of pro-life imagery. In their material, em-phasis on the fetus as "the unborn child" constitutes a "root meta-phor," a paradigm "from which many subsequent structures may be 'unpacked'" (Turner 1974: 51). Such symbolic frames produce

> a certain kind of polarization of meaning in which the subsidiary subject is
> really a depth world of prophetic, half-glimpsed images, and the principal
> subject, the visible, fully known (or thought to be fully known compo-
> nent) at the opposite pole to it, acquires new and surprising contours and
> valences from its dark companion. . . . Because the poles are "active to-
> gether" the unknown is brought just a little more into the light by the
> known. (Turner 1974: 51)

Right-to-life visual material offers two representations of the fetus that are continually "active together." The principal subject is the magnified image of the fetus—for example, floating intact inside the womb, or focused on tiny perfectly formed feet held between the thumb and forefinger of an adult. These pictures are usually in warm amber tones, suffused with soft light, rendered more myste-rious by their separation from the mother's body. Juxtaposed to these photographs are gruesome, harshly lit, clinical shots of muti-lated and bloody fetal remains "killed by abortions—what pro-life activists refer to as "the war pictures." Thus, the qualities evoked by the representations of the principal subject—the mystery of conception, warmth, unconditional nurturance, radical innocence, and maternity—are continually contrasted with visions of their possible violent destruction.

In the 1983 version of a popular slide show produced by National Right-to-Life Committee President Jack Wilke, the associations to these images were expanded to take on more explicit political meaning. The "war pictures" of the fetus are intercut with old news photos of Southeast Asian civilians burnt by napalm. These slides are accompanied by the following narration.

Do you remember Cambodia?

We ignored the genocide then until our nation saw the horror through our media. These horrible pictures woke people up.

There is another war going on today. This nation should also see the horror of that reality. Every citizen of this country should see what we call "the war pictures."

[The slide used at this point shows dead fetuses from late abortions piled in garbage cans; it then switches to a shot of a twenty-one-week-old fetus aborted by a saline injection[7] which turns the skin a shiny red color.]

We call this the candy-apple baby. The saline must feel like napalm. Neither the abortionist nor the bombardier saw their victim.

Through such symbolic constructions, the pro-life campaign casts those who ignore, support, or participate in abortion as unwitting war criminals. Through these analogies to war, the aborted fetus becomes a sacrifice offered for the redemption of America. This is demonstrated not only in verbal and visual media, but in other forms of symbolic action. At the 1985 North Dakota Right-to-Life Convention, a permanent memorial for "all of our nation's children who have died by abortion" was erected next to the War Veterans' Memorial. A local pro-life leader observed:

The symbolism was clear. More babies have died through abortion than in all the wars our country has fought. Abortion on demand is clearly the war on our unborn children. The veterans died to protect freedom everywhere, yet for the unborn there are no rights. A few yards from the grave-site also stands the flagpole with the American flag overhead.

Similarly, this analogy drawn between the aborted fetus and the fallen soldier as sources of redemptive power informed the following comments made to me by a sidewalk counselor on the Fourth of July:

Ask yourself this question. On the Fourth of July we celebrate all the people who died that we might have freedom. And I'm wondering if some of these children aren't dying so that we will appreciate life, marriage, and relationships more fully. To keep a sixteen-year-old from getting pregnant, she needs a good self-concept. If she has that, she won't get pregnant. If it makes us go back and think of that, it may not be in vain.

While the life and death polarities fixed on the fetus are expanded and conflated with historically specific meanings, they are often then taken out of historical time and place by analogy to Christian religious imagery. Explicitly or implicitly, the fetus is linked frequently to Jesus and the woman with the unwanted pregnancy is likened to Mary, as in a December 1986 article in the *AAA Problem Pregnancy Center Newsletter*, "Jesus Became a Fetus."

Luke's Gospel tells us that an angel named Gabriel visited a virgin named Mary and said, "Rejoice, O highly favored daughter. The Lord is with you . . . (Luke 1:28). . . .

How does Jesus feel about an abortion? Might Jesus have said, "For I was unborn and you killed me. I became a fetus, a little one, and you turned me into property." (Michael Gaworski, Pro-Life Action Ministries)

Thus, the battle over abortion is cast as one in which the sacrifices entailed in bearing an unwanted child will redeem those suffering from the unfortunate circumstances that are viewed as the cause of unwanted pregnancy. Through such processes, as is the case in any culture, meaning is constructed out of the struggles and everyday difficulties of social life.

The Liminal Subject: The Pregnant Woman

Given the increasing focus on "problem pregnancy" as the object of political struggle and social redefinition, the relatively small number of images of pregnant women in pro-life visual material is striking. This absence, I believe, is an index of the problematic position and shifting status of pregnancy in the abortion debate, and in understandings of female gender identity in America more generally. My argument draws on some well-known work in anthropological theory.

In American culture, as in many others, first birth is often consid-

ered a significant mark of a woman's transition to social adulthood. As
a condition that announces the pending transition, pregnancy has a
liminal status as a temporary condition placing a subject between
two structural states. The pregnant woman, especially in the case
of first conception, is "betwixt and between fixed points of classification," temporarily set apart from the structural arrangements of
the culture (Turner 1974: 232).

In the classic examples of rites of passage, the liminal subject or
initiate is usually secluded, hidden from public view, and only re-
gains visibility when he or she reenters the social system with a
new status—one that is more or less culturally predetermined. Re-
incorporation of the liminal person into the appropriate role serves
to legitimate, for the subject and observers, a particular interpretation of social reality as both necessary and irrefutable. A deviation
from that outcome is a serious violation because it exposes that
there could be alternative interpretations of not only a particular
situation, but the whole cultural order as well. Unexpected occurrences present the possibility that cultural categories and social arrangements could, in fact, be different.

For the pregnant woman, when abortion was illegal, the assumption was that her liminality would end when the woman gives
birth and is given the ascribed status of motherhood. Because de-
viations from that script were either hidden or punished, they confirmed the dominant discourse. With abortion legal and available,
the liminality of pregnancy carries a new and contested semantic
load. The state that the pregnant woman should enter can no longer
be assumed; rather than become a mother, she may choose to end
the pregnancy and return to her former state. Legal abortion, im-
plying birth need not be the inevitable outcome of pregnancy, subverts the prior associational chain that pregnancy "must" result in
childbirth and motherhood.

With the collective acceptance of abortion, the dominant and
oppositional discourses regarding the place of pregnancy and abortion in women's lives were suddenly reversed. Although abortion is
now legal, right-to-life advocates clearly do not consider termination of pregnancy as an option. Yet their view now exists within the
new set of conditions created by abortion's legalization. To succeed,
right-to-life activists cannot simply defend past arrangements but
must construct their own position in positive terms that address

the current situation. In pro-life action and discourse, particularly in the focus on women with problem pregnancies, one can see how this accommodation has been made. The decision to keep the pregnancy *despite* adverse circumstances becomes an achievement, rather than the inexorable if begrudging fulfillment of a predetermined ascriptive role. The woman who decides to carry an unwanted pregnancy comes to signify an assertion of a particular construction of female identity—now experienced as oppositional by pro-life activists—in which nurturance, achieved through accepting pregnancy and birth, is of paramount value.

From this viewpoint, the absence of pregnant women in pro-life imagery is less of a paradox. The legalization and availability of abortion not only pose the possibility that pregnancy need not lead to motherhood, but also give authority to an alternative cultural scenario for women's lives. The right-to-life focus on the fetus in their visual materials stresses motherhood as the outcome of pregnancy and emphasizes this as an achievement, unambiguously overshadowing other contingencies that a representation of a pregnant woman might evoke, especially when abortion is legal.

Abortion and Metaphors of Social Reproduction

In the associations that are drawn to the fetus, some of which I have spelled out, biological reproduction becomes a representation of the continuity of cultural life as well. By extension, abortion comes to signify, in the right-to-life view, not only a withdrawal of unconditional, self-sacrificing nurturance, the devaluation of human life, but also a denial of the reproduction of the culture itself. Hence, it is not sufficient simply to hope to recriminalize abortion. Using the metaphor of the home being destroyed by outside forces, one LIFE Coalition activist wrote in a recent Newsletter:

Matthew, Chapter 12, verse 29 says, "Or how can anyone enter the strong man's house and carry off his property or goods, unless he first bind the strong man? And then he will plunder his house?" Could it be that we have allowed idols of materialism, drugs, alcohol, money, sex, power or success to bind us . . . and now our children and our families are being destroyed and taken away captive by satan?

We must return to the God of the Bible and I believe that II Chronicles

7 : 14 speaks clearly what we must do to reclaim our land and our beloved State of North Dakota from the enemy. ACTION WITHOUT PRAYER IS ARROGANCE BUT PRAYER WITHOUT ACTION IS HYPOCRISY!!! (*Life Coalition Newsletter*, April 1987)

For these pro-life activists, political action is seen as ineffective if separated from the refiguring of a gendered landscape through prayer, demonstration, and efforts to convert others, particularly women in the vulnerable and liminal position of carrying an un- wanted pregnancy.

It is significant that conflict over abortion emerges not simply when the act occurs, since its practice is not new. Passions are aroused when it becomes publicly tolerated. If one rejects legal abortion as a reasonable choice, it must be seen as a symptom of a more general disorder, in this case a disruption of women's domain and moral authority based on an understanding of nurturance tied to motherhood. In their vigils, sidewalk counseling, prayers, and meetings, right-to-life activists reframe the termination of preg- nancy as beyond a boundary of femininity as they would define it. Through their actions, the physical and metaphorical terrain that legal abortion claims as an acceptable choice becomes taboo. At the same time, these pro-life advocates redefine the difficulties of pregnancy, sexual relationships, and motherhood as positive tests of female identity in terms appropriate to the current histori- cal circumstances.

In the pro-life view, women who choose, in the face of problem- atic circumstances, to keep an unwanted pregnancy when abortion is a choice, are "truly" female. Pregnancy is now understood simul- taneously as a decision not to abort, a kind of heroic passage in which their capacity for nurturance has been tested. By contrast, women who abort or advocate abortion are marked as "unfemale" or at least fallen away and weak, perhaps to be redeemed at a later date. The development of pro-life ideology in the abortion debate in the 1980s, then, is more than a political debate over reproduc- tive and fetal rights. In it one sees a renegotiation of pregnancy, childbirth, and nurturance as they are transformed from ascribed to achieved features in the construction of female gender identity in American culture.

Chapter Seven

Angles of Incidence,
Angles of Reflection

Sometimes I think I'm too sympathetic. Isn't that terrible? I just think there has to be somebody that can say what needs to be said better than I can. Like on the radio show I thought, you know, I just hadn't represented anything right. I remember going into the bathroom and just bawling. I just think there's gotta be people, you know, that have the words for things. I mean, who am I? I sit there trying to think of the word for something and I know my being there is right, and I know somebody has to speak out, but it's still very difficult for me to do. I think I understand the other side too well. I see their arguments and I understand them. (Fargo pro-life leader, 1983)

As the focus of pro-life activity narrowed increasingly to the clinic and its clientele, activists on both sides developed a sense of familiarity with each other that grew out of their constant physical proximity and a close monitoring of each other's behavior. For abortion clinic personnel, the presence of the right-to-life protesters had become a part of their routine; on the rare days when prayer vigilantes and sidewalk counselors were absent, the staff expressed the kind of unease that accompanies an unexpected change in pattern. They knew individuals by name and even had "favorites" with whom they exchanged pleasantries. Similarly, the pro-life women knew the habits of their opponents, the hours they came and went, whether they were married or had children, the bumper stickers on their cars—a "Save the Whales" sticker, for example, was the source of constant remark. They even knew individual voices, since someone from LIFE called every week to make a fictitious appointment in order to know the day that abortions would be performed.

After two years of this activity, it appeared that the habituation of the two sides to one another enhanced the stabilization of the conflict. Occasionally, the familiarity and knowledge that activists on each side had of each other broke through the structure of opposition that normally held these women apart, defined their differences, constrained their action, and charged the field around the clinic.

Small incidents stood out as brief moments that momentarily altered the proscenium of the ongoing social drama. When an abortion counselor slipped on the front stairs, Linda Anderson who had been on a prayer vigil in front of the clinic ran over to help her. When it was clear the woman was not hurt, Linda quickly returned to her post on the sidewalk, suddenly cognizant of the boundary she had crossed. The recognition of commonality was, occasionally, more self-conscious and discursive, stressing a sense of shared community, both spiritual and physical. When a pro-choice leader who counseled at the clinic published a piece in the newspaper about a sexual assault she had experienced, one of the sidewalk counselors sent her the following note:

After walking out in front of the clinic for two months and seeing and praying for you, I felt a closeness in the spirit. I've had a longing to talk with you but that is impossible under the circumstances. I lift you before the Lord daily. We also live in the same neighborhood, so there is a closeness there.

Very rarely, the one point of actual convergence in each side's mission, their common concern for the woman with the unwanted pregnancy, actually became apparent, as the following story Kay told me illustrates:

This woman came in and said she wanted to pay for an abortion in advance and when I told her the clinic doesn't accept personal checks, she returned in the half hour with the money. She looked pretty down and out and gave her address as the transient hotel downtown. She never showed up on Wednesday for her abortion and then she called on Thursday to say she was having second thoughts.

I asked her if her concerns were financial and she said yes, that if she could afford it, she'd keep the pregnancy. So I said "Stay there, I'll have someone get back to you." And I picked up the phone and I called the

LIFE Coalition office. The phone rang. Someone picked it up and said, "Hello," and I said, "Hi. This is Kay Bellevue from Fargo Women's Health." There was a long pause at the other end and then the voice says, "Yes?" And I said, "I understand you want to help out women who are carrying a problem pregnancy and don't want an abortion." There was another pause and she says, "Yes?" "Well, I have someone who is in financial straits and I would appreciate it if you could give her a call and see if there's anything you can do." Another pause. "Sure." So I gave her the name and number.

While this was, in one sense, a recognition of common purpose, an overcoming of difference, Kay's decision to call LIFE was also expressive of her determination not to let the pro-life side claim that the clinic coerced ambivalent women into having abortions.

When I spoke with a LIFE leader regarding this incident, her comments revealed the difference between the public rhetoric of activists and their privately expressed understanding of their opponents:

I truly believe that Kay cares very, very much about the woman. She believes it is one way, that she wants them to have the option of abortion. And she sees it as more lucrative, not for herself but for the woman, better for her, and we disagree with that. But I think it's out of her caring for that woman that she is doing what she's doing. And it's out of our caring that we're doing what we're doing. So I'd say that's the common ground.

Constructing a political identity around an issue defined oppositionally is always a complex, dialectical process; pro-life women in particular require the "other" to exist because they are fighting to change the status quo. In a setting like Fargo where face-to-face contact is always possible, the "other" is constantly present in daily interaction. One pro-life organizer explained:

You know, there's something about a small community. If we would paint Kay as a monster we would lose, and that's what it boils down to, to some degree. Because people know them. People know they aren't monsters. They are people who are trying to do the right thing too. So maybe that forces us to be more tolerant, to try and understand their thinking so that we can accept them better or whatever. It's not that we'll ever agree. But it's nice to know we can disagree and not be totally polarized.

As the quote indicates, activists are well aware of the way in which the local arena shapes their behavior. Given the dense and overlapping social networks as well as certain shared concerns, it is not surprising that pro-life and pro-choice women feel constrained by local knowledge. They occasionally encounter one another in other settings. Activists might and do run into each other at PTA meetings, the YWCA, in Lamaze classes, as volunteers at the rape center, on church committees, and at political party meetings. One woman described how her friendship developed with a pro-life woman with whom she serves on a board of a community service organization.

I remember when I met Myra and I was really enjoying her and when I found out her position I was really surprised, you know, but I was able to say, OK, I understand. I respect Myra's position and she respects mine and neither of us have any fantasies about changing the other. And I think we both recognize that it's a very complex and difficult issue. I find with Myra that there is unity on other values, or at least nothing that leads to conflict.

These comments show how the crossover in ideological concerns that exists but is often glossed in public debate has a correlate in the organization of everyday life. The commonalities between pro-choice and pro-life women emerge as well in aspects of the larger social critique to which abortion activism is linked. To ignore the humanity of their opposition violates a fundamental code of social life that activists on both sides value.

By the spring of 1983, the sense of intense crisis that characterized the period of the opening of the clinic had passed. The conflict had settled into a socially recognized and predictable schism between the two parties. LIFE members were focusing their activity more and more on the Problem Pregnancy Center. Just as the conflict appeared to be stabilizing, however, developments at the national level triggered an unanticipated, more violent phase of the local drama over abortion that mobilized actors who, previously, had been only peripherally involved.

Revival of the Spirit: Regression to Crisis

In June 1983, the Supreme Court ruled that various local ordinances intended to restrict the use of abortion clinics were unconstitutional, essentially reiterating the position it took supporting elective abortion in the 1973 rulings. Shortly afterwards, Fargo's moderate right-to-life activists—committed to working within the political system, cultivating a public image of compassion and civility, and stressing public education and alternatives to abortion—were challenged by the emergence of a pro-life group that played by different rules.[1] This group, organized by Richard Hilgard, one of the former Partners in Vision,[2] introduced a confrontational style of harassment of abortion patients and providers that revived the conflict in new form.

Like Partners in Vision, the new group was looked upon with some suspicion by people in Fargo, including some members of LIFE Coalition. Although it managed to draw a well-respected Fargo family into its ranks, its local base and sources of support were not clear. For example, these activists originally called themselves Save-A-Baby, the name used by the Moral Majority for its antiabortion efforts; yet the Fargo group disclaimed any direct connection with Jerry Falwell's organization.[3] Similarly, the resemblance of the tactics of these new activists to those of Joseph Scheidler, the charismatic figurehead of the more radical right-to-life groups, was not coincidental, although any direct connection was denied by group members. Several of the leaders of Fargo's Save-A-Baby group were inspired to start their protests after hearing him speak in Chicago, and later invited him to Fargo.[4] While nearly all of the people in Save-A-Baby belonged to or attended the conservative evangelical First Assemblies of God congregation, both the group and the church denied more than a circumstantial connection. No local clergy associated themselves directly with the group, at least in public.

The relationship between this new group and LIFE Coalition was uneasy at best. In contrast to the relatively quiet, moderate tactics of LIFE, the Save-A-Baby activists stopped just short of violence in their weekly demonstrations. They gathered outside the clinic in groups as large as thirty and screamed at women entering the building not to kill their babies, displaying large signs with Biblical quotes and pictures of whole and mutilated fetuses. They blocked traffic, followed patients leaving the facility, and even picketed the homes of the clinic's administrator and physician, carrying signs with slogans likening them to Hitler. In addition, they held press conferences to call for investigations of the clinic's activities, such as the disposal of fetal remains. They "exposed" local social service counselors who refer women to abortion services, and challenged the clinic's compliance with city regulations, such as the fire code. On Christian, national, or "abortion" holidays, such as the *Roe* v. *Wade* anniversary on January 22, they staged dramatic presentations in front of the clinic. On one Good Friday, they hired a hearse and parked it in front of the clinic. Two women dressed in black got out, began to pray and speak in tongues, and laid roses and a tiny coffin on the clinic lawn.

In November 1984, a stone was thrown through the window of the clinic and, although the culprit turned out to be unaffiliated with any of the local right-to-life groups, this event dramatized the growing concern on all sides that the escalation of harassment by the new group might lead to serious violence. The Fargo Police Department, which had more or less ignored the clinic until this point, assigned a special officer to the grounds on days when abortions were scheduled.

The clinic and its supporters responded to the new right-to-life harassment with lawsuits, security guards, and a steady round of volunteers to escort patients through the intimidating line of protesters in front of the facility. In contrast to the more cordial feelings that clinic personnel expressed toward LIFE Coalition's sidewalk counselors, the actions of the new group have placed the clinic staff under enormous stress. As bombings and arson escalated at clinics across the country, the fear that this could happen at any moment in Fargo became a regular feature in the clinic's daily routine.[5]

Surprisingly, the presence of the more aggressive protesters seemed to have little negative effect on patients. The numbers of women using the clinic remained more or less constant. Prior to the escalation in pro-life activity outside the clinic, the waiting room had often been quiet, with only an occasional hushed conversation to break the silence. By contrast, patients who endured the more vociferous pickets joked or expressed their anger, trading stories with one another about retorts they made or the ways they evaded the demonstrators. Apparently, the common experience of crossing the picket line created a momentary bond.[6]

Interventions in the Dramatic Field: The Impact of National Media

For LIFE Coalition, the emergence of the new group created a quandary. Save-A-Baby seemed to represent only about fifty people, hardly a match for LIFE's well-organized thirteen hundred members. Yet the former group captured local and even national attention with its tactics. Given how central the creation of a particular public image is to the various pro-life factions, as one would expect, there is considerable struggle within the movement for access to the resource of print and electronic media coverage. The presence of these forms of communication in community conflicts can have a critical effect on the local political arena.

The nature of this competitive process was demonstrated when a national television network produced a segment on the abortion conflict centering on Fargo. The following brief analysis of how the show was developed and the local reaction to it raises a range of questions regarding the symbiotic relationship between mass media and the efficacy of extreme political styles in the twentieth century. By picking up violent or near-violent action as "newsworthy," to the neglect of the less dramatic but more representative work, most coverage of the abortion issue unwittingly colludes with the radical behavior of a vocal minority—for whom visibility is a prominent goal—even when condemning it.

In the fall of 1984, producers for ABC's "20/20," a magazine-style news show with high public visibility, began to explore the idea of producing a locally based story that would exemplify the increase in violent pro-life activity that had been occurring across the United States during the prior year. Because Fargo had received publicity regarding escalating right-to-life activity, they chose Fargo as one of their locations and began to do research. Since I was one of their sources of information, I knew that the producers were aware of the presence of a well-organized, broadly based, moderate pro-life group, the LIFE Coalition, as well as the pro-choice organization, Citizens for a Real Choice.

The story that was produced, however, although it claimed to be showing how the controversy looked in one locale, offered almost no evidence that either of these more moderate groups even existed. The producers chose to focus instead on the socially and politically marginal but highly visible year-old Save-A-Baby group. In fact, that group accommodated the presence of network camera crews by staging even more dramatic demonstrations than usual. Around Christmas, Richard Hilgard dressed up as Santa Claus and tried to get into the clinic to deliver "toys to the unborn." These actions received coverage; unlike those of the moderates, they provided "good TV," to use a producer's phrase.

On the 1985 anniversary of the *Roe* v. *Wade* ruling (January 22), a day usually marked by right-to-life demonstrations, local pro-choice activists were so concerned about the potential for violence in the escalated activity engendered by the presence of television crews, that they kept a vigil around the clinic for thirty-six hours, despite record cold temperatures. Their presence as an organized group was not mentioned in the show. The ABC focus on the Save-A-Baby group was not sympathetic and included an exposé of deceptive practices used in their efforts to keep women from using the clinic; however, by excluding more moderate activists, the show seriously misrepresented the actual shape the conflict takes, as well as the motivations and behavior of abortion activists on both sides.

Telephone calls and letters written to me after the show reveal the helplessness and frustration grass-roots activists on both sides felt in encountering the media on a national scale and the sort of distortions created by the interventions of these representations. A leader of LIFE Coalition, who was not interviewed by "20/20," wrote me:

ABC's "20/20" just got done filming here for their program in January. I am disgusted and disappointed. Almost everyone interviewed was from the same church, The First Assembly of God. They seemed to be trying to make a connection with the Moral Majority and Jerry Falwell. They cancelled two interviews with me while they were here, and none of the following groups [all part of LIFE Coalition] were represented in their interviews. 1) N.D. Right-to-Life; 2) Lutherans for Life; 3) Minnesota Citizens Concerned for Life; 4) Fargo Right to Life; 5) National Right to Life Committee; 6) the Pro-Life Office of the Catholic Diocese; 7) Birthright; 8) The Problem Pregnancy Center. They called it "fair" since seven interviews were done on the anti-abortion side and three on the pro-abortion side. They also *paid* women money to interview anonymously and tell how their needs had not been met when working with the pro-life groups!

The disproportionate attention won by the new group created confusion and loss of morale for LIFE Coalition. One staff member expressed her frustration at being identified with what she considered to be an extremist right-to-life group at odds with her own, regardless of mutual concerns.

There is nothing we can do. We don't own the pro-life position or the sidewalk in front of the clinic. They are the radicals and we the moderates. They are just a few people but they are turning others away from us by their tactics. They are out of control.

Despite such friction, the moderate right-to-life activists refused to reveal internal dissent publicly. They continued with their prayer vigil, unwilling to relinquish turf, even if it meant being misidentified. Because the two groups of activists were seen together in front of the clinic on a regular basis engaged against a common enemy, it is not surprising that passersby and even local journalists saw little difference between them. The internal distinction and external confusion between "mainstream" pro-life activists and the more extreme "no compromise" groups existed both locally and at the national level. This conflation of distinct pro-life constituencies was created in part by the activists themselves, as well as by the media's portrayal of them as monolithic, equivalent to the most vocal exponents.

Pro-choice activists were also frustrated with the media representation. The leader of the pro-choice group, who was not interviewed, explained to me:

I was just really mad because I felt like all that effort didn't even matter. I know that it does, but it was really frustrating that they didn't even mention our work. I never realized how much we are at the mercy of the media. Suddenly, I really feel out of control.

The clinic administrator, who was in the show, felt that though it was distorted, it had at least alerted people to the hostility she had been confronting on a daily basis:

It was distorted, but it outraged a lot of people in the community who hadn't known what was going on. And when I look at who is causing distress for us now, it *is* the people they showed. The problem is, it gives them credibility and coverage that they don't deserve.

In fact, the "20/20" program helped the clinic insofar as it generated local hostility against the activities of Richard Hilgard and the Save-A-Baby group, while increasing the clinic's credibility with police and the judiciary. These sentiments were manifest, directly and indirectly, in a number of legal cases in 1985 that curtailed the activities of the more radical pro-life activists.[7]

Redressive Action

Whatever its distortions, the visibility that the show gave to extremist tactics—forms of action contrary to Fargo mores—helped initiate a new stage in the social drama. Soon after the broadcast, the abortion clinic—the Fargo Women's Health Organization—

won a preliminary injunction from the District Court against the Hilgards' pro-life pregnancy counseling center, The Women's Help Clinic of Fargo, for false advertising. The charges against the pro-life group claimed that the imitative name, advertisements, and "counseling" misled potential clients into thinking that the Women's Help Clinic offered or made referrals for abortions. The Court's injunction required that they change their name and publicity, and inform callers that they do not perform abortions. The pro-life group immediately appealed, claiming that the false advertising restrictions violated their free speech rights. The Court also ruled in favor of the abortion clinic in its case against Richard Hilgard for entering the clinic dressed as Santa Claus. He was charged with intent to harass and sentenced to two days in jail, a $200 fine, and a year on probation during which he could not be near the abortion clinic. In addition, the Fargo City Commission approved a ban on picketing of private residences that had been proposed in response to the Save-A-Baby group's picketing of Kay Bellevue's home.[8]

Finally, as a direct result of the "20/20" show, the Planning Commission of Fargo realized that the Hilgards' Women's Help Clinic was operating a business in a residential neighborhood without a permit and required them to obtain one. The Hilgards, ever-resourceful in the face of adversity, leased a former boarding house as an alternate base for their activities, in case they might have to close their clinic. With legal limits confining their other forms of protest behavior, they escalated their efforts in the "problem pregnancy industry" instead. The house was turned into a pro-life home for unwed mothers named The Perry Love and Caring Center, in memory of two prominent Fargo pro-life activists who died tragically in a car crash. A benefit for the Center held in September 1985 at the First Assemblies of God Church raised $4,700 in start up funds and $9,000 in pledges. The featured guest was Beverly LaHaye of Concerned Women of America, who gave a talk on "Positive Alternatives to the Militant Feminism That Threatens the Future of America." Eventually, the Hilgards moved their problem pregnancy center, renamed The Women's Care Clinic and now offering "Christian Family Life Services," around the corner from the Perry Center.

In January 1988, a Cass County District Court jury affirmed the 1985 decision against the Hilgards' "Women's Help Clinic" in favor of the Fargo abortion clinic, assessing $23,500 in special damages.

These, along with other rulings, served as redressive actions that drew authoritative limits to the range of acceptable behaviors that would be tolerated in the battle over the abortion clinic. Essentially, the judgments declared Richard's more overtly rule-breaking pro-life efforts to be unacceptable. As local people like to say, "North Dakotans believe in a philosophy of live and let live." The rulings asserted this understanding of community standards against counterclaims, as the framework within which differences could be addressed.

Synopsis of a Social Drama

What is at stake in community battles such as the one in Fargo is more than the issue of abortion services in one's own backyard, so to speak. The development of right-to-life protests over the abortion clinic during its first six years provided dramatic enactments and claims for control of abortion's meaning for the local body politic. The director of the National Women's Health Organization assessed the protests in Fargo as similar to those she has encountered in setting up other facilities.

Opening a clinic in a nonmetropolitan area is about like getting on a roller-coaster ride. You have to take the ups and downs before you come to the end and that's usually when the community begins to accept you. A tremendous amount of emotion surfaces over these votes and reversals, as if people have to show that the clinic was established over their protest. I've seen it over and over again.

In analytic terms, her comments emphasize how the Fargo controversy—and other local protests over abortion clinics—took shape in the sequence of phased conflicts typical of "social dramas": breach, crisis, redress, regression to crisis, and eventually stabilization either through schism or reintegration. Using this framework, one can see such conflict not as chaotic deviation or predetermined script, but as a potentially transformative period in which social actors are engaged in reformulating the meaning and practice of local social life.

For pro-life activists in Fargo, the first rumors in 1981 of plans for an abortion clinic in their community created a breach, an intrusion into their local world of what they perceived as a radically different aspect of American society and culture. A crisis developed with the formation of LIFE Coalition to stop the abortion clinic in

1981. Actions ranged from the use of formal legal processes in the
campaign to revoke the clinic's permit, to the failed attempt at informal pressure by Partners in Vision's letter-writing campaign, to
the public stigmatizing of the clinic through the prayer vigil. In response, local pro-choice supporters mobilized CRC to defend the
clinic in all the arenas where it was under attack. The City Commission's reinstatement of the clinic's permit served as a temporary
redress. The schism that had emerged as a result of the clinic,
marked by the new local pro-life and pro-choice groups, seemed to
have stabilized. LIFE Coalition, recognizing that it was not succeeding in the political arena, began to shift its focus from the clinic
per se to its clientele through a program of "sidewalk counseling"
and plans for a "problem pregnancy center."

Unexpectedly, in late 1983, Supreme Court rulings and Congressional actions endorsed the pro-choice status quo. Divisions in
the ranks of the national pro-life movement became more apparent, while violence against abortion clinics escalated around the
country. Locally, a similar "regression to crisis" occurred with the
emergence of the "direct action" Save-A-Baby group and its confrontational tactics: harassing clinic patients, picketing the clinic
administrator's home, and opening their own problem pregnancy
center.

The intervention of and distortion by national television in Fargo
in the fall of 1984 had paradoxical effects: while the program that
was produced exaggerated the role of Save-A-Baby, it also helped
to generate local hostility to the group's expansion. Although such
sentiment was not necessarily causal, it contributed to the range of
legal curtailments placed on this more radical pro-life group in
1985. The rulings were a redressive action against the violation of
more deeply valued norms of behavior, halting, at least temporarily, further escalation of crises over the clinic. It is at this phase of a
social drama that the social unit is at its most self-conscious and the
Fargo legal system clearly ruled in favor of moderation as the ground
rule for debate. In Fargo, as in other social dramas, redressive action was followed by "legitimization of irreparable schism between
contesting parties" (Turner 1974: 41).[9] In the language used by citizens of Fargo (and many Americans), they had "agreed to disagree."

What is significant about the phases of the conflict in Fargo is
that they clarify how, as new players enter the scene and claims for

legitimacy shift, the scope and range of the contested domain—in this case the conflict for control over the definition and practice of abortion and its attendant meanings—are altered in the process.[10] The struggle over the clinic created as much as it revealed those previously unvoiced social and cultural divisions. The obvious rift was between the pro-life and pro-choice forces. However, the rulings implicitly emphasized distinctions within right-to-life ranks as well, especially between the more moderate and the more radical activists. By 1985, the divisions that first had emerged in 1981 had divided into several enduring pro-life groups—Birthright, Life Coalition, Save-A-Baby—each carrying on with their own agendas, hoping eventually to put the clinic out of business, one way or another. By 1986, these pro-life groups seemed less competitive with each other, even sharing some resources, such as donated maternity clothes or the cost of a pro-life billboard on Main Street advertising their phone numbers.

Although the contest seems most visible in the area around the clinic, where protesters from different groups—pickets, prayer vigilantes, sidewalk counselors, and even a group of out-of-town nuns—still appear with great regularity, the focus of the conflict has shifted from direct attacks on the clinic. Energy is increasingly focused on developing "alternatives to abortion" through a variety of "problem pregnancy centers." The battles that are creating lawsuits are being fought over advertisements in newspapers and phone directories to attract women with unwanted pregnancies to one or another service in the "problem pregnancy industry."[11] Attention of all parties in the abortion debate is focused increasingly on winning the minds, bodies, and the right to define women who might choose or advocate the legitimacy of the alternate script implied by abortion.

Female Grass-roots Activists: Local Voices in a National Debate

Activists on both sides of the Fargo conflict base their legitimacy partly on their concerns for the society at large, but also on their claims to represent the true interests of the community. This attachment to and pride in the local community is voiced in the claims they make, the groups they organize, and the institutions they form; it gives particular shape to their activism. It is expressed clearly in the independence each group maintains from national affiliations and mandates.

Although efforts at pro-choice organizing in the late 1970s had some support from NARAL, CRC was formed as a distinctly, even aggressively, local entity, refusing to affiliate as a chapter of a larger, national network. All its funds and support are generated locally. Its focus has been the defense of the Fargo abortion clinic, which includes public speaking, petition campaigns, helping with financial assistance for poor women seeking abortions, and providing escort services for abortion clinic patients facing intimidating protesters. As long as the clinic seems safe, the group operates more as a "reserve army" ready to be mobilized in case of attack, but not actively engaged in battle or building its forces.

The orientation of LIFE Coalition has remained self-consciously local and nonpartisan as well. The organization focuses on educational efforts in churches and classrooms, and on alternative counseling and aid programs for women with problem pregnancies in the Fargo area. Although many of LIFE's members are involved in the National Right-to-Life Committee, the Coalition is not directly affiliated with that group or with any other national antiabortion organization. LIFE receives financial and organizational support from local Catholic and Evangelical churches, yet it cannot be reduced to an expression of either of those institutions. Approximately 40 percent of the Coalition's members are Catholic and 25 to 30 percent are Lutheran; the remainder come from a range of other Protestant churches, particularly the growing Pentecostal and Evangelical congregations, a distribution close to that of the area in general.[12]

In addition to the adamant local focus of Fargo's pro-life and pro-choice organizations, the *ideas* of these grass-roots activists are distinctive as well, suggesting variation to generalities drawn from national surveys.

In their rhetoric, I found that activists in CRC appealed to traditional liberal arguments in favor of legal abortion that are commonly voiced in the national debates—for example, the right to privacy, or the need for safe, legal abortion services to prevent an illegal black market. However, these points were almost always couched in terms of the importance of legal abortion to family life, community, and raising children. In short, abortion was justified in terms of the domain of female nurturance and domesticity in American culture. In so doing, pro-choice activists were claiming and reshaping the agenda of the national women's movement to fit the North Dakota context. This accommodation was managed ideologically through what Fargo activists called "Midwestern feminism," an idea that was critical in framing the scope and meaning of pro-choice activism in the local arena. When I asked what they meant by the term, one woman described it in the following way:

It's a sense of connectedness, a valuing of life, kindness and gentleness and all the qualities that I think are important in human beings.

Another was more concrete:

Well, it's why I don't really even read *MS.* magazine anymore. It just doesn't talk about my life or other women in Fargo. You know, we still have potlucks here. We're worried about our community, raising decent kids, our marriages, getting old with or without a man. These are basic priorities that we all have to work together on.

In other words, the commitment of Fargo pro-choice activists to local concerns is expressed as part of a larger defense of the cultural values that, in their view, women represent (but need not monopolize). A CRC leader shows how this is managed:

It's important that we remember our place, that we remember we are the caregivers, that we remember that nurturing is important, that we maintain the value system that has been given to us and that has resided in us and that we bring it with us into that new structure. . . . It's important that we bring to that world the recognition that eighty-hour weeks aren't healthy for anyone—that children suffer if they miss relationships with their fathers and that fathers suffer from missing relationships with their children. . . . This society has got to begin recognizing its responsibility for caring for its children.

What is striking in the connections this woman draws to her abortion rights position is not their difference from her opponents, but the similarities. However, for most pro-choice women the enactment of these goals was dispersed over a range of other activities. This distinguishes them from pro-life women and may be due, in part, to the fact that the pro-choice position is, at least legally, the status quo.

When the social and historical construction of these ideas is taken into account, the concerns shared by female grass-roots activists are not so surprising. Many of the pro-life women I interviewed who had identified as liberal on other issues felt that as a consequence of their position on this one issue, they had been wrongly dismissed by their colleagues and erroneously placed in a right-wing camp. A Fargo right-to-life activist described the dilemma:

They say they're open-minded. I was a Democrat and labeled as being liberal all along and all of a sudden I took a stand on that issue and I was put in with everybody else like Phyllis Schlafly. Some kinds of things she says I really have trouble with, like she strongly believes in a fortified nation and I don't know about that. That's why I didn't like the idea that they [Schlafly et al.] completely took control. You all get lumped up; you are all considered a part of the right wing, you know. I used to criticize conservative people but when you're put into things with them, you start seeing some good things about them, too. You know, liberal and conservative doesn't make sense anymore. It really doesn't.

A 1980 survey conducted by Daniel Granberg (1981) offers statistical support for such anecdotal evidence. The Granberg study reveals a complex pattern that distinguishes views of gender and politics of pro-life activists from the sharp antifeminism of the New Right.[13] The answers given to survey questions on female sexuality and political power subvert stereotypes that link "conservative" views of sex with the acceptance of a subordinate status for women. Based on the NRLC sample, 87 percent disapprove of premarital sex; 75 percent oppose giving birth control information to teens without parental consent (and one-third of those object even with parental consent); and 80 percent feel it is too easy to get a divorce in America. However, 90 percent feel that women "should not leave running the country up to men" and 83 percent approve of women working regardless of marital status and husband's income.

The responses indicate support for women's economic and political power but reflect concern over the loss of two of the major bargaining strategies women have traditionally used for leverage in the "domestic sphere." Briefly put, these are the individual woman's refusal to engage in sex without marriage, which implicitly links female sexuality to procreation, domesticity, and male support of families; and collective pressure, formal or informal, on men to get and stay married and share in the responsibilities for children. Judith Blake and Jorge del Pinal, in a comprehensive study of abortion attitudes in the United States, give the following explanation of such findings:

To have total discretion over abortion may trivialize the cosmic impor-tance of motherhood for women who wish to use pregnancy as an instru-mentality in their relations with their husbands and their lovers. [In this view] easy access to abortion lessens rather than increases feminine power. A pregnancy that has been embarked upon for the purpose of precipitat-ing a marriage or holding one together no longer has the clout that it once did. (1980: 49)

Are right-to-life women simply trying to maintain a disappear-ing way of life, as Blake and Pinal would maintain? Implicit in this view is an equally flat depiction of pro-choice women as the van-guard of "modernity."[14] From my research in Fargo, it appeared that this representation is a misreading of the movements and the effects they are having in the contemporary United States.[15] Re-ducing the positions of each side to a defense of motherhood or "liberation" fails to recognize either the structural conditions that limit women's access to other resources or the larger philosophy that links such viewpoints to critiques of the culture in general.

"I think there is a general breakdown of sorts in moral values and I don't say abortion has caused it all," explained one activist, a grandmother and feisty organizer in the local Democratic party.

The idea that we can say somebody can live and somebody can die for just any reason—I think is all tied up with the kind of thinking that's going on today.

You know, we went through about fifty magazines to find baby pictures to decorate donation cans for our annual right-to-life fund-raiser and we couldn't find any. Babies aren't in style today anymore. Babies are trouble. They cry; they get sick in the middle of the night. They wake up and in-terrupt a lot of things. Babies used to sell products, but not anymore. Now it's the nice luscious young gals.

Testimony to her perception is provided by the array of women's magazines at the corner drugstore. The covers of *Savvy, Working Woman, Glamour,* and *Self* all feature beautiful women aspiring to the goals of upwardly mobile, corporate men (with considerable disposable income), for whom the care of infants and children seems a secondary concern at best. Most LIFE members are aware that such imagery of the "liberated woman" is fabricated on Madison Avenue. Nonetheless, the effect of this mass media imagery is insidious. One woman, a strong and dynamic partner in a family farm, told me that reading these magazines was like "looking into a black mirror."

Many pro-life women I worked with saw these images on a continuum with abortion, as symptoms of an increasingly selfish and materialistic society, a vision from which their own moral identity is drawn by contrast. To write off such response as simply "defensive" or "reactionary" sidesteps analysis of the widespread appeal and power of their position, as well as the assumptions and goals held in common by activists on both sides. Many of the pro-*choice* women were equally disturbed by, and saw their work as a corrective to, cultural currents that promote, in their view, narcissistic attitudes in which the individual denies any responsibility to kin, community, and the larger social order.

It is not only abortion activists—pro-choice or pro-life—who wonder whether domesticity and nurturance can stand up to the ever-increasing presence of women in wage labor, the rising divorce rate, a mushrooming service economy, the end of even the illusion of a family wage, inadequate daycare facilities, and the specter of drive-in sperm banks ready to be franchised. Many women in Fargo, and America, are invested in a cultural and social system—by choice and by circumstance—that connects their understanding of the desirable female life course not only to childbearing and a husband but to a society that values the work involved in the nurturance of others. Writing in 1981, the feminist Deirdre English noted:

Most women who want to have children still cannot make it without a man. . . . Giving up children for a glamorous career may be one thing (although this is an either/or choice that men rarely face) but it may not be a decent trade for a dead-end job in a pink-collar ghetto. (1981: 58)

Certainly, at the level of practical consciousness, many women find themselves caught in the place English describes between the ideals and limits of domesticity on the one hand, and the social realities of inflation and limited opportunity in wage labor and careers on the other.[16]

As I spent time with activists in Fargo, it became apparent to me that their battle was more than an enactment of the sex inequalities in and contradictions between wage labor and motherhood in American culture. These activists viewed their work as part of a larger effort for full-scale social reform. They were engaged in a culture-reconstructing agenda that allowed them to refashion their own lives. Abortion activism offered a frame for and interpretation and critique of the culture and one's place in it. Thus, the relationship of activism to self-construction has critical implications for understanding the nature of commitment to the abortion issue, and why it is embraced with such passion.

Part Three

"Procreation Stories"

Chapter Eight

Interpreting Life Stories

Introduction

When I went to Fargo initially, I wanted to see how the abortion controversy operates, not only for the national leadership and policy makers who have received the most attention, but in the lives of individual grass-roots activists who provide the constituency on which the movement is currently built. The social drama over the clinic opening had the feel of a Manichean battle, the image commonly associated with the public side of the abortion battle. In following the daily lives of those involved in the struggle over the Fargo clinic, however, I came to know them outside of the dramatic enactments of their positions, and a different level of discourse, one with more interesting possibilities, became apparent. This other level required looking for alternative ways of understanding the situation.

Neither daily participant observation in the field nor larger scale macroanalysis provided answers for central questions I had regarding the significance that activism assumed in people's lives. Accordingly, I asked people in Fargo to work with me in clarifying the connections they saw between their sense of personal identity and abortion activism, to help me understand their "world view," an organization of ideas in which the self is the axis (Redfield 1953: 86).[1] My approach was simple. How, I asked activists, did they see their own lives in relation to their current activism on the abortion issue? The result was a set of life stories[2]—narratively shaped fragments of more comprehensive life histories.

I am calling these narratives, in which women use their activism to frame and interpret their historical and biographical experiences, "procreation stories." In them, activists constitute provisional solutions to disruptions in a coherent cultural model for the place of reproduction, motherhood, and work in the female life course in contemporary America. They illuminate how those dimensions of experience considered "private"—particular to the self—intersect with particular social and historical conditions that distinguish the memberships of each group.

Let me emphasize here that I chose to work with activists not for their "representativeness" but because they see themselves and often act as agents of social change. By looking at several dimensions of their involvement in the abortion contest, one can see how the meaning of cultural constructs and social rights and obligations—such as the relationships between individualism, nurturance, and dependency—are challenged and redefined at particular junctures in American culture. This work, then, is intended to illuminate a more general process of cultural transformation, showing not only how such actors shape and are shaped by the local and supralocal contexts (as I have in the preceding chapters) but also how they themselves are changed in the very act of engagement in a social movement. In this chapter I will lay out the methodological and theoretical frameworks I used to analyze and interpret the "procreation stories" presented in the following two chapters.

The Interviews: Method

Activists in the interview setting, talking outside the context of political meetings and events, were at ease to discuss in depth and breadth what they felt were their motivations for activism without resorting to movement rhetoric. In lengthy, one-on-one interviews, they could voice doubts and dissent as well as felt contradictions.

I chose activists who had taken, during the period of my fieldwork, the most prominent roles in local activity and who, by my observation, reflected the range of diversity encompassed in the active membership of each group in terms of age, socioeconomic status, religious affiliation, household and marriage arrangements, and style of activism. Most of my interviews were with women since the membership of both groups is primarily female, as is the case throughout the country. Altogether, I collected twenty-one life stories from right-to-life activists and fourteen life stories from pro-choice activists. Most of these people continue to be active; however, memberships on each side undergo rapid permutations both locally and nationally. The activists considered here represent, necessarily, only one scene in a continually unfolding drama. Thus, the benefits of in-depth participant-observation research must be balanced against the debits of a small sample bound by the conditions of a particular time and setting. However, other studies of abortion activists have also found their activism linked to a more general integrative process (e.g., Callahan and Callahan 1984; Luker 1984a).

Restrictions of space require that I be selective. I have chosen from thirty-five interviews those cases that are both compelling as texts and illustrative of themes found in all the interviews and in my research more generally. I have tried as well to present sufficient interview material from each case to give the reader a sense of its coherence as a narrative. In the presentation of the data, I have changed names and obvious identifying features as I agreed to do at the time of the interview.

From the beginning of my research, I explained that my interests were to understand why women were so divided on the abortion issue and to provide an accurate portrayal of grass-roots abortion activists since they tend to be overlooked or misrepresented. Most of the activists shared my interest in these questions, and the interviews appeared to be of equal concern and significance to them. We were, in a sense, interested in figuring out the same problems. Because my objective was to interfere as little as possible in the creation of the narrative, I only asked directed questions when something was unclear and to be sure that I had relatively comparable material from each person.[3]

The actual interview proceeded in a straightforward manner. People were interviewed for four to five hours, sometimes twice at a location of their choice where we knew we would not be interrupted. This was often at the home of the interviewee; sometimes the session took place at a workplace at the end of the day; or, occasionally, during the long car trips that are a common part of everyday life on the northern prairies. Most responded to my initial inquiry as to what motivated them to become an abortion activist by recollecting key events that, in their view, led them to their present activity. Generally these were placed in a loose chronological frame—experiences with natal families; education and work; courtship, marriage, and reproduction. In almost all cases, I was a familiar figure to people so that we both assumed a certain amount of prior knowledge. There were no objections to my tape-recording sessions.

I also made clear that I would be having similar "visits" (as Fargo residents referred to the interviews) with their opponents. This arrangement presented no problem due to the circumstances that first brought me to Fargo in 1981–82—my job as a producer for a television documentary about the opening of the clinic and the controversy that ensued. Both sides apparently felt the program accurately portrayed their position since both pro-life and pro-choice groups were using the show in public presentations. As a result, when I returned to do more fieldwork in 1983, my credibility as someone who would listen open-mindedly to people on both sides of the debate was not an issue.

In addition to negotiating my personal and social identity, I was worried that people would find the interview process itself to be an intrusion. Relative to other regions of the country such as the urban Northeast or West Coast, self-disclosure is not a common form of discourse. From my observations in the Upper Midwest, personal revelation occurs infrequently, even in settings that require disclosure, for example in the taking of medical histories. When it does occur, it is generally in highly stylized forms, such as at Alcoholics Anonymous meetings, in religious testimonies, at charismatic prayer group meetings, or in feminist consciousness-raising sessions. People are aware of their own laconic tendencies and readily poke fun at the more extreme forms it takes. For example, a joke I heard often while in the field, part of the "Sven and Ollie" genre of Scandinavian humor common to the area, captures the quality of the emotive style I am describing, as well as their own self-awareness of its limits.

(Sven to Ollie): You know, Ollie, I love my wife so much I almost told her once.

Despite all my worries, after the first few interviews it appeared that my concerns were misplaced. People seemed to be talking freely to me and even enjoying the process. I continued to see people, of course, after the interviews and frequently they would recall things they had forgotten to tell me. In a sense then the interview was not bounded but was part of an ongoing dialogue that preceded and endured beyond the framed event itself.

Life Crises, Cultural Models, and Social Change

The desire of people to continue telling me their life story indicated to me that the interview was part of an ongoing reconstruction of experience, providing continuity between the past and current action and belief. Anthropologist Barbara Myerhoff noted this process in explaining the delight taken by one of her elderly informants, Jacob, in articulating his life history:

He created for himself continuity by integrating all the phases of his long life into a single narrative account, contemplated by a single sentient being, aware of having been other beings at other points in the life cycle. And he incorporated external historical events into his life account, thus establishing continuity between himself and the times in which he lived, meshing inner and outer history into a unified tale. . . . Jacob was not only constructing a myth, an orderly and moral tale about himself, he was constructing a Self. (1978: 221)

Myerhoff and others focused on the importance of this sort of life review to the process of aging (Myerhoff 1978: 222). However, this critical ordering and reconstructing is not confined to the old—though it may be more marked at that stage of the life cycle—but is part of a more general process of recollection. In his classic work *Remembering*, F. C. Bartlett writes to this point:

Alike with the individual and with the group, the past is continually being remade, reconstructed in the events of the present, and in both cases, certain outstanding events or details may play a leading part in setting the course of this reaction. (1932: 309)

In other words, life reviews may be equally compelling during critical shifts that occur throughout the life course, particularly when there is dissonance between such moments and cultural definitions for them. These "life crises"—"transitions from one culturally defined stage of life to another at which there is regularly ex-

perienced individual stress" (Silverman 1975: 309)—may reveal
contention over cultural definitions. This sense of life crisis may be
even more likely in situations of rapid change when the social rules
for an assumed life trajectory are called into question.

This view stands in contradistinction to most early anthropological studies of transitional life events. In the tradition of Arnold Van
Gennep's 1908 classic, *The Rites of Passage*, "life crises" were seen
as a key to understanding the culturally *typical,* rather than the
problematic.[4] Life histories, similarly, were considered ideal models, meant to illustrate "standard" socialization processes. In this
framework, anthropologists have since come to realize, the individual is constructed as a passive recipient of timeless and unchanging
cultural norms. Such a perspective on the human life cycle takes
little account of subjective experience in its frame, creating "a
blindness to possible discontinuities in the ritual process and disso-
nances in the ritual experience" (Crapanzano 1980a: 17).

A more complex picture emerges when inquiry begins with the
experiential vantage point of participants. Erik Erikson's pioneering
studies of Luther and Ghandi, for example, suggested a broader
model of "life crises" as moments of moratorium or creative re-
orientation for individuals whose experiences do not mesh with
presumably "typical" biographies, particularly in rapidly changing
socioeconomic conditions (1958; 1969). The view that "life crises"
might indicate a lack of fit between a cultural ideal for the life
course and individual experience has informed some of the most
interesting recent work in demography and social history.[5] It also
has influenced studies of life histories in anthropology since the
1970s that draw on more interpretive paradigms such as phenome-
nology and psychoanalysis. Stressing the native's interpretation of
cultural events, the emphasis has been on *difference from* as well
as conformity to normative models, and the way the two are dia-
lectically structured (e.g., Crapanzano 1980a; 1980b; Shostak 1981).
Other works have addressed specifically the question of how dis-
junctions between the individual life course, cultural expectations,
and new historical conditions enable individuals to become agents
of social change (e.g., Mandelbaum 1973; Mintz 1981).

This sort of orientation, in which the experiences of the actors
are seen in tension with the larger cultural and social context, provides the framework I use to interpret the narratives of abortion

activists. Their procreation stories reveal the generative relationship between political engagement and discontinuities in the life course—for an individual or a generation—when cultural models for their interpretation are in contention. The narratives of those engaged in such struggles show how change is incorporated, ordered, and assigned meaning. Looked at in this way, it is more apparent how battles such as that over abortion emerge as loci for potential cultural and social innovation.

In each story, the narrator links her activism to the intersection of specific life transitions—considered "private" in American culture—with larger cultural and historical situations. These nexuses are represented as pivotal points that changed or reinforced the course of an assumed life trajectory. The reasons given and directions taken distinguish the memberships of each group.

Specifically, difficult reproductive events, shifts in household composition and kin arrangements, and tensions between the work of wage labor and mothering are prominent in the narratives as sources of critical conflict at both the individual and collective level. When narrators formulate these transitions as life crises, it reveals a gap between the experiences of discontinuous changes in their own biographies and the available cultural models for marking them, both cognitively and socially. Abortion activism, I argue, creates both an interpretation and arena of action that activists use to reframe in social terms what they had experienced initially as problematic shifts specific to their individual lives.

Historical Shifts and Generational Markers

As I tried to explain the differences between women on opposite sides of the issue, the seeming convergences in catalyzing experiences, social backgrounds, and sentiments only seemed to confound the problem. If one simply attended to the *referential* aspects of stories, it would be hard to predict whether women would end up pro-choice or pro-life in their views. The life stories frequently contradicted popular stereotypes: working-class Catholics became ardent pro-choice activists whereas middle-class, college-educated Protestants became staunch pro-life advocates. However, as I puzzled over the qualities activists shared—most see themselves as working toward the reform of society as a whole—I began to notice that they seemed to fall into generational groupings that marked their narratives in significantly different ways. From this perspective, it became clearer how women on opposite sides of the abortion issue, despite their different agendas, see themselves as acting in the best interests of women.

Almost all of the pro-choice women (80 percent) were born between 1942 and 1952. In terms of their reproductive histories, they were either at the end of a phase of their life cycle devoted to motherhood, or were unmarried, divorced, or childless. For the most part, these women had reached adulthood—which in most cases meant marriage and children—in the late 1960s and early 1970s at a time when feminism and reproductive rights activity were culturally ascendant. When these women sought new cognitive resources with which to understand and frame their experiences, feminism provided an analysis, a community of others, and a means for engaging in social change that legitimated their own dissonant experiences and revised interpretations of them.

Of the pro-life women, on the other hand, the women who were both most active and in the majority (77 percent) were born between 1950 and 1964, with a small cluster born in the 1920s. Almost all the younger women had youngsters at home, worked prior to having children, and left wage labor when they became mothers. For most, this transition occurred in the late 1970s or even more recently, a period when feminism was on the wane as an active social movement and pro-life and anti-ERA activity were on the rise.

Let me clarify that I am not arguing that all abortion activists fall neatly into one or another historical cohort. As is the case in most anthropological studies in complex societies, mine is small and local, allowing for fine-grained, long-term research that can suggest or reveal new understandings but not necessarily prove broad generalizations. In this case, the appearance of a generational shift, even in this small sample, is intended less as explanation and more as a reminder of the importance of temporal factors in the dialectics of social movements.

That social activists may hold different positions is due not only to social and ideological differences; differing views may also be produced by historical changes that include the experience social actors have of the opposition at different points over the life course. Indeed, my own research suggests that this might be particularly relevant in conflicts tied so closely to life-cycle events. In the narratives, *all* the women are struggling to come to terms with difficult life-cycle transitions, but in each group, the way they experience those transitions as problematic is associated with very particular historical situations. Abortion activism seems to mediate between these two domains, as a frame for action and for interpretation of the self in relation to cultural understandings. For most of these women, their life stories create coherent narratives out of the dissonance of history, both personal and generational. Insofar as the intersections of such "biological" and historical events figure as key moments, the narratives are marked by a sense of generation.

The importance of generational shifts in the formation of political consciousness has been noted in studies of other social movements. In an essay exploring this topic, entitled "The Problem of Generations," Karl Mannheim underscored this point in ways that are relevant to understanding activists in the contemporary abortion controversy. Mannheim wrote:

Our culture is developed by individuals who come into contact anew with the accumulated heritage. . . . We can accordingly differentiate between two types of "fresh contact": one based on a shift in social relations, and the other in vital factors (the change from one generation to another). The latter type is *potentially* much more radical, since with the advent of the new participant in the process of culture, the change of attitude takes place in a different individual whose attitude toward the heritage handed down by his predecessors is a novel one (1970: 383-84)

Such conditions of "fresh contact"—the moment of intersection of the individual life cycle and rapidly changing historical and social conditions—that Mannheim viewed as critical in the formation of new social movements are apparent in the procreation stories of abortion activists. They reveal how the embracing of a pro-life or pro-choice position emerges out of a confluence of generationally marked experiences and individual life-cycle events, often related to reproduction.

Narrative Strategies: Procreation Stories as Counter-Discourse

The point of the stories and my analysis of them is not to show that specific experiences *determine* whether an individual will become an activist. Rather, my interest is in the formal strategies activists use to structure and give meaning to the recounting of life stories that distinguish the women of each group. If these indeed reflect the efforts of social actors to constitute order and cultural transformations at "disjunctive" historical moments, then this activity must be apparent in concrete forms of symbolic action.

In their narratives, activists use the stories of their lives to construct a plot in which the social consequences of different definitions of the female life course in contemporary America are selected, rejected, reordered, and reproduced in new form. This plot-story distinction is based loosely on the framework developed by the Russian formalist Viktor Šklovskij for analyzing narrative. He distinguished between the story (*fabula*), the "raw" temporal-causal sequence of narrated events, and the plot (*sjužet*), the way in which these "raw materials" are formally manipulated in unconventional ways that make the audience reconsider the usual ordering of events (Steiner 1984: 51). It is the plot that provides the defamiliarization (*ostranenie*) considered essential by Šklovskij and others to creating new understandings of everyday life (Bennett 1979: 53). So, for example, for activists the "story" is the expected arrangement of a woman's biography according to Western narrative and social conventions (birth, childhood, marriage, motherhood); the "plot" emerges from the unexpected twists in the narrative that draw attention to differences from the conventional story, thus "defamiliarizing" the taken-for-granted assumptions, for example, of a "typical" biography. Activists are aware of the tension between their own plot and the expected story and indicate that awareness by a variety of devices, often as simple as a prefatory comment such as "I guess I'm different because . . ." preceding an unconventional anecdote.

I found consistent patterns to the plot twists of the "procreation stories" of each group. A summary of the "plot line" that, in general, distinguishes the pro-choice and pro-life narratives should clarify the point. For pro-choice women, these are, typically, a differentiation of self from family in early life; a questioning of the confines of motherhood, usually after first birth; a "conversion" brought about by contact with feminism and other social movements of the 1960s and 1970s; and a subsequent reframing of understandings of self, women's interests, and ideals of nurturance in terms of the broader domain we call "the public" through their activism on the abortion issue.

For the younger pro-life activists who were the key players at the time I was in the field, the plot takes shape as an "awakening" to pro-life activism from what they would consider a feminist position, usually after having left the work force to have a baby. Unlike the pro-choice women, these activists came of age in a world reframed by the second wave of feminism, the existence of legal abortion, and at least a surface acceptance of women working. The key twist lies in the construction of nurturance as an *achievement*. Their stories of pregnancy, birth, and mothering are not told as a matter of course but as dramas of overcoming hardship and doubt. This plot exists in complex tension with changing understandings of the "proper" female biography in America. On the one hand, it subverts the conventional story of reproduction as "natural" to women's lives. On the other hand, it reasserts the primacy of reproduction and mothering for women's identity and authority, but it does so on the grounds that female nurturance offers an alternative model and powerful critique of increasingly materialistic and individualistic trends in American culture.

In analyzing activists' life stories, one sees how narrators' verbal and self-conscious understanding of their society develops out of their own historical experiences as social actors and also inflects the way they communicate this knowledge—what Giddens would call the "discursive penetration" of "practical consciousness" (1979: 5). However, the narratives are more than simply discursive knowledge. In them, activists reframe experiences they originally felt were dissonant with social expectations by constituting them as new cultural possibilities. The plots articulate a "counter-discourse"[6] that has "the capacity to *situate*: to relativize the authority and stability of a dominant system" (Terdiman 1985: 16)—in this case, presumed models of the female life course in America. The tension between plot and story in the narratives shows how their knowledge of the culture is embedded in critiques of it that are drawn from the practices and problems of everyday life (Marcus 1986).[7]

For almost all of the activists, reproduction is central to these critiques at a number of levels. In their constructions, reproduction is a key turning point, not as a biological occurrence but as a class of life-cycle events that forced an encounter with the inequali-

ties of a gendered social world. These encounters, as told in the
stories, lead the women to reconsider their relationship to and
understanding of their assigned place in society. Subsequently,
their activism took discursive shape as a concern not only with the
place of procreation in women's lives, but with the reproduction of
the culture as a whole. Whether pro-life or pro-choice, activists express their motivation for social action as a desire to alter the meaning and circumstances of procreation in order to make conditions
better for the next generation. In other words, they are concerned,
as female activists, with their role in reproducing the culture, but
in terms different from the present. Because procreation in American culture is so deeply connected to asymetrical understandings of
male and female, any question raised about procreation is, necessarily, also one about gender identity and cultural reproduction.
Thus, the narratives are "procreation stories" in the narrowest and
broadest senses of the word.

In the procreation stories, then, speakers from each side use the
abortion issue as a plot element connecting different but interrelated understandings of gender, sexuality, and reproduction. Abortion activism consistently provides a central narrative turning point
in the life course of activists, confirming or changing their subjective relationship to their own past and future. In this narrative refiguring, activists create alternative "life scripts" to what they consider to be a conventional cultural form for a female life trajectory.
The disjunctive transitions accommodated in their plots illuminate
sources of dissonance between cultural codes, social process, and
individual transformation. As a counter-discourse, they take on
particular power now, a historical moment when there is no clear
hegemonic model for the shape of the female life course in America.

When the definitions of a particular life event such as pregnancy
or abortion become the object of a contentious political struggle, it
reveals a larger disruption occurring in the social order as well. In
the narratives I collected, *every* plot rests on some sense of tension
between domesticity and the workplace. Responsibilities of women
in relationship to nurturance is the salient issue and contradiction
for women on both sides of the debate.

Such concern reflects the critical yet contested place nurturance
holds as a central feature marking feminine identity in this culture.
In America, nurturance links the category female to biological re-

production, childrearing, and heterosexually organized households and families. Given this system, women can claim nurturance simultaneously as a source of female moral authority *and* reject it as a cultural frame that puts women at a disadvantage socially, economically, and politically, confining them to the culturally and materially devalued tasks of caring for dependent people. These two mappings of the "proper" place of reproduction and nurturance in the female life course are the poles around which activists' biographical narratives are constituted; they mark and claim the terrain of the abortion conflict.[8] More generally, the construction of female identity through such social action suggests a model for understanding how women activists in the American context use their actions to mediate the construction of self and gender with larger social, political, and cultural processes.

Chapter Nine

The Pro-Choice Narratives

Introduction

In my search to gain insight into why local activists became involved in the abortion issue, it was soon apparent to me that there
was no easy or obvious explanation. I turned to life stories because
they offered a different order of knowledge than linear notions of
cause and effect. In the following chapters, I present material from
these elicited narratives and analyze the processes by which understanding of the self was reconstituted and aligned with a new social
identity as actors were engaged increasingly in the pro-life or pro-
choice movements. Due to limitations of space, I have made selec-
tions from six of the fourteen pro-choice narratives that are exemplary of the shared overall themes while retaining what I hope is a
sense of the integrity of individual life stories.

In the pro-choice narratives, certain themes emerged consistently in the plots. In almost every case, the speaker's recounting of
her birth or childhood stressed her difference and independence
from others in her family or her social milieu early in life. Similarly,
the speaker's encounter with the protest movements of the late
1960s and early 1970s is told as a key transformative event, a second moment of differentiation from either natal family or local community. In all the pro-choice plots, contact with the feminist movement is central, an event that turned each one toward activism, a
new social identity, and a particular understanding of the culture
and her place in it. In most cases, that encounter is tied into what
one might loosely call a transition to adult female identity—often a

story of an abortion, pregnancy, or birth. This is not only apparent to the analyst but also is clearly framed as a transformative element by the pro-choice narrators.

As is the case for *all* the activists, a tension between their participation in domestic and public domains is prominent. Pro-choice women, however, stress the latter domain. While nurturance, caring, and communal concern are presented as natural to women, emerging from female domestic activities, they are seen as values to be carried *outside* that domestic domain and into a more broadly defined social arena. In this way, the separation between motherhood and the workplace and their culturally assigned attributes is blurred or violated. The narratives suggest that this question of the moral authority of nurturance attributed to domesticity and its relationship to both female identity and action is critical to understanding the nature and larger significance of the contemporary abortion controversy for American history and culture.

The "Pioneer"

In Fargo, a few older women had been pioneers in the first wave of efforts to legalize abortion in the late 1960s and early 1970s. Notable among these early advocates to change abortion legislation was Ronna Hartman. Now in her late sixties, she introduced North Dakota's first bill to reform abortion laws in 1967, her freshman term in the State House of Representatives. She saw the issue as a natural extension of women's concerns, something she decided to represent after having spent three decades of her life as a full-time homemaker and mother. Of the handful of state legislators who were women (there were five her first term), Ronna was the only one, until recently, who espoused causes popularly identified as feminist. On the abortion issue, she had been opposed by some of her female colleagues.

Ronna attributes her distinctive perspective to her mother's influence: the plot of her narrative begins with her own birth as an event differentiating her from the rest of the family. In her narrative, Ronna claims her own inconoclasm as a trait she acquired from her mother.

My mother was a very unusual woman. She decided to divorce my father when I was born in 1916 and that was unheard of. . . . My father was very well off and good to my mother as far as material things went. When I was due, he parked her in the hospital and he went over to the Superior which was really a whorehouse. She had a very strict Baptist upbringing and was sorely upset. And she decided she wasn't going to bring her children up with that sort of thing. . . . When she got home, she convinced him she wanted to have a business, a beauty parlor. . . . He went along with that, bought all the equipment and got everything set up and then when he went off on his next big toot, she moved it all to Bemidgi. She planned it all out. She knew she had no skills and four children. She'd been married, like all girls then, right out of high school. So then she married a miner, but she was independent as a breeze and did what she wanted to do. . . .

But I think my mother always had a certain amount of guilt because she did the divorce soon after I was born. So she always treated me differently. I was the family pet.

Ronna's view of her special relationship to her mother that marked her as unusual early in life crystallizes in the story of her menarche.

As I look back, I had a lot of troubles menstruating. I have only one ovary and was told I would never have children. So my mother decided that if that was true, I better have a career and it shouldn't be just anything. Wouldn't I like to be a lawyer? So I guess I would have to say that all that was planted in me early on.

The dreams of a public career, however, were deferred for five decades by historical and economic circumstance. Caught in the pinch of the Depression, Ronna went to nursing school rather than college, then quit to marry a man who eventually became manager of an insurance company. By her own description, she lead a "very traditional life." She raised three children and was involved in the PTA, Cub Scouts, and women's groups of the Republican party and the Presbyterian Church.

In her forties, Ronna joined the local chapter of the League of Women Voters, a women's voluntary organization engaged in research and education to improve the political process. When she was nominated to be president of that group, she asked her husband's permission to take the position, fully expecting him to say no. Instead he encouraged her, noting she was "getting crotchety" since their last child left home that year; she accepted the offer, a moment she describes as "the beginning of her liberation." Several years later, two friends suggested she run for office. The idea took root immediately and eventually flowered into eighteen continuous years as a state representative, an unexpected second career to the first phase of her life spent as homemaker and mother, and a fulfillment of both her own and her mother's early ambitions.

Between 1967 and 1973, Ronna introduced abortion reform bills three times into the state legislature, and was met with increasing opposition at each attempt. Ronna continued with her agenda to represent the interests of women and children on other fronts besides abortion, indicating her connection of the abortion issue with the protection and promotion of what she sees as women's interests in the domestic domain. She introduced bills to improve treatment of juvenile offenders, enforce child support payments, support displaced homemakers, and criminalize spousal rape. While Ronna recognizes the legislative progress for women that she helped to implement, she nonetheless is concerned about young women today who she feels are unappreciative of the battles fought by an older generation, people like herself.

I worry a little about what's happening now. I read something about the kids in college and how conservative they are . . . and I get angry because I know so many young women lawyers and doctors and they are the smuggest bunch of people. And I think, "Oh my God they haven't the faintest idea how people fought so that they could get into that kind of law school. I wish it had been that easy for me."

This shift in attitudes that worried Ronna is what Mannheim called "the problem of generations." Mannheim writes:

Whether a new *generation style* emerges every year, every thirty, or every 100 years . . . depends entirely on the trigger action of social and cultural process (1970: 403).

Ronna's concern is, in a sense, how to reproduce in the present a particular stance regarding gender and politics given that the particular historical and cultural conditions that shaped most of the pro-choice activists no longer exist.

It's too easy to reach maturity when this [legal abortion] is an accomplished fact, like it's always been there for you. And that is the mentality you are talking about on the abortion issue that this group coming up is going to have. How long has it been? 1969 to 1983? A lot of people became adults during that time and I guess we have to accept that's the way life is.

From her own experience, Ronna understands that activism on issues such as abortion that are so deeply shaped by particular life experiences is therefore particularly contingent on historically shifting conditions. Thus, ironically, she worries that the gains she made as an activist have encouraged quiescence among young women. With good reason, Ronna fears that a new generation, presuming that the feminist goals she fought for are the status quo, will not maintain support for abortion rights. It is a worry she shares with other abortion advocates, many of whom are twenty years junior to her.

Pro-Choice Activists of the 1970s and 1980s

The women activists who organized the pro-choice efforts to defend the Fargo abortion clinic in 1981 were born, for the most part, between 1942 and 1952. They represent a range of backgrounds in terms of their natal families, and their current household, conjugal, and work arrangements differ. However, in all their stories, the strong commitment to pro-choice activism was connected to particular personal and political experiences: on the one hand, they all drew connections to specific life-cycle events, generally having to do with experiences and difficulties around sexuality, pregnancy, and childbearing, including the choice not to have children. On the other hand, the social unrest of the late 1960s and early 1970s, and the women's movement in particular, are critical turning points in their plots as they define themselves oppositionally in relation to the culture. For some, their encounter with these social movements as young adults was experienced as a moment of "conversion" from ideas and values with which they had been raised. For others it was expressed more as an "awakening" of some truth felt but never fully realized.

Kay

The central figure of the current controversy in Fargo is Kay Bellevue, the woman who opened the abortion clinic in 1981. Kay grew up in the Midwest, the oldest of seven children, the daughter of a Baptist minister and a woman who was a homemaker and part-time worker in the public school system. As is the case for most of the pro-choice activists, Kay began her narrative with the biographical "reasons" that, in her view, made her different. The plot begins with this early sense of differentiation, the source of identification with a key family member who served as a model for what she sees as her later oppositional stance toward the culture.

I always perceived myself as different from other kids. As a preacher's kid, whether it was true or not, I always felt people expected me to be perfect and to behave in a ladylike manner. . . . My dad was always interested in what was going on politically and took a keen interest in the antiwar movement and rights for blacks. I was the apple of his eye and he's always been proud of the things I've done. My dad's a real independent person and I see a lot of that in me.

Although she stopped going to church when she got married— something she feels could stigmatize her in a community noted for its church attendance—Kay nonetheless connects her activism to religious principles of social justice learned in her natal family. Again, like other pro-choice women, the stress on caring and nurturance as part of their concern is prominent.

I have always acted on what to me are Judeo-Christian principles. The Ten Commandments plus love thy neighbor. I was raised by my family to have a very very strong sense of ethics and it's still with me. I have a strong concern about people and social issues. I've had a tough time stomaching what goes on in the churches in the name of Christianity. I've found my sense of community elsewhere. . . . It's very distressing to me that [people,] particularly the people opposed to abortion, will attempt to say their moral beliefs are the only correct ones. . . . I think pro-choice people have a very strong basis in theology for the caring, loving perspective they have on abortion as do the antiabortion people have a basis in theology for their strong, loving caring perspective about the fetus.

In her senior year of college, Kay got pregnant and married and soon after moved to Denver where her husband was pursuing graduate studies. Like almost *all* of the women activists, regardless of their position on abortion, Kay's transition to motherhood was an event surrounded by ambivalence. Although her behavior was not, in fact, that different from that of many right-to-life women—for example, as a young mother she worked part-time and became involved in community associations—Kay's *interpretation* of her actions stresses the limitations of motherhood. Kay's plot turns on her unexpected reaction to her assigned and chosen role as mother.

I enjoyed being home, but I could never stay home all the time. I have never done that in my life. After being home one year and taking care of a kid, I felt my mind was a wasteland. And we were so poor we could almost never go out together.

Dividing childcare with her husband and babysitter, Kay started substitute teaching and taking classes. In her early twenties, she became active in a local chapter of La Leche League, an international organization promoting breastfeeding and natural childbirth. She marks this as a key event. Her quote demonstrates how, through her activities, she refigured both her social world and her initial dissonant experience of childbirth into a critique of the medical system's treatment of women.

My first child had not been a pleasant birth experience so I went [to La Leche] and I was really intrigued. There were people talking about this childbirth experience like it was the most fantastic thing you'd ever been through. I certainly didn't feel that way. I had a very hard labor. I screamed, I moaned. . . . My husband thought I was dying.

So anyway, this group introduced me to a whole different conception of childbirth and my second experience was so different I couldn't believe it.

And the way I came to feminism was that through all of this, I became acutely aware of how little physicians who were supposed to be doctors for women actually knew about women's bodies. So I became a real advocate for women to stand up for their rights, starting with breastfeeding.

In many ways, her concerns are not so different than those articulated by her neighbors and fellow citizens who so vehemently oppose her work. Not surprisingly, for both groups of women, voluntary work for a "cause" was an acceptable and satisfying way of managing to balance the pleasures and duties of motherhood with the structural isolation of that work as it is organized in America. La Leche League, for example, is a group where one stands an equal chance of running into a pro-life or pro-choice woman. In Kay's case, she met a woman who introduced her to feminism, a critical twist in the plot that sets it in tension with the "story."

Through La Leche League, I made a really good friend and she had read Judith Holes's book, *The Rebirth of Feminism*. It was at the time when, well feminism in New York was several years into its development, but in the Midwest, it certainly was not, so she and I started talking about some things I had never thought about and that was my introduction to the whole feminist perspective.

The preceding and following fragments reveal the kind of intersection of life cycle and historical circumstance that Mannheim underscored as critical to the formation of political movements in complex societies. Kay's growing sense of consciousness concerning the way women's reproductive needs were mishandled by the medical profession crystallized during her third pregnancy. She remembers being influenced in particular by the Sherry Finkbine case.

She was trying to get an abortion in the country because she was carrying a thalidomide child. At that time, I had never had any connection to abortion and as I read these stories, I began to feel very strongly that this woman had the right to make this decision and who in the world has the right to tell someone that they have to bring a deformed child into the world. I just remember feeling that so very strongly. So the funny thing is, when I look back on it, from my involvement with La Leche League and my strong feelings about a woman's right not to have a child, I felt strongly enough that this was important to me when I chose my physician, even though I had no experience with abortion in any way shape or form.

In 1972, Kay moved to Fargo with her husband and children. She continued as a leader in La Leche and got pregnant again. Kay marks this period as one of crisis. Her parents were divorcing and one of her children was having problems.

Then I ended up having an abortion myself. My youngest was eighteen months old and I accidentally got pregnant. We had four small kids at the time and we decided if we were going to make it a family unit, we had all the stress we could tolerate if we were going to survive.

Kay went to a clinic in another state for her abortion and, due to complications, stayed in touch with the staff there. A year later, they gave Kay's name to a NARAL organizer who was looking for people to start chapters in the Upper Midwest.

I talked it over with my husband and he said "Kay, what are you asking me? This is your choice. You do what you want to do."

In her life story Kay consistently linked her activism to a commitment to maintaining strong family ties, whether it concerned her public role or her personal decisions regarding abortion. This was, in part, a self-conscious response to right-to-life claims that pro-choice advocates are opposed to marriage, family, and children. This stereotype, to which most of the pro-choice women in Fargo were extremely sensitive, may account for the lack of open public support for pro-choice efforts in Fargo, even among feminists and liberals. Kay's comments below indicate not only her resentment of the casting of pro-choice by right-to-life advocates as being "antifamily" but shows how each side reformulates its stance in relation to the opposition, giving the debate both its dialectical and dialogical qualities.

I think it's easy for them to stereotype us as having values very different than theirs and that's not the case at all. Many of the people who get abortions have values very similar to the antiabortion people. The right-to-life people don't know how deeply I care for my own family and how involved I am since I have four children and spent the early years of my life working for a breastfeeding organization.

The perspective that abortion is "destroying the family" is a very, very narrow one. In my experience, people who have made the choice to have an abortion made it because they want a strong family. How bringing an unwanted child into a family strengthens it is something I have never been able to understand.

Kay's story of how she came to be an abortion rights advocate unfolds as she and I drive past expanses of rich black prairie topsoil being readied for spring wheat planting. It was her concern for the lives of the women who live out here that motivated her to open the first clinic in the state. By 1977, Kay was providing abortion referrals from her home and was growing increasingly disturbed at the lack of abortion services for women in the area. Two years later, when Kay was asked to be on the national board of NARAL, she met Sharon and with her help began plans in earnest to open a clinic in Fargo. Kay's comments show a symbiosis between her social action and emerging sense of self.

During that time, my perspective began to change about the kinds of things I was willing to do with my time. I no longer felt the need to argue the issue with anybody. I think it's a natural progression of anyone involved in a cause. You change your perspective as you grow with it. And once the clinic got going, I was real aware I could no longer be spokesperson for abortion rights because my role would be confused. So I stepped back from the political end of things with some regrets because I enjoyed it. I was frequently tense and yet I found it was something I could do, and I was seen as effective and that was rewarding, especially in a state like this because you can really have an impact on the process here.

In making the shift from activist to professional, Kay has faced new frustrations. As plans for the clinic progressed, and right-to-life groups began to mobilize to stop it, Kay became increasingly worried that something she wanted so badly and had worked for so long to achieve would fall through. Since the clinic opened, facing protesters has become an almost regular part of Kay's work. Pickets are there weekly on the day that abortions are performed. The reward of her work, not surprisingly, comes from the moments that remind her of the initial impulse that sent her off on the trajectory of pro-choice activism in the first place, her desire to make safe and legal abortions available to women who need them.

The very most satisfying thing of all has been when the patients are ready to leave here and they come up and put their arms around me or one of my staff people and say, "Thank you so much. You don't know what a difference this has made to my life. I expected something very different, [but] everyone here was so warm and so caring and nonjudgmental." And that in itself is a real reward.

The scenario Kay evokes in this "ideal" compliment indicates her goal is not simply the provision of safe abortion services but also the creation of a medical environment for women that is nurturant, warm, and caring.

While Kay is grateful that a pro-choice group formed to defend the clinic, her relationship to the entry of new activists has been difficult. Like Ronna, she sees them as unseasoned and shaped by newly emerging concerns that differentiate them historically from herself and other "veterans" of the movement.

I see the other people who have stepped forward as being at the starting growth stages I have passed through and gone beyond. And choices the new leaders have made are not choices I agree with about what needs to be done. But I have been able to say they have to grow the way I had to grow and the best thing I can do is be there for them if they want advice but allow them to grow at their own pace. There aren't a whole lot of people left from the early days.

Cathy

One of the pro-choice activists from the "early days" who helped organize the 1981 defense of the clinic was Cathy. Born in the late 1940s, she and Kay became friends working together on feminist causes in Fargo in the mid 1970s.

I believe strongly in the issue but might not have chosen to put as much energy into it if Kay hadn't asked me to help. I think being there with her all along, talking about the idea, looking at this building, talking about that contract. And when they thought they might close the clinic, I was the one who spoke up at the Commission meetings and helped organize Citizens for a Real Choice [the pro-choice support group] . . . and my God, I believe in privacy and respect for a person's body.

After years of activism, Cathy finds, like Kay, that her relationship to new recruits is problematic, due not only to a sense of generational difference from the younger women. She sees her "activist fatigue" in terms of her own life cycle as well.

Intellectually and philosophically, I am much more comfortable with women who are older and have a feminist value system. I'm getting tired of doing it all. The mid-thirties settling down is striking. And there is a part of me that would like to be involved in a relationship and change my life a little. In a sense, either I'm withdrawing or have already achieved a sort of "senior statesman" status.

Although she claims she is slowing down, the range of Cathy's current activities is nonetheless extensive, perhaps even exceeding the schedules filled with commitments that are typical of female activists on both sides. Cathy teaches full-time at the university and serves on several faculty committees. In addition to working for CRC, she is a board member of several feminist groups she helped found in the mid-1970s: The Women's Center, The Rape and Abuse Crisis Center, and the state chapter of NOW. She is also active in the local art museum. Her long-standing support for the region's artistic talent is reflected in her home, a tastefully decorated apartment whose walls are covered with local artists' renderings of North Dakota's icons: grain elevators, prairie pioneers, and images of native Americans. The enthusiasm she has for this art mirrors her interpretation of the activist work that engages her: it is a way to envision the local landscape anew.

I believe you work in your own environment. I grew up in a small town that largely identified itself as Republican. I don't know if I learned this from my mother—I suspect I did—but early on, the lesson was if you have the ability to affect it and you don't use that ability then don't bitch about it. And I've always been a mouthy sort. I internalized the myths of democracy and religion early on in terms of justice and fairness and I learned real well that's how things should be. Republicans talk a lot about individual freedom and choice and that's what I believe. Because of that I was a strong Goldwater supporter.

In each arena she works in, Cathy strives to reorder symbolically and materially the cultural milieu she claims as her own, without destroying what she values in it. This is apparent in Cathy's description of her encounter with the antiwar movement in the late 1960s.

And looking at my political development, about the time I started graduate school in 1968, I met some people who were very involved in the antiwar movement, and I started thinking, "What in the hell are we doing there?" [in Vietnam]. It finally clicked in my little noggin and I became one of them. I was the token Republican. I was very involved in the Lutheran Church; and I had more liberal ideas but I fought for them there too. I always felt that was part of the battle.

Cathy worked for several years in government and, out of a "sense of powerlessness" at her job, decided to go to law school in 1973. In much the same way that pro-life women speak of their mothering as a vocation they were "born to," Cathy describes her talents as a lawyer as "innate."

I had a strong social-justice orientation and I wanted those credentials. The law comes easily to me. I'm a natural-born bureaucrat. I didn't have a long-range goal. It was just the direction I moved in. In law school, I reentered the political arena as a Democrat and became involved in that party, and in forming NOW, the Women's Center, the Law Women's Caucus, and served in the Lutheran Church.

Cathy's engagement with feminism at that point in her life became and continues to be a major part of her identity, expressive of her earliest memories of her self. In her narrative, her involvement with the second wave of feminism has the quality of an awakening.

I have a kind of a strange feeling about my role in the women's movement. I mean, to me it's just coming home to where I belong. Working with women and with issues that have an impact on women's lives. . . . And I know that was part of my total being and growing up with it that there's no distinction between the personal and the political. I would assume it's analogous to a black growing up in white culture.

Her analogy of the experience of being female to that of being black in America indicates how she places herself oppositionally to what she considers to be the dominant culture.

Much of Cathy's life currently fits the right-to-life (and some researchers') stereotypes of pro-choice women. She is a single, professional, feminist woman, currently middle class, liberal in her political philosophy, and sophisticated in her cultural tastes. However, her early history fits as easily into equally unsuitable stereotypes of pro-life women in terms of class, religion, politics, or community background. Cathy grew up in a small town within a hundred-mile radius of Fargo. Her mother, widowed when Cathy was seven, worked as a waitress to support her daughter and herself with the help of a local network of aunts and cousins. Along with most of the women in this pro-choice group, Cathy stresses her own independence from conventions of gender, class, and regional values and attributes these qualities to similar traits in her mother.

I think that my mother had started making strong decisions on her own when she was in high school. And her mother remarried a man she didn't like. She [Cathy's mother] earned her way through high school doing everything on the farm and walking to school to get her education. All that says something about her being a fairly strong and autonomous woman. Part of that means I missed a lot of female socialization because she didn't buy into it. There has never been pressure on me to marry. . . . The only pressure I felt was academic performance. . . . I grew up never having a sense that there was a career I couldn't go into. Never having any role expectations placed on me in my own environment. And those I'm sure were important shaping forces.

Cathy sees herself as continuing her mother's distinctive stance in her work to create a more just social order within a local framework. Her identity is bound to the everyday qualities that she feels distinguishes a place like Fargo from a large metropolis.

We have an assumption about knowing a person as a person, not just as someone who delivers the paper or whatever. Here you know everybody because they live down the street and their third cousin is from your hometown. And that's what I like about here . . . that I don't know anybody that knows me only by one of my labels.

Janice

When the clinic was first attacked in 1981, it was Janice Sundstrom who stepped forward to organize a pro-choice group to defend it. A peer and friend of Cathy and of Kay, Janice was one of the first women to run for a high state office in North Dakota. Because she campaigned as a feminist and a Democrat in a conservative Republican state, her loss with 48 percent of the vote is as remarkable as the course her life has taken since her Catholic girlhood. Janice grew up in a family of seven children that struggled in the shadow of poverty when their farm was foreclosed in the early 1950s. Her plot begins with her unusual role in her family to which she attributes her iconoclasm in later life.

In 1945, shortly after I was born, my mom and dad moved here and brought me along and left all the other children with relations back in Illinois. I think I'm different from the rest of them because I had the experience of being the only child at a time when they had far too many children to deal with.

The transformations she eventually experienced are cast, in her story, as almost predictable. However, to the observer, they hardly seem the inevitable outcome of her youth and adolescence: twelve years in parochial school and marriage to her high school sweetheart a year after graduation followed immediately by a pregnancy and birth of her first child.

[My husband and I] were both in school and working and there we were with this kid. And then, three months later, I was pregnant again. We were both nineteen then and I didn't want to have another child. But I didn't have any choice. There was no option for me about birth control because I was still strongly committed to the Church's teaching. After Jodie was born I started taking pills and that's what ended the Church for me.

Janice's encounters with reproduction and contraception that made her question her church are key events in her plot. They are central pivoting moments in her life, which turned her toward alternative cultural models. Now a lawyer, political activist, mother of two, and wife of a professional, Janice considers her contact with the social movements of the late 1960s as critical.

It was around that time I remember watching the Senate Foreign Relations Hearings on television in these tin huts on campus [student dormitories] with these two little kids and wondering why this man wanted to turn this little Southeast Asian country over to the communists. And then my oldest sister came home and I remember asking her that question and she gave me a whole new way to look at Vietnam.

That sister left home and became active in politics, working on Eugene McCarthy's staff in Washington. She is both Janice's senior by ten years and the figure with whom Janice identifies as "a model" for unusual female behavior in her plot.

My sister was an important role model for me. I knew her to be involved in politics when I was eight and she was eighteen. There are a lot of girls who grow to womanhood never thinking of themselves as "political" because in their experience no one like them ever was. I grew up knowing that political activity was an appropriate province for a female.

With her sister's encouragement, Janice became involved in McCarthy's presidential campaign and was on the state delegation to the Democratic Convention in Chicago in 1968.

I went to Chicago. I demonstrated with the people on the streets. I didn't have any idea what was going on. Of course, in North Dakota they thought of me as a radical. I remember having my hair done and I was in this little pink and white bra dress and little white sandals and they were shouting "Free Huey" and I had no idea who Huey was. . . .

Here I am a telephone operator from North Dakota and I have two small children and I've never done anything like this before. And my conclusion about Chicago is it's too late when they're this old. You've gotta get them while they're younger. I decided to go back to school and graduated with a teaching degree.

Janice continued in her political work when she returned to college and was introduced to feminism by friends who by 1970 were involved with the women's movement "and opened it to me and me to it as the case may be. I learned real fast and basically it seemed the lesson was that through law I could help effect change for women. I decided to go to law school and worked to save for that."

While she stresses the importance for women of activities outside the home, that emphasis is always couched in terms of defending female interests. Janice's hopes for her college-age daughters are prominent for her at this point in her life. She hopes that unlike her, they will postpone marriage and prepare themselves for fulfilling wage work before they have family obligations; these concerns are linked to her pro-choice activism.

It seems to me it's restrictions on abortion coupled with a failure of sex education and a general social milieu that points to sexual activity as some means of personal fulfillment, whatever else it is supposed to mean to children, that leads to the increased rate of unwed parenthood among young women.

Sherry

This negotiation of a pro-choice position that establishes connections to family and community, as they understand them, is prominent for pro-choice women both in their narratives and in the public performance of their activism. Sherry, for example, president of CRC from 1981 to 1984, was baffled to find herself attacked as a "women's libber" because of this public role. Her sense of obligation to women's interests is not confined to what are identified as feminist groups. She was president of the Elkettes (the women's branch of the Elks Club) in 1982, a position she took on in part to remain close to her mother. In addition, she serves as an alumni collegiate advisor for her college sorority, a position she enjoys for the contact and influence with younger women it affords her.

I just can't say no to things that are important to me . . . most things that have to do with women's issues. And I can't really pick one over the other. The abortion issue is more important to me probably because it affected me personally in so many ways, so many times. I just feel it's a duty.

Sitting in the cramped kitchen of Sherry's modest two-story house, I remember a description of her given by another activist as "every Fargo woman's ideal. Slim, blonde, attractive with a decent job and a husband who travels a lot." Dressed in faded jeans and a man's shirt, Sherry looks and sounds unpretentious. She finds the images others have of her disturbing, a misreading of her life. Her marriage is a rocky one and she describes her work as an office administrator as "a ridiculous job I hate with men who are impossible to deal with." She is trying with difficulty to maintain the life course that was expected of her—marriage, family, children, church, and community—while accommodating experiences of the last decade that have taken her in different directions. In her plot, it is the progressive sense of dissonance from an "ideal female biography" that led her, eventually, to political activism.

Sherry was the first of two girls born to a couple who met at the utility company where they worked their whole lives. She describes herself as having been a dutiful daughter, attending Lutheran church activities four times a week until she was seventeen, and as a teenager more interested in fun than politics. Like the other pro-choice women, she marks her contact with the social movements of the late 1960s as a time when she began to look at things differently, the roots of a view of the world that she feels differentiates her from right-to-life women.

When I left high school and got to college, the whole hippie generation, the campus unrest, the Vietnam war made a lot of people question. . . .

You have to answer things for yourself. . . . I realized it's dangerous to believe in something beyond being able to ask a question. I don't feel the right-to-life position is invalid. I understand what they're saying. And if they honestly believe life begins at conception, I don't see any other choice for them. It only makes me angry that they don't realize other people don't believe that. And that they can't determine what's gonna happen in other people's lives.

I mean people react in ways that you don't expect them to all the time, every day. Who am I to say they're right or wrong?

The unexpected events in Sherry's life in the late 1960s and early 1970s are almost a catalog of what right-to-life activists call "the hard cases," the most persuasive of the pro-choice arguments, beginning with the horror of illegal abortion.

I never thought about abortion at all until my first year in college. In high school, I believed no one had sex, so I didn't. And then my friends started getting pregnant. We had no sex education. I had friends with whom I went to have abortions before it was legal. One got pregnant at my eighteenth birthday party and I felt this incredible sense of responsibility.

The first time, I went to Winnipeg to a woman's home, I sat out in the living room and looked out the window for the police. I was sure she was going to die. It was really terrifying. It wasn't a subject I could discuss with them and say, "I don't think you should do this." . . . It was their decision and they were my friends and I cared about them. It was a growing up story for all of us. I just about flunked out of college because of it.

Angered by this personal encounter with the inequities women faced in reproduction, Sherry became interested in feminism and a passive pro-choice supporter. In 1976, she married and began teaching in the local parochial school and, to her surprise, was pregnant within a year. The child was very much desired, but there were unexpected complications.

It wasn't a pregnancy I planned. I was teaching and my husband was beginning as a salesman so our financial position wasn't great. It didn't occur to me to have an abortion. I would work it out no matter what I had to do. Finally, my daughter was born and I was thrilled. For about thirty seconds. And then the doctor said, "There's something wrong here. There's an opening in the spine." I don't know if I can explain the feelings that I had. . . . I didn't know if I really had had a baby, and then, the doctor came in and told us our daughter was born with spina bifida. She would never have been able to control her bowels or her bladder. She would never have been able to walk. And all of a sudden we heard her start to choke and the hospital social worker said, "Don't worry it's going to be all right," and I said, "No it's not. It's never going to be all right again." And we just stood there and watched our daughter die. And what I can say mostly about that time is that I don't feel anyone has the right to force me to go through that again.

Shortly after the death of her daughter, Sherry was sexually assaulted one evening on her way home from work. It was the combination of these experiences, especially the traumatic pregnancy and birth of a severely handicapped infant, along with the growing right-to-life activity that effectively restricted abortion locally, that finally spurred Sherry to pro-choice activism.

Right after Melissa died in 1978, I saw something in the paper about how they intended not to allow health insurance to cover abortions and we had thousands of dollars in medical expenses because we had no health insurance. So I wrote a letter to the newspaper and then Kay contacted me and that's how I first got involved in the pro-choice movement.

Once Sherry took a public stand, she began to encounter right-to-life proponents directly at the legislature, in city commission meetings, and in speaking engagements at Sunday schools, businessmen's luncheons, and homemaker's associations. Her comments show how through the process of engagement in abortion activism, she began to articulate more sharply her own identity in relation to it, what she calls her own evolution.

The way I began to feel about these people who are so antiabortion for any reason is that it wasn't their experience. They weren't there for me when I needed support. They're out there talking and they're out there complaining and carrying on about the life of the fetus and not one of them is concerned about me. If I don't say something for myself, it might not get said. I don't want to have to leave the country because my own country has made it illegal for me to do what is best for my life.

I really believe that you evolve from a point of trying to control someone else's life into a point that you realize circumstances are so different for everyone that you can't possibly say there's no divorce, there's no abortion. I mean nothing is absolute. And I guess I feel I have evolved to that position and the anti-choice people haven't.

Sherry's characterization of the pro-choice and pro-life positions reflect critical differences in their philosophies of human nature and show how these abstractions are integrated into individual experience.

I think that if this were a perfect society, everyone could know about birth control and about sex and they would take the proper precautions and they would all work. All pregnancies would be planned or people would say this is fine, I'll deal with this. But that's not the way things are.

She is critical of the pro-life belief that people should behave in the present according to ideals of a future society in which abortion would be considered unnecessary. From the pro-choice point of view, life is seen as essentially problematic. Abortion is understood as an act of compassion, a way of helping women solve dilemmas according to the solutions they themselves have decided upon in difficult circumstances.

I think it's really more important that you do good things and you care about people. Sometimes those of us who already exist are more important. Even if someone who is anti-choice said I was well intentioned but misguided . . . well, I think, then how could you possibly be found wanting when it came to Judgment Day?

In this way, Sherry and her colleagues see their activism as part of a broader goal for improving the conditions of women's lives in conditions of sexual inequality. Because abortion is legal, they are often active in a variety of organizations devoted to social change on other fronts. Most of the pro-choice activists saw their work in CRC as a defensive measure; activism peaked, in general, around its defense of the clinic in 1981 and 1982. As Cathy put it,

CRC is a vehicle that is there to be used at the time that is appropriate but I'm not going to get all concerned about it. The question is, who's got the energy in their life and the drive to do it. Then let them use it. Let that vehicle be their life.

Jan

During 1983, one young woman, Jan Larsen, saw CRC as just such a vehicle.

After the initial hullabaloo, CRC became an organization that reacted instead of acted. Whenever the anti-choice people would do something, CRC would have to respond rather than take an active role in the community. Personally it means more to me than just the right to abortion. I would very much like to expand out to provide birth control information, referrals to doctors, advocate service for minors, postabortion counseling.

So I figured the only way to do it was to get on the board of CRC. The reason I got elected was I organized a picket at the Right-to-Life convention in 1982, so people knew me at the meeting. I felt it was an important thing to do. So what I'm doing is really asking CRC to become something very different than what its purpose was at its inception.

Bringing new vision and energy to CRC, Jan eventually became president of the group in 1984. When pro-life picketing of the clinic picked up in late 1983, she developed a service to escort patients through the regular line of right-to-life protesters. The energy Jan generated, as well as the escalation of antiabortion activities in Fargo, momentarily revived CRC, attracting new members to the group for the first time since 1981.

Jan is atypical in a number of ways from the other pro-choice activists in Fargo. She is nearly a decade younger than most of the other women, and she is motivated by an extraordinary, almost religious commitment to improving medical care for women. As she phrased it, "If there were a school to minister to women's health, I'd start my own church."

She traces her distinctive interests in part to medical circumstances she faced as an adolescent when she underwent extensive orthopedic surgery.

I think it started for me with my knee. My knee has nothing to do with women's health in the sense that it has nothing to do with my reproductive organs. But I felt terrified of doctors because I was powerless. They gave me morphine for eight days and I went through withdrawal. I freaked out.

Feminist writings of the 1970s provided Jan with a framework to order her own difficult encounter with the medical profession.

Feeling that so personally, I started reading about how women have been defined by doctors in terms of hysteria. They would take out her ovaries, cut off her clitoris, and send her home. When I started reading about that, things started falling into place in terms of my personal reaction and fears and anger about my doctors and just how women in general had been treated. It all seemed to fit really well.

And then I guess I started hearing about individual women I knew. About DES. And my friend had an ovarian cyst and was treated horribly by her doctor. And women who have had hysterectomies who don't need them. It just started dawning on me. And abortion. I started reading about what it was like when it wasn't legal.

Jan's illness, occurring right after high school, coincided with late adolescence, a period framed as liminal—a transitional state between social categories (see chapter 6)—both in her narrative, and in American culture more generally.

After the operation, I didn't know what I wanted, so I inquired into VISTA and went to Kansas City for two years to work as a community organizer. We're so homogeneous here that going anywhere else is an incredible shock and something everybody should do. It's so important in order to get a sense of who you are and what you want to do. You have to go somewhere else. I grew up in a kind of sterile political environment. VISTA is the place where I learned about politics at its fundamental level, which is the community.

That experience, along with her illness, created for Jan a strong identification with feminism and liberal left-wing social justice causes unusual among her peers in their twenties.

When she returned to Fargo in 1978 to go to college, she became involved in a range of grass-roots political activities: organizing senior citizens; defending Native American land claims; and volunteer work on Dalkon shield litigation, representing women who had been harmed by using that form of birth control. The last project turned into a full-time job as a legal assistant when she finished school in 1982. This period marks the end of Jan's liminality, a "turning," a point when she takes on "a new set of cultural roles, enters into fresh relations with a new set of people and acquires a new self-concept" (Mandelbaum 1973: 181).

As Jan's activism brought her into the public eye, her relations with her family changed.

I need to let my family know that I am going to forge my own life and own space in this town. That I'm going to do what I want to do. I don't want to do it to hurt them. I do it because it's what I believe. In a way, it's a credit to them. They raised me to think and know that I have a right to say what I believe. They don't look at it that way.

The oldest of four children, Jan spent the first seventeen years of her life in North Dakota in what she describes as a "nontraditional household." Her mother is a career woman with outspoken views about sexuality, which she passed on to her daughter. Homemaking became her father's responsibility.

If we were gonna have dinner, my dad and I would have to cook it. My mother is real nontraditional in a lot of other ways too. When I was in the eighth grade and went on my first date, I came home and my mother sat me down and told me that saving myself for marriage was a bunch of bullshit. And I should get it over with as soon as I could. Consequently, after every date, I was asked if it had happened. And when in fact it did, when I was nineteen years old, and I told her, she sent me a dozen roses in congratulations. From the time of that first date, I was also told that if I ever got pregnant, I would be at the abortionist—that's what she called it. I knew that if I became pregnant that, in a sense, I would have no control over it.

While Jan attributes her position on abortion to her mother's unconventional views of male and female behavior, her desire to establish a separate identity from her mother is an equally prominent theme in her activism and the plot of her story.

My mom and I aren't very close. And I think that is connected to her need for me to have a different perspective on sex, and her drive to make me exactly what she wanted me to be. She would like me to be in law school now. I know she loves me. It's just that she wanted me to do everything that she didn't do. It bothers her that I put myself out on a limb. What I have to do is counteract the influence of my mother.

Her relationships with an older generation of pro-choice activists—Kay, Cathy, and Janice, for example—provided Jan with alternative models of women who share Jan's strong commitment to social justice and women's rights. Unlike these older women, however, who view their lives and activism as unexpected responses to personal and historical experiences, Jan expresses much more intentionality in relation to her activism.

I thought a lot about how I wanted to deal with my life when I finished school. Just working wasn't going to be enough, so I decided—it sort of sounds dumb—but I just pinpointed some things I really needed to get involved with on my own, that I wanted to be part of, that I wanted to have an impact on, and CRC was a real logical choice for me for a number of reasons. First of all, I am really committed, thanks to my mother, to a woman's right to choose. And also, I have had clients that were victims of illegal abortions. And I see a very positive role for CRC and an influence that it can have in this area that is real well defined for me.

In addition to the intrinsic rewards of activism, Jan's pro-choice engagement is linked to two critical questions for her at this point in her life cycle, as she contemplates the possibility of having children.

I honestly am not comfortable saying that my bottom-line reasoning for being pro-choice is because I don't believe that life begins at conception. The very most fundamental right [for women], fortunately or unfortunately, is the right to bear children. That's what makes us different. It's our cross and it's also what raises us above. To not be able to control that single most unique part of us would devastate our entire sense of independence in every other aspect of our lives.

It is important to understand how Jan's use of the word "independence" is coded in the abortion debate. For right-to-life proponents, Jan's use of the term represents a desire for self-indulgence and a lack of responsibility for one's procreative potential. For Jan and most of her fellow activists, it stands, in fact, for the opposite of narcissism. It is not simply a fear that an unplanned pregnancy will interfere with what Luker characterizes as "their abilities to use the valuable 'male' resources—education, labor-market experience—which [pro-choice] women have in such abundance" (1984b: 110). Rather, doubts about bearing children are intertwined with questions about the social and cultural order that will be reproduced. In Jan's case, she worries that she will inevitably duplicate the familial and cultural relationships that are so problematic for her, and which she hopes, in her activism, to alter in new form.

Jan is an example of Mannheim's point that a generation is not necessarily age stratified. Jan shares a world view identified with a specific set of social and historical conditions experienced by a cohort a decade or more older than she is.

The fact that people are born at the same time, or that their youth, adulthood and old age coincide, does not in itself involve similarity of location [in the social and historical process]; what does create a similar location is that they are in a position to experience the same events and data. (Mannheim 1970: 388)

Although Jan is ten to twenty years younger than most of the other pro-choice activists, her vicarious encounter with feminism at a particular moment of crisis in her life has, in a sense, replicated for her—even at a generation's remove—their historical, political, and cultural experiences. In Jan's vision of the future in her life story, her thoughts about her own potential for procreation are inextricably bound with her present preoccupation with the social and economic inequities women face.

Biological parents have the greatest potential for destroying or creating a potential individual. If I have a biological child, if she's female, there are so many things that I'll do to her and deal with her similarly to how my mother dealt with me that I would never want to deal with a child like that. The expectations, the things we pass on that we don't want to. But they're in us. It is impossible to expect that they aren't going to influence that young person. I may want to be a biological parent. I'm twenty-five now and I'm no nearer to feeling I could deal with the responsibility of creating and molding an individual than when I was a teenager. God, what a thing to take a chance on.

In this passage, one can see how Jan, through her activism on the abortion issue, is seeking to rewrite the biographical and cultural scripts that she feels were bequeathed to her. In so doing, she is attempting to locate and create, in the environments she takes as her own, a social order that she would want to reproduce: a world more hospitable to the qualities and tasks she and other pro-choice activists identify as female.

Narrative Themes in Pro-Choice Life Stories

In the plots of their life stories, pro-choice activists stress their work and activities outside the home over motherhood, but always in terms of the values of caretaking that are identified with motherhood and domesticity. Thus, their defense of abortion rights is linked to a larger goal of (re)producing on a larger social scale what they would call female cultural values and what I am calling nurturance. This is apparent in the way their life stories uphold nurturance as a valued quality that is considered natural to women as well as the basis of their cultural authority; however, they reject it as an attribute that might confine them to childbearing, caretaking, and domesticity.

In most cases, the narrator portrays as unusual her involvement

in the breaking of the boundaries between home and the workplace, arenas conventionally held apart in American culture. Her
plot traces her convictions and behavior to a sequence of biographical encounters that emphasize her differentiation from cultural expectations of an ideal female biography: in the plot of a pro-choice
life story, these events might include an unusual birth or childhood, identification with iconoclastic and outspoken family members, the experience of life-cycle events related to reproduction
that brought her to question the institutions and received wisdom
she had always known, and a conversionlike encounter with the social movements of the late 1960s. For almost every pro-choice activist, this historical moment is deployed in the plot of her narrative as a transitional marker. Its central meaning for the narrator
is shaped by the fact that this encounter occurred, in most cases,
when the speaker was a young adult, what Mannheim termed a period of "fresh contact" when new actors enter into the cultural
order (1970: 383). Because of this, the stories suggest that generational shifts are of some significance in understanding not only
abortion activism, but also the emergence of social movements in
general.

For the Fargo pro-choice activists, their marking of their own
ideology as "Midwestern feminism" specifies both the regional and
temporal location of these women, yet also gives a particular uto-
pian subtext to their stories. It emerges narratively in the repeated
insistence that their activism is not for personal gain or individual
indulgence but serves the interests of women and social justice. In
this way, nurturance takes on a broad definition: although it is
viewed as rooted in particular female experience, it is seen as a
guide to action and a goal for social change in general. In other
words, nurturance is understood as an oppositional stance to a
world that is viewed as materialistic, male defined, and lacking in
compassion. Activists express this stance as a desire to create generative, loving, or at least tolerant relationships between family,
friends, members of the community, people in the workplace, and
even the nation as a whole.

These themes emerge not only in pro-choice life stories. Their
more general agenda is to use legal and political means to extend
the boundaries of the domain of women's interests into the culture

as a whole through their abortion activism as well as other activities. Both in their self-definition and social action, then, these women are attempting to transform the cultural meaning and social organization of human reproduction and dependency, so that they are not confined to arenas defined as female, but are viewed as conditions to be met collectively.

Chapter Ten

The Pro-Life Narratives

Introduction

Like their pro-choice colleagues, right-to-life activists also express
a concern for the preservation of what I am calling nurturance, but
their interpretation differs. Although nurturance is understood to
be a source of cultural value and female authority, as it is in the
pro-choice narratives, it is linked more directly to biological reproduction. In all the stories of pregnancy and birth told by right-to-
life women, the ambivalence of the speaker toward that condition
is invoked and then overcome, either through reference to her own
or her mother's experience. Frequently, the narrative resolution of
problematic pregnancy is managed through the protagonist's acceptance of the responsibilities of nurturance *despite* problematic
circumstances. Sometimes the conquest of the difficulties of and
doubts about pregnancy and birth seem almost heroic. In this way,
nurturant qualities and behavior appropriate to female identity are
something to be won through effort. Paradoxically, despite the
stress of this link to the physical body, nurturance as a characteris-
tic on mothering and the domestic domain is not seen as a natural
moral quality but one that is achieved.

Like the pro-choice life stories, the pro-life narratives reveal
how these activists are continually reworking ideologies[1] about the
place of women in American culture so that they are contextualized
in their historically specific experiences of everyday life. However,
for many pro-life activists who came of age in the 1970s and left the

work force to have children, this encounter with feminism is worked into the plot as a misguided identity they have transcended. This sort of generational shift in interpretations of female experience is a reminder of Mannheim's idea of "fresh contact," which stresses the temporal elements—both life cycle and historical—that affect political consciousness. This shift also shows how the controversy develops as a dialectic in time; the plots of pro-life procreation stories address and attempt to incorporate historically prior pro-choice positions.

I have selected seven cases from the twenty-one extensive interviews that are both exemplary of themes present in all the stories and that offer a sense of the shape of individual narratives as well. Again, the material and analysis presented here is not a definitive explanation of right-to-life sentiment in general; rather, it shows how women activists in this social movement are engaged in a process of cultural transformation.

The First Wave

Shirley

I met John when he first got back from the service and he decided he wanted to be an engineer. He had one year left when we were married on December 6, 1946, and I worked up until the day Jane was born, November 12, 1947. I wasn't even a bride a year. Well, our Senator, he's not pro-life, sent me a congratulations letter when Jane got a teacher of the year award in 1980. I wanted to take the letter back to him and say, "It was very inconvenient to have this daughter. My husband was in school and I was working. We thought we needed other things besides a child. And had abortion been available to me, I might have aborted the girl who was teacher of the year. What a loss to society that would have been." What losses are we having in society now?

The speaker is Shirley, a pleasant-looking sixty-three-year-old widow dressed in a gray and white plaid dress with a jaunty, knee-length hem, her hair in a soft short bouffant popular among older women in Fargo. Our interview took place at her dining room table where Shirley has set out—next to my tape recorder—coffee, juice, and fresh flowers. These touches, along with the neat and

comfortable furnishings—a couch, a barcalounger, a television
going in the background to entertain a resident pregnant teen—
are consistent with the unpretentious, warm hospitality that characterizes so many of the homes I visited. This middle-class section
of Fargo where Shirley lives stretches north along the Red River,
spreading east and west in indistinguishable streets lined with
ranch houses and dotted with the sort of young trees that indicate
that this is a recently built-up area. Shirley moved here a few years
ago when her last child left home. After her husband's death in
1971, she became involved in right-to-life efforts and has remained
active in the movement ever since.

The women in their sixties whom I interviewed shared with
young right-to-life women a range of ideologies, religious and political affiliations, and work and economic histories. They were distinctive, as a group, in the ways their lives have intersected with
historical experiences: like many other women born between 1920
and 1925, Shirley went to work as soon as she was able, to help out
a large extended family still reeling from the Depression. Although
she dreamed of becoming a stewardess, she trained as a nurse and
eventually married the brother of a high school chum right after
World War II when she was in her late twenties. She quit work
after the birth of her first child and went on to raise six children.
(Three others died in birth or infancy.) In her forties, with the encouragement of her husband and the support of the Manpower
Training Act, she took a refresher course in nursing and has been
working twenty hours a week since then, and also selling cosmetics
from her home to supplement her insurance income. She is, and
always has been, a devout Catholic, active in her church. For
years, she was a leader in the PTA and the Elkettes where she still
enjoys playing bingo and having a few drinks with long-standing female friends. Alert to national, local, and familial events that signal
a world changing around her—a son recently divorced, a daughter
with a baby out of wedlock—she measures herself with thoughtful
good humor.

I think we're bad on TV, I mean the morals that our children are watching,
these soap operas, what's right and what's wrong. There's a lack of commitment, of religion. They cheat and lie and steal and only bad people get
ahead. There's one I watch, my daughters got me hooked on it, called
"General Hospital," and I ask them, "Do you think this is normal? Gad, it

must be awful to think you all come from the same mother and the same father. What a dull life you must think I had when I could have been out living it up."

Shirley is entering what might be considered a typical phase of the contemporary American female adult life cycle for her cohort: the early stages of old age and the anticipated changes accompanying that, coping with the loss of a spouse or a husband entering retirement and the death of one's own parents, and adjusting to the exodus of children from the household and the recognition of their adult status with its attendant joys and sorrows.

What is consistent in the narratives of the women in their sixties is the way they link their pro-life position to their gender identity. That connection is made not through abstract formulations, but through interpretation of specific events. Whereas younger women focused more on the present, those in the older cohort traced a trajectory back to earliest memories, even to the circumstances of their own birth. The following excerpt shows how Shirley, for example, sees her pro-life work, her career as a nurse, her community activities, and her work as a mother as intertwined. Note how motherhood is presented not as natural to women but is "earned" and "deserved," a vocation requiring lifelong learning.

You know, a mother is a mother and if you deserve the title, you better work at it and earn it. . . . I started mothering when I was growing up on the farm. When the sheep would be lambing in the snow, my dad would bring the little ones to me and I'd put them in the oven door and give them a little bottle of milk. That's how I started. They said I was a nurse forever; I was always bringing things back to life.

Shirley first became involved in the right-to-life movement in 1972, during the referendum proposing reform of state abortion laws. After the referendum she helped found and then became president of a local chapter of Birthright, an international organization set up to provide alternatives to abortion by providing material and emotional support for women with unwanted pregnancies. The first wave of right-to-life activity in Fargo received much of its support from women of Shirley's cohort, many of whom had recently been widowed and were facing the departure of children from their households as well.

Well, the referendum was over and we ended up at a Birthright meeting
and all of us women, and five of us, were widows in the first year to year
and a half. It was really a grief session. And I took my first unwed mother
into my home the year after my husband died.

Shirley's account provides an instance of the critical intersection of
life cycle and historical event that shapes so many of the activists'
life stories. At a moment in her life cycle when the household and
kin context for a lifelong vocation of motherhood was diminishing,
pro-life work provided an arena for extending that work beyond the
boundaries of home and family. That is not to say that the actual
shift in the life cycle determined her activism. As the passage indicates, it is the narrative link she draws between the events that is
critical. In the plot of her story, Shirley reframes a problematic
transition through her activism so that it is infused with new meaning and draws her into a new social identity.

Recently, Shirley applied for the day shift at the student health
center where she works and did not get the job. She thinks this was
because they were afraid that she would not give information on
birth control. Like many female grass-roots activists, even staunch
Catholics such as Shirley, this is not the case.

I have no qualms about counseling for birth control. I won't counsel for
abortion. . . . I believe that a life that is started should be completed. If
they want to be sexually active, let them get on the pill. Let them prevent
pregnancy rather than destroy it.

Because of this incident, Shirley feels she has met with discrimination for holding her point of view. This theme is even more prominent in the narrative of another right-to-life woman of this cohort,
Corinne.

Corinne

Although she is also in her sixties, Corinne is as feisty as Shirley is
sedate, up-to-date on the latest trends and dressed in the current
fashion. Slim and wiry, twice divorced and once widowed, she
raised her three children on her clerical worker's salary, with some
help from her parents. Now, she lives with and cares for her ailing
ninety-four-year-old mother. While she has been active in pro-life
work for the past decade, Democratic politics has been a lifelong
passion, a family legacy.

My dad was always a Democrat. Joe Lewis, Joe DiMaggio and FDR and God were all on the same level. I grew up on it, but as I got active myself, it was a philosophy I supported, you know, legislation for the common ordinary man. I have some really good friends in town who were strong Democrats until they opened their businesses and turned Republican.

Given her dedication to the Democratic party, Corinne's pro-life activism has had a high price. Like other pro-life activists, Corinne's plot turns on a prior identification with the women's movement that eventually ended when her feminist colleagues rejected her for embracing pro-life views.

I joined the National Women's Political Caucus when it first started here, locally. This was in 1974 and pro-life was an issue here, although I wasn't that involved yet. I still felt there were a lot of things I wanted to work for in the women's movement. I was pretty good friends with [another local feminist leader] until the abortion thing really split us. She was pretty vicious with me when she found out I was pro-life. So then in 1975, the woman who was running the local right-to-life chapter asked me if I would take over for her and, even though I didn't feel qualified, I said OK. Since then, I've testified at the legislature for pro-life issues.

In her recounting, one sees how her identification with the right-to-life cause and ideology is not a reflection of preexistent identity but shifts over time as she experiences the effects of her incipient activism.

Six years after her first interest in pro-life activity, Corinne was one of the four women who pulled together the local right-to-life opposition to the abortion clinic. Two years later she was expelled from the local Democratic party for supporting a right-to-life candidate who ran on the Republican ticket. When I asked her what motivated her to take a position that has cost her so much, Corinne made an immediate connection to her own first and very difficult pregnancy.

I was pregnant, my daughter was six months old when I became pregnant again. My husband had just left me. I was three months along when he left. I didn't want that baby. I would never have thought of abortion although I knew it was available. . . . I believe in choice, in picking a career, or whether to buy this or that. But I don't believe anyone has the right to kill another human being. There are many women, including maybe your mother and my mother that hadn't planned on us and weren't happy with the idea of being pregnant. Look at my son. I was desolated when I found out I was pregnant. I was left in a real tough position. . . .

Life itself is no longer sacred. I said it in a speech in 1974. Abortion isn't anything new. I had friends years ago that went and did it. But we've made it legal, so therefore it's easy.

For Corinne, her right-to-life position gives symbolic order and meaning to difficult moments not only in her own reproductive history, but provides a link to her daughter's experience as well. When Corinne's daughter Anna recently had a miscarriage in the sixth month of pregnancy, the nurses encouraged both Anna and Corinne to hold the dead baby in order to "say goodbye." Although Corinne went into a severe depression after doing so, she felt the experience had

affirmed what I've always believed and what I've always known. The baby is a human being, a part of the human race from conception on.

The theme uniting these plot elements stresses the difficulties and sacrifices that women manage in carrying on "the human race."

Helen

A third woman of that cohort, Helen, also linked her pro-life commitment to overcoming ambivalence toward pregnancy. In this case, her story focuses on her mother's experience. Her "conversion" to the right-to-life movement is the plot element linking her experience of being "born again," and a repudiation of a prior sense of self that had separated her from her mother who recently passed away. Narratively, she connects all of these to the circumstances of her own birth and her mother's death.

You see, I had a sister killed in a car accident before I was born and you can imagine what that did to my family. I don't know if I ever would have been if she hadn't died. That's been something I never talked to my family about but I talk to myself a lot about it. My mother was so sick when she was pregnant with me because she was still grieving. She couldn't eat and they said if you don't eat we're gonna have to take that baby because you're gonna die. They wanted to abort her and she said, "No way."

So when she died last year and all these checks came in, I gave them to LIFE Coalition and as a thank you note to people, I told them about her story, how they wanted to abort her when she was pregnant with me and I am eternally grateful that they didn't. This is a coalition of people who love life and want to preserve the life of unborn babies. It's very exciting to do that. It brought life to me that at her death this could go on.

Helen was raised in one of Fargo's elite Lutheran families, the daughter of a physician and a mother who "always wanted nice things for her daughter," including an education at a prestigious college. Helen fulfilled her mother's dream; she attended and did well at an Eastern "seven sisters school" and went on for a master's degree in social work. "I always thought I'd marry somebody out there and lead a very different kind of life." Instead, she fell in love with the boy next door when he visited her out east after the war. They returned to Fargo together, married, and had three children. For most of her adult years, she has led the life appropriate to an upper middle-class wife of a local retail magnate. She has been a leader in the Junior League, the Fine Arts Club, the Lutheran Church, and enjoys bowling and birdwatching in her spare time. In the early 1970s, as a volunteer, she helped establish a private social service agency in town that became the primary adoption placement program for the area. At that time, she was a pro-choice advocate. In the construction of her plot, she connects this view with separation from her mother. Her claims to the prior position help give her current views greater authority.

Years ago, as a social worker, even though I reverenced life, I can still see some of those families and how they lived. . . . I remember this one lady who had nine children and the man she was living with wasn't her husband.

So when the thought of the Supreme Court ruling came, I was really for it, I was pro-choice because I thought of those little children and how they lived. And I remember my mother saying "Helena" (she always called me Helena when it was serious), "That's murder." And I said, "Better those children were never born, mother. They live a hell on earth." And she never talked about it to me after that but I'm sure it hurt her.

By 1975, Helen became a devotee of Yoga and dabbled in the occult. Soon after, she began attending interdenominational charismatic prayer group meetings and became a devout "born-again" Christian, active in formal organizations such as Women Aglow (see chapter 5) and several ad hoc women's prayer groups. This new commitment has affected her life on many levels from the mundane—she likes to speak in tongues while driving on her motorized lawn mower—to the more serious. Since her conversion she has changed her views on many issues, including abortion.

When the clinic opened in 1981, Helen was approached by a member of one of her prayer groups to join the pro-life coalition against the clinic. She joined the group and now is one of their more active board members, praying regularly in front of the clinic and using her social influence to gain friends and legitimacy for the group.

When they asked me to join, it was the first I ever really thought about it consciously, other than feeling guilty that I had changed my mind personally on abortion. . . . You know there is one scripture in Isaiah 44 that I especially pray for my family and that says "I knew you before you were formed in your mother's womb. Fear not, for you are my witness." So I'm sure unconsciously this change was coming about.

Helen's passage describing how she became involved with the pro-life movement has the quality of a conversion story, not only because of the use of the religious idiom but also because of the sense of transformation of self.[2] In the preceding fragment, Helen establishes metaphorical continuity between her pro-life conviction and the opening story of her narrative, in which she reconstructs her own sojourn in her mother's womb. In the plot, Helen's own birth becomes a story of her mother's heroic determination to carry the pregnancy to term, despite all expert advice to the contrary. Helen thus identifies herself simultaneously with her earliest moments of existence and with her mother's trauma as well. In Helen's retelling, the denial and acceptance of mother and daughter of each other's lives are merged, and then given larger significance as Helen connects both events, figuratively and materially to her commitment to the right-to-life movement.

The Generational Bridge

Peggy

These connections of the right-to-life position with overcoming ambivalence toward pregnancy, a transformed sense of one's own values, and the merging of divergent generational identities in the act of recollection are present in the narratives of younger pro-life women as well. Peggy Jones is a devout Catholic woman, born in 1942 and raised on a farm in a family of nine. Her narrative begins with a recollection of her initial difference from her mother on the issue of abortion when she was a teenager. Her comment that "so much has changed since then" indicates the twist in the plot marking her conversion to the pro-life position. She was persuaded by the pictures of aborted fetuses.

You know, when I was in my teens, I remember my mother saying she was against abortion, how it could lead to euthanasia and I always used to disclaim that and say, "Oh mother, you're so out of date." I can just hear myself saying that. And so much has changed since then.

I remember in 1972 when there was that referendum here and I bought a book, *The Handbook on Abortion*, and I remember being shocked by the pictures of the aborted babies. My own children were five and two, so that was even more shocking to have gone through pregnancy and know that it's a life and all that.

I first met Peggy at the Fargo parochial high school where she had programmed a day of events on the tenth anniversary of the 1973 *Roe* v. *Wade* decision legalizing abortion. On that occasion, as coordinator of the pro-life section of the local Catholic diocese, she introduced the play she had written based on the Supreme Court testimony. The staging, with the teachers cast as Justices, costumed in choir robes and seated at long tables draped with cloth, was meant to mimic the decorum of the high court but seemed to me to resemble more closely a *tableau vivant* of the Last Supper. What impressed me was that Peggy had retained in her stage version the most compelling speeches in defense of abortion argued before the court, a recognition of an opposing point of view I had not expected.

Peggy greeted me at her office wearing loden green corduroy trousers and jacket, a white turtleneck sweater, with her red hair in a short stylish cut. Her manner reinforced my earlier impression of her as an open, intelligent, and compassionate person. Peggy is one of the small number of pro-life activists in Fargo from the same group from which much of the pro-choice support is drawn— women born between 1940 and 1945.

In the narratives of the right-to-life women of this age group, their concern with abortion reflected issues prominent for them at this point in their life cycles: they are contemplating the changes ahead as they move back into the paid work force and out of a decade or more spent as full-time mothers and homemakers. They are evaluating their marriages in relation to these shifts, particularly as they witness marital trouble among many of their peers. They worry over the effect on their teenage children of the ubiq-

uitous temptations of the American adolescent subculture that
have made their way into Fargo life. This last concern was one of
the first that Peggy mentioned when I asked her why she became
active in the pro-life movement.

Well, I didn't get that involved until the last two years. And one thing I
feel keenly about now, and it's probably because my oldest son is fifteen
and a freshman in high school, but I just firmly believe that the more we
can talk to high-school-age students about what abortions are, and the realities of abortion and its alternatives, that there are people who care. . . .
I've personally been speaking in the schools now for these last two years.

I guess I see abortion as being linked in terms of . . . well, if we can
respect ourselves enough that we can say no to outside pressures kids are
getting today, and I know they are tremendous, then we can feel good
enough about ourselves that if we become pregnant, its OK to go through
with that. I think a lot of it has to do with the fact that we don't feel good
enough. . . . We're pushed from the outside. I mean every magazine you
pick up today talks about sexuality and 98 percent of the teens have had
sex by the time they're nineteen. So you think you're some kind of freak if
you don't.

    As lay pro-life coordinator for the Catholic Church, Peggy was
involved with public education and made it her personal goal to
develop outreach programs to high schools, along with keeping up
on legislation, staying in contact with other national, state, and local
right-to-life groups, and maintaining ties with parishes throughout
the area, each of which has its own pro-life contact. Peggy, like many
other right-to-life women, sees the abortion issue as inseparable
from a need for sex education that goes beyond "explaining the
plumbing," an obligation that she feels should be shared jointly by
family, school, church, and state.

I always considered our generation would certainly be open about talking
with our kids about sex, and I've tried to be with my family. I think part of
the problem is we haven't talked nearly enough about being responsible
for our actions. You spill a glass of water then you wipe it up. There are
natural and logical consequences. That's the risk. It's like getting in the
car. One of the risks you take is having an accident.

Peggy worries especially that abortion fosters a sense of irresponsibility for the reproductive consequences of sexual activity and
makes a concerted effort to discuss these things with her son. She
prides herself that now (after practicing by talking to her plants)

they can sit at the kitchen table and discuss wet dreams, or the sudden mood shifts of his thirteen-year-old sister.

When Peggy finished high school in a small town north of Fargo at age seventeen "it was assumed you would get married and have kids." Within two years, Peggy did just that, marrying a man she met at her job as a grocery clerk. He now works in middle management for a utility company. She is grateful that it took her two years (even without birth control) to get pregnant so that they had time to get to know each other "before the kids came." Since then, they have had two and adopted a third, a biracial child.

In their late twenties, the Joneses became actively involved in church-sponsored marriage reform movements, starting with an activity called Marriage Encounter. Initiated by the Catholic Church, it has become quite popular in the Fargo–Moorhead area (and throughout the country) and is now imitated by other denominations. In Peggy's view, the energy they have put into their marriage through these activities (including pro-life work) has enabled them to focus on common goals as a couple and helped them keep their marriage together through what they recognize can be a very stressful period in the family cycle. In her narrative, "women's growth" is seen as particularly dangerous to the survival of marriages.

We've noticed, my husband and I, with our friends, that now that we're all through our thirties, there's been a heck of a lot of growth, especially for the women. A lot of us have gone back to work or to school. A lot of our friends, about five couples this last year, are experiencing serious marital difficulties because of [the woman's] growth. My husband and I just really care about each other and how the other is growing and I think our spiritual life together has helped us a lot too, the time we spend in prayer together, that's given us hope when it's been tough. Gosh, I just think that our own marriage is a lot healthier than it was ten years ago. We're a lot more willing to compromise and talk things out.

As was the case for most of the right-to-life women I worked with, successful marriages are seen as the product of much time and effort.

Karen

Karen, a pro-life activist and mother of three, while not involved in "marriage reform" groups, viewed her relationship with her husband as an achievement. She explained her views on marriage.

One of the problems now is that everyone thinks that marriage should just be easy. Well it's not. It's a lot of hard work, and if you have differences to start with, it's even harder.

For pro-life activists, strong marriages are supported by the ideologies and social organization of movement activities. Karen and her husband consider each other to be best friends, and he is a staunch supporter of her activism; although he has less time than she does to devote to the cause, the pro-life philosophy meshes with his view of the world. Karen views her husband as atypical, because of his concern with the "domestic sphere."

I think he's unusual in that he's devoted to home and family. To him it doesn't make sense that we would not allow life a chance, and I see it as an optimistic viewpoint because what you're saying is all things are possible. He's in horticulture research and he works with plants and likes to grow things. We have almost a quarter of an acre out here in a garden. And it carries over into his life. He sees growth rather than destruction. And it isn't just a single issue. He doesn't see the reason for war either.

Karen was born in 1944, the day after her father died, on a farm in Nebraska. To support the family, her mother moved back to her natal home and worked as a schoolteacher until she remarried seven years later. Karen met her husband in college and married him the same year she completed an advanced degree in home economics. Due to her husband's work as a research agronomist, she has lived overseas until recently, and has devoted herself to running the household and raising her three children. The family moved to the Upper Midwest three years ago, to a development on the outskirts of Fargo, between farms to the north and the sugar beet processing plant to the south that dominates the landscape and economy.

Karen's home, which I first visited during a right-to-life board meeting two weeks before the interview, is filled with an unusual combination of Americana and foreign art objects collected during her time abroad. When she returned to the United States, she recognized that her years as a homemaker, like her sojourns overseas, were ending. Karen went back to school in 1981 to take a refresher course in home economics and shortly after that, became involved in LIFE Coalition. Returning to the work force is a salient concern at this point in her life and shapes her current understanding of self, her social position, and her critique of the culture. All these are integrated and given meaning through her right-to-life activism through which she articulates a critique of materialism and sexual inequality in American society. For her, abortion signifies a social denial of nurturance defined as a quality acquired through the activities of caretaking.

I think we've accepted abortion because we're a very materialist society and there is less time for caring. To me it's all related. Housewives don't mean much because we do the caring and the mothering kinds of things which are not as important as a nice house or a new car. I think it's a basic attitude we've had for some time now.

You know, the whole thing got me to thinking about displaced homemakers and they are the most undervalued people in the whole world. The things that a mother does, if she's a good one, a conscientious caring mother, there's no one in the whole world who can take her place. But because she's not paid we don't appreciate her. So when you go out into the world, people say, "What have you been doing all these years?" when you're interviewed for a job. And they have no feeling or compassion. It doesn't pay so it doesn't count.

Contrary to the popular stereotype and consistent with many other right-to-life advocates, Karen does not believe women should only be at home with children. In fact, she endorses women working; her criticism is of the dehumanizing effects that wage work has on both men and women. In her program, the current sexual division of labor would change, making work and parenthood easier to combine for both men and women. As she sees it, liberalized abortion is an obstacle to the changes she has in mind.

I think there should be flexible hours so that a mother and father can each have a part-time job. I think there should be shared jobs, consideration made so that daily life can provide as much as possible. That doesn't mean that the child never has a babysitter. But companies should hire people in ways that will allow mothers and fathers to take care of their children. No one loves them like a mother and dad love those children.

People . . . women who are married can get maternity leave and go right back. But if we destroy it by getting abortions, we're not going to change it as fast as when we change it by allowing people who are pregnant to have their babies and helping them.

The public acceptance of abortion, then, stands for what she sees as the growing devaluation of the work of caring for dependents in American culture, a problem that, in her view, hurts not only women and children but men as well.

Men are liberated in a sense when women are liberated because it's liberating to be able to nurture and care for children and it's not that confining when you don't have to do it all the time. . . . I mean a woman who has a job or career and a family and a man who has a career and a family find they will balance each other if they work together at it instead of turning the job over to daycare.

Although Karen sits on the board of LIFE Coalition, she does not consider herself as serious an activist as other local leaders. She became involved, she explained, at the insistence of friends and because of the sense of urgency she felt when the clinic opened. Similarly, Peggy took her position because she was bored with clerical work and had been asked by the diocese to replace the former pro-life coordinator who left to have a baby. These women, while committed to the pro-life cause, are unlike others in that they describe their activism as evolving more out of circumstance than passion. The statement with which Peggy closed the interview suggests how their activism intersects with their life-cycle positions.

I had been working as a secretary for an insurance firm about twenty hours a week and it was getting tedious. I wanted to move into something else, and I found this to be really healthy for me because it has allowed me to be creative, to have much more self-confidence. I like what it's done for me as a person. I don't see that I'm going to do it for my whole life—for example, I don't think I would have gotten into politics if it hadn't been for my pro-life work. It's really been a life-broadening experience in a lot of ways. I think my next step is to go to college. At age forty. Imagine that. (laughs).

The Younger Activists

Sally

While the move from motherhood to marketplace was absorbing these women in their late thirties, those born a decade later were facing the opposite transition. Sally Nordsen is part of a group of women born between 1952 and 1958 who made up the majority of Fargo's activists involved in the fight against the clinic and were the most dedicated members. Like most of the other pro-life women of this group, Sally went to college where she met her husband who now works in wholesale marketing. They married soon after her graduation; she worked for seven years as a social worker. In her late twenties, she got pregnant and decided to leave the work force in order to raise her children. This is a critical element in her plot, a difficult passage. Although she regards the choice as a positive one, it was nonetheless marked by ambivalence.

I had two days left of work before my resignation was official but Dick was born earlier than expected. So I left the work on my desk and never went back to it. There were so many things that were abrupt. When I went into the hospital it was raining, and when I came out it was snowing. A change of seasons, a change of work habits, a new baby in my life. It was hard. I was so anxious to get home and show this baby off. And when I walked in the door, it was like the weight of the world and I thought, "What am I going to do with him now?" Well, these fears faded.

So it was a change. When Ken would come home, I would practically meet him at the door with my coat and purse cause I wanted to get out of there. I couldn't stand it, you know. And that's still the case sometimes. But the joys outweigh the desire to go back to work.

Like other pro-life activists, Sally is articulate about the difficulties of motherhood, the work involved, and her acceptance of that identity despite the hardships. Balancing motherhood with voluntary work provides a temporary resolution for the difficulties of this period in her life cycle, much as it did for some of the pro-choice activists. In contrast to the pro-choice narrators, however, Sally stresses her need to be at home.

I had some hobbies at one time (laughs) but with the pro-life work and my family and church—it's really all I've been able to manage. And there have been times when I've just spread myself too thin. And the kids are the ones that suffer if I get too involved.

The Nordsen home, located in an older neighborhood not far from downtown Fargo, reflects the more gracious era when it was first built: wood moldings, stained glass windows in the foyer, a hospitable porch well trafficked by friends and family who drop by frequently and unexpectedly. On the spring day of my visit, the block was its own world. Children at play tested the boundaries between sidewalk and street while mothers watched under the graceful arches of Fargo's prized elms, joined occasionally by some college boys who rent rooms in their homes or an elderly parent out for fresh air.

I first met Sally during a health fair at the local shopping mall where she and a neighbor spent the day at a pro-life information table handing out literature to passersby. For those who stopped, she explained the life of the unborn with the aid of plastic models of fetal development loaned by a sympathetic obstetrician. Later, at her home, she explained how she became "converted" to the right-to-life cause. A reevaluation of the meaning of her continuing belief in "women's rights" and "freedom" are critical to this twist of her plot.

When the abortion chamber came to town, it just hit me that I was responsible for this. I was walking in front of the clinic and all of a sudden, many things just came crashing down, you might say, about my attitudes and values and things. . . .

I go around acting like I had to be the champion for women's rights. But I honestly have a hard time with some of the screaming that goes on because some of those women also feel that abortion is one of those rights and they call it reproductive freedom. To me, yes, it is your freedom to choose to reproduce or not to reproduce. But once that's done, you've already made that choice. So when those things get lumped together with women's rights, like equal pay, I get really upset. There are some things, such as abortion, that can actually be destructive to other people. If we are so right, let's not repeat the same mistakes that other people have made. Let's not repeat the mistakes that men have been making.

Her statement was interrupted briefly by a crying child, the younger of her two boys aged three and one who, until this moment, had been snoozing amid recently abandoned toys in a comfortable heap on the floor with the family husky.

Sally is extremely warm, with an engaging and available sense of humor even in the presence of two demanding toddlers. Her blonde hair, blue eyes, and broad bone structure bear testimony to her second-generation Norwegian heritage. Her clothes—old jeans and a turtleneck—are the daily uniform of a young mother. For Sally and the other pro-life activists her age, the move from wage labor to motherhood occurred in the late 1970s or more recently. This critical moment in their life histories intersected a paradoxical moment for American feminism. Much of what the prior cohort of feminist activists of the 1960s and 1970s had struggled for appeared to have been achieved. Sally's developing plot indicates the hidden toll of feminism's rapid successes. In her narrative, she progressively differentiates herself from feminist rhetoric that was so powerful ten years earlier yet did not reflect her experience in the late 1970s.

Some of these things I equated with being a free woman were not necessarily good and did not necessarily have to do with freedom. Women's rights were important to me. But sometimes I acted as if I was downtrodden. I have a husband who respects me completely, who shares in the work around the house. I have no reason to complain. I didn't live in a home where I was belittled for being female.

Women like Sally who have decided to leave the work force for a "reproductive phase" of their life cycle are keenly aware of the disjunction of their choice with the images that surround them. Sally's colleague, Roberta, made the case succinctly.

Roberta

I first met Roberta at a pro-life banquet and fund-raiser. Born in 1953, Roberta is now married to an auto mechanic. Before giving birth to her first child, she worked as a college teacher and a graphic designer. In 1984, she was a full-time homemaker, raising two children, expecting a third, and active in the pro-life movement as well as Democratic politics.

They paint the job world as so glamorous, as if women are all in executive positions. But really, what is the average woman doing? Mostly office work, secretarial stuff. Even teaching gets routine after a while. When you watch TV, there aren't women pictured working at grocery store checkouts.

I just don't see homemaking as any worse than eight to five. I really like homemaking. It's something I've chosen. I can, I bake, I garden, I sew, I see it as an art. I don't say everyone should do it that way. And my husband likes to do it too. People should be able to do what they like to do. That's the part of the women's movement I've really been in favor of.

In Roberta's construction, this is not simply a defense of homemaking as a choice of vocation. Her description of her own life is embedded in a critique of what she considers to be the dominant culture. What she *does* defend is the social and economic consequences of having made a decision that she senses as unpopular.

There are a lot of pro-life people who choose to stay at home with their children like me. A secondary income is not that important to us. My income would be pretty darn good if I took off for the work force again. My husband alone can support us but we have to pinch and budget and so we don't go to the fundraisers. And now that my husband and I have become evangelicals, we don't really believe in drinking for the sake of drinking. So we're severely criticized for that. Anyway, to completely exclude us for that one reason, being pro-life, just blows my mind.

In choosing to leave the work force, Roberta knew she would be greatly reducing the disposable income for her household. The economic consequences of her ideological choice, then, have restricted the activities in which she and her husband can participate.

It is important to remember that the pro-choice women only ten years senior to Roberta felt that their decision to do the opposite, leave motherhood for the workforce, was similarly controversial. What this indicates is how rapidly the definition of "normal female behavior" has changed. For example, Roberta sees in the lack of recognition for domestic work an extension of a more pervasive condition: the increasing commercialization of human relations, especially those involving dependents.

You know, the picture painted these days is how much kids cost. These are the reasons given for most abortions. How much work kids are, how much they can change your lifestyle, how they interrupt the timing of your goals. What is ten years out of a seventy-year life span? You know, I've done a lot of volunteer work in nursing homes and it's just a lonely world to see women who don't have families. If you don't have your family, if you don't have your values, then what's money, you know?

In her narrative, abortion is threatening because it suggests the public acceptance of sexuality disengaged from family formation and the values the latter supposedly entails. Metaphorically, Roberta represents this as the triumph of material interests over the care of human beings, a loss of a locus of unconditional nurturance in the social order. A similar theme emerges in Sally's narrative, but here the link is made to men's sexual behavior. From her perspective, abortion weakens social pressure on men to take responsibility for the reproductive consequences of intercourse.

I think men can get away with certain things that women can't, like infidelity, and I don't want to count that in my package of rights. To me sexual freedom is a loving relationship with one person. It came to me at that prayer vigil that all these things follow in a chain. There are consequences we're not ready for and that plays a big part in legalized abortion. And really, the other way I was living, I was really bored. I just wanted more and more and more.

The plots of these pro-life activists stress the negative consequences for women of the dismantling of a system that links male sexuality to childrearing and marriage. Sally, for example, uses her experiences as a social worker as evidence that abortion undercuts women's ability to gain the support of a man.

In my work, I saw a lot of people who were part of the middle class and then because of a divorce or having a child out of wedlock, they became part of the welfare system. I saw how really necessary, how many reasons there were to really maintain that relationship. There's a very real world out there. I feel sorry for men that they can't have the same feelings I do about pregnancy. But in the situation of a woman, where all of a sudden after twenty years of a marriage, she has nothing, and he at least has a business or a job or whatever . . . women just have a different kind of investment in the marriage situation.

Ironically, the same sort of cases are used by pro-choice activists who attribute the viewpoints of their opponents to ignorance of the difficulties many women face. Almost all of the Fargo pro-life activists were aware of these stereotypes and addressed them in a dialectical fashion, using them to confirm their own position. Roberta, for example, expressed it in the following way:

If you take the pro-life stand, you're labeled as being against anything else that women stand for. And ironically, it's mostly women in our movement. The pro-choice people say about us, "Well, they must have feelings but they're so put down they can't make up their own minds, you know." And they think we're just saying what we do because that's what men have taught us. Well, if the men have taught us, why aren't the men helping us?

To write off the views of a Sally or Roberta as naive is as much a misreading as are their claims that pro-choice women are unconcerned with raising families. They, along with other right-to-life activists, are well aware of the fragility of traditional marriage arrangements and recognize the lack of other social forms that might ensure the emotional and material support of women with children or other dependents.

The women I have been talking to are strong and independent, hardly
weak women, homemakers by choice because they value that. They support equal pay for equal work. I know about that because I sued the company I worked for and won. . . . No, we aren't quiet. You know, we
couldn't have a movement if we were all the way we're stereotyped.

Roberta's view of the place of women in the sexual division of
labor has a complex relationship to a new-found religious commitment, a connection typical of many right-to-life activists. Seen in
the diachronic perspective of a life history, the relationship between religiosity and right-to-life activism is not a simple case of
cause and effect, with religious faith a prior condition for pro-life
belief, as Roberta's case makes clear.

Like Sally and Helen, Roberta had not been particularly interested in religion most of her life and had been attending a mainstream Lutheran church in Fargo, more for social reasons than out
of spiritual conviction.

The church we had been going to didn't take a pro-life stand. I was over
at the church one day—in fact, that's where this all really got going for
me. I was one of those, what you would call a sleeper. I mean the issue
could have been shot in my face and I wouldn't have noticed. But there
was an article in the paper about this girl who had an abortion and I was
having coffee with some women in the church and I said, "How on earth
could anyone ever consider that? What happened to motherhood?" . . .
Well, at the church where we went, we had hoped to get a discussion
going because the lady in charge of Planned Parenthood was a member . . . and they said, "It's such a controversial issue, it will divide the
congregation."

Roberta and her husband decided to leave their mainline church to
find a community of peers who would support a range of decisions
they made as individuals, and as a couple. In moving to an evangelical Lutheran congregation, they found a setting and a group of
people whose values are consistent with those they had been for-
mulating over the past few years.

So we joined this Lutheran Free Evangelical Church where they just pure
and simple said that they thought abortion is wrong. And we have grown
into thinking that it's the best thing that ever happened to us. And it's
quite a bit changed our lifestyle. And at the same time, the evangelical
community was changing to be more openly pro-life. Some people consider that the Church is so demanding that people have a hard time sustaining commitments to other things. We have Bible Study and church on

Sunday morning, evening, and night. And I have Tuesday morning Bible study too. And I'm a speaker for pro-life and I take calls. But with the two kids, that's where I draw the line.

Roberta's shift from wage labor to homemaking, her commitment to the right-to-life cause, and her conversion to born-again Christianity emerged more or less in sequence. Contrary to stereotype, she was not urged by religious leaders to join the pro-life movement. Rather, she has been urging the minister at her new church, as she did at her former congregation, to take a pro-life stand.

For the most recent wave of right-to-life activists in particular, the pro-life movement speaks to their concerns. Through it, their own dilemmas are framed as part of a larger struggle to reform the culture in the interests of women. For Roberta, the right-to-life cause legitimates choices she has made—as a woman, mother, and political activist. As she explained to me while I cleared my tape recorder from her kitchen table to make room for freshly baked bread:

The image that's presented of us as having a lot of kids hanging around and that's all you do at home and you don't get anything else done, that's really untrue. In fact, when we do mailings here, my little one stands between my legs and I use her tongue as a sponge. She loves it and that's the heart of grass-roots involvement. That's the bottom. That's the stuff and the substance that makes it all worth it. Kids are what it boils down to. My husband and I really prize them; they are our future and that is what we feel is the root of the whole pro-life thing.

Narrative Themes in Pro-Life Life Stories

The collective portrait that emerges from these stories is much more complex than the stereotype that portrays pro-life women as reactionary housewives and mothers passed by in the sweep of social change. They are astute, alert to social and political developments, and on many issues are not antifeminist. They approve of and endorse women seeking political power and economic equity. Roberta, for example, brought a comparable-worth suit against a former employer. Most held or had held jobs and some had careers. In the marriage relationships I observed, husbands helped out regularly in domestic duties and were pragmatically and emotionally supportive of their wives' political work.

What is striking in the narratives is how most of these women had assimilated some version of feminist thought and woven it into their life choices. The plot of almost every story hinges on how the narrator either repudiated or reorganized these ideas into a right-to-life framework. Sally's narrative of how her ideas have changed as she joined the pro-life movement is illustrative.

You're looking at somebody who used to think the opposite. I used to think that sex outside of marriage was fine. Now I see I don't believe that anymore. I believe when you practice sex outside of marriage you are taking all kinds of chances, including walking out on each other and not having to accept the responsibility of children or whatever. And to me, once you engage in the act of sex, it's a big emotional commitment. If my boyfriend walked out on me I would be devastated. I think the world preaches you can have it all . . . doing lots of things without getting caught and I guess over the last few years, I've really changed my mind about a lot of things. And when I see the abortion clinic, there's proof positive to me that my values are right and an innocent human being is paying the price for all this.

It is this sort of negotiation of feminism into their life story that distinguishes the younger right-to-life women in particular, although it is present in more muted form with older activists such as Corinne and Helen. Rather than simply defining themselves in opposition to what they understand feminist ideology and practice to be, many, like Sally, claim to have held that position, and to have transcended it. Sally, for example, describes her former "liberated" ideas about sexuality and heterosexual relationships as a repression of her true self.

I think there was part of me that never fully agreed. It wasn't a complete turnaround. It was kind of like inside you know it's not right but you make yourself think it's OK. When I was in college, I loved to read *Cosmopolitan* magazine, all kinds of magazines and I thought, "This is the kind of life I was meant to lead." You know, I think part of it is rebellion.

This sort of appropriation of other identities by rejection occurs in political rhetoric as well; for example, a pro-life lecture popular in 1984 Fargo is entitled, "I Was a Pro-Choice Feminist, but Now I'm Pro-Life."

What the pro-life women consider feminism to be is another issue. The point here is that in their narratives they assert the prior alliance; this assertion is usually described as a period of (ideological) separation from the narrator's mother. The "conversion" to the pro-life position often follows a first birth or pregnancy; this becomes the basis, in the plot, for a reexamination of the previously held position. Thus, they narratively subsume their opponents' ideology into their own and thus claim authority over it.

Their position on abortion is not defined simply by repudiation of the other. In their narratives, their commitment to the right-to-life cause is connected to experiences of pregnancy and motherhood. The plots of these "procreation stories" told by right-to-life women hang on the ambivalence of the mother toward that condition, which is invoked and then transcended. In this way, the narrator becomes a mother not automatically but by *effort*. In the context of legal abortion, pro-life activists reframe the transition to motherhood as an achieved rather than a natural state. At the same time, the heroic cast of these "procreation" stories offers an embedded critique, the challenge of nurturance to the values of materialism and competitive individualism that they see as negative social forces.

Much in the same way that pro-choice women embraced feminism, this younger cohort of pro-life women find in their movement a particular symbolic frame that integrates their experience of work, reproduction, and marriage with the shifting ideas of gender and politics that they encounter around them. It is not that they discovered an ideology that "fit" what they had always been. Their sense of identification evolves in the very process of voicing their views against abortion. In the regular performance of their activism, they are, simultaneously, transforming themselves and their community, projecting their vision of the culture into the future, both pragmatically and symbolically.

Conclusion: The Narratives as Dialogue

What underlies these narratives is a partially shared world of reference—the sociohistorical context of American women's lives and the social and cultural understandings of procreation and sexuality in particular. One can hear in the different emphases of activists' stories the range of problematics that the work–family opposition presents for specific groups of female actors in ways that mark them as "generations." Two "life scripts" emerge, each of which gives dramatic shape to contradictions experienced by American women

over the female life cycle, in particular, between motherhood and
wage work.

Their proposed solutions to this dilemma are being created
in the abortion debate, a social arena marked as a contested domain. Therefore, to succeed, each side must see and present its
understanding of the cultural and personal meaning of reproduction as "natural" and correct. To legitimate their own position, proponents must make a persuasive case so that the formulations of
the opposition appear unnatural, immoral, or false. On an individual and organizational level, then, each side constitutes itself in
dialogue with the "enemy," real and imagined. The opposition is
both incorporated and repudiated, understood and denied. This
process is what gives the "procreation stories" and the abortion
debate their dialectical qualities. The "other" becomes a critical
counterpoint on which one's own stance depends.

While activists' actions and "life scripts" are cast against each
other, both provide ways for managing the structural opposition in
America between wage work and parenthood that still shapes and
differentiates the lives of most women from men in this culture.
Nurturance, reformulated to mesh with different historical and biographical experiences, is prominent in both positions as a source of
both female authority and a critique of "masculine" values. As the
historian Linda Gordon points out,

[Right-to-lifers] fear a completely individualized society with all services
based on cash nexus relationships, without the influence of nurturing
women counteracting the completely egoistic principles of the economy,
and without any forms in which children can learn about lasting human commitments to other people. Many feminists have the same fear.
(1982: 51)

Additionally, nurturance provides a link in the narratives that ties
critical moments in the narrator's life course—the transition to
motherhood—to the central philosophical questions of each side:
the pro-life concern with the protection of nascent life, and the
pro-choice concern with the rights and obligations of women to
whom the care of that nascent life is culturally assigned. The plots
constructed by women on each side suggest different interpretations of the place of procreation in women's lives, and the place of
women in reproducing the culture.

In the procreation stories, one sees how an ever-shifting social environment is measured, reformulated, and given new meaning. Moral and ethical questions of concern to abortion activists are intertwined in the construction of self, social action, and historical experience.[3] The signification attached to abortion thus provides each position with opposed but interrelated paradigms that reconstitute and claim a possible vision of being female. This process is not confined to the abortion controversy but is a manifestation of problematics in American society and culture that have generated similar struggles for the past two centuries over conflicting views of the interpretation of gender.

Part Four

Reconstructing
Gender in America

Chapter Eleven

La Longue Durée

Introduction

One of the striking features of the life stories was the way in which activists claimed nurturance as a source of moral authority, even as they were working to revise it in terms that would not be disadvantageous to women by raising its cultural status or enlarging its social placement. The salience of this theme suggested that I explore further the critical and contested place of nurturance for women engaged in other American social movements concerned with transforming gender arrangements, past and present. The utility for anthropologists of examining historical material, especially in a study of one's own society, is that patterns emerge over time that are not immediately apparent from a synchronic perspective.

As I read the works on female-led moral reform movements in the United States, I saw that the cultural preoccupations, social profile, organizing style, and agenda for social change of contemporary abortion activists had significant precedents. On the basis of the rich and ever-increasing scholarship of women's history that has flowered since the 1970s, I view the current abortion controversy as the most recent expression of a two-hundred-year tradition of female reform movements engaged in defending what activists consider to be the best interests of women. In them, certain cultural themes regarding gender identity have had remarkable endurance as they have been continually addressed and revised by women activists for over two centuries. Briefly put, "home" and "commerce" and particular values attached to them have been cast as separate but interrelated male and female spheres from Colonial times to the present. Regardless of the different issues that have engaged activists, the relegation of women to the "domestic sphere" is of critical concern, as it is continually challenged by activists and frequently reinstated in new form.

This glance at "la longue durée" (Braudel 1958) helps illuminate the dynamics of the abortion controversy not only in terms of the current situation, but as part of more long-term social and cultural processes that generate female-based social movements in America.[1] While each case develops along different lines, each is characterized by a particular situating of the opposition between male and female domains. In casting female concerns as unified (despite divisions among them) in opposition to those of men and the market, women activists have called on the moral authority of nurturant qualities and roles associated with women. Thus, paradoxically, the traits associated with domesticity became the basis for establishing the legitimacy of female activism in advocating change in and moving beyond the boundaries of that domain.

Female Activism and the Cultural Construction of Separate Spheres

Many scholars of American history view the material and cultural distinctions of male and female arenas in this culture as intertwined processes, elaborated with the growth of industrialization and commercial capitalism beginning in the eighteenth-century colonies. Speaking generally, the home was the workplace for both men and women in preindustrial America, although the appearance of economic independence in this "domestic mode of production" relied on a network of international trade and mercantile exchange.

The threshold period between the eighteenth and nineteenth centuries was a time of intensive economic growth and industrialization. The ensuing social and economic differentiation of the wage labor "workplace" as separate from "the home" lead to a sexual division of labor in which housework, childrearing, and family care—labor that remained in the household and was nonmonetized—became, ideally, a female domain.[2] In the ideologies that developed along with such arrangements by the early nineteenth century, women were considered morally superior to men, exempt from commercial concerns and more interested in motherhood and the welfare of others than in their own needs, a phenomenon termed the "cult of true womanhood" by historian Barbara Welter (1966).[3] Regardless of the actual differences among women, the classing of all females together around the ideology of nurturance and the vocation of domesticity intensified women's gender group identity and their oppositional stance toward what was more and more identified as a male world of commerce, self-interest, and wage work. As historian Nancy Cott observes:

Women's sphere was "separate" not only because it was at home but also because it seemed to elude rationalization and the cash nexus, and to integrate labor with life. The home and occupations in it represented an alternative to the emerging pace and division of labor. . . . To be idealized yet rejected by men—the object of yearning, and yet of scorn—was the fate of the home-as-workplace. (1977: 62)

Whereas cooperation, nurturance, and selflessness were identified with women and the household, competition, materialism, and self-interest, considered essential to the growth of the economy, were viewed as natural to the male character. Thus, separate social and political domains for men and women were viewed as the "natural" outcome of differentiated gender attributes that simultaneously defined, required, and repudiated one another.

The organization of production based on these understandings of gender created a particular ideal for the sexual division of labor in which men and women could not be culturally or socioeconomically complete without each other. The combination, in marriage, of male wage work and female domesticity considered necessary to the production of goods and services and the reproduction of the work force in households and families has been seen as essential for the continuity of the culture as well.

Given the expansive nature of capital in relation to other exchange systems, it was almost inevitable that, over time, the material base of the "domain of domesticity" would be steadily reduced. Through the production of commodities, "the market" increasingly subsumed the productive functions of what had been, in preindustrial America, a relatively nonmonetized household economy. With the growth of industry, internal markets, and specialized production for commercial exchange, domestic manufacture gradually was replaced by commodities produced in factories. Thus, the dependency of households and the women in them on a cash and wage labor system increased.[4] The effects on the social organization of gender were multiple. Increasingly, middle class mothers and children were isolated in the home, separate from, yet dependent on, male wage labor. Whatever the opportunities or needs for such women to participate in wage labor, most did so only for limited periods of their life cycle or out of economic necessity. At the same time, single, childless, and poor women were entering wage labor work as laborers in textile factories, in teaching, or in domestic service or, in the case of Afro-American women, were working as slaves.

It is, in part, in response to such changes that movements for social change led by women took on definition. I interpret these campaigns as an ongoing effort on the part of women both to expand and to defend their social domains and their cultural understandings of self against what have been experienced and symbolically identified as opposed, intrusive, and ever-expanding masculine interests. The issues that have mobilized women are not arbitrary. To my understanding, they often represent those aspects of the domestic sphere thought to be most threatened by the expansion of the market at a given historical moment. Moreover, particular rallying symbols—from alcohol to abortion—were used to claim alliances with sources of authority whose interests intersect at points with those of women—for example, the church, the state, and the helping professions.

In the following section, I present a few illustrative sketches of female activism that provide a historical context for the contemporary case of abortion activists. Through their activism in moral reform movements—from the evangelical revivals of the late eighteenth century to the temperance and social purity movements of the nineteenth, to current activism around abortion—women have tried to reformulate culturally given understandings of gender identity in their own terms. For readers interested in more than the brief sketches provided in the text, I have included a more fully documented overview in the Appendix.

Antebellum Evangelical and Moral Reform Movements

The historian Barbara Epstein traces the roots of American female activism to what she calls "the first great mass movement in American history" (Epstein 1981: 11), the Protestant religious revivals known as the First and Second Great Awakenings. These movements, which began in the 1740s and reached a peak in the early nineteenth century, were characterized by mass conversions and strong female participation. On the basis of her reading of male and female testimonies from the Second Great Awakening, Epstein concludes:

The divergence in world views of men and women that emerges from their conversion accounts reflects the actual divergence of their worlds. Though they lived in the same houses, men and women spent their days doing very different things, which required different outlooks—not only different but conflicting, for men's and women's values represented competing social orders. In order to succeed in the world of commercial capitalism, men had to learn to separate morality and sentiment from self-interest, while women, in legitimizing their own domestic activity, called upon the values of the society that commercial capitalism was engaged in destroying. (1981: 62)

In Epstein's view, prayer campaigns provided women with a vehicle for challenging male authority while emphasizing their own through appeals to divine power to protect their interests against what they saw as the depredations of men and the market.

Women's experience of common purpose, separate from male interests, in evangelical religious activity may well have provided the social and cultural bases for female collective action in the nineteenth century. Prominent among these were the benevolent societies active during the first few decades. In them, women took on tasks of charity, supplying provisions and education to poor women and their children along the western frontier and in the expanding urban areas of New England and the mid-Atlantic region (Berg 1978). Later in the century, the more overtly political temperance, suffrage, and social purity groups drew a larger number of mostly married middle-class women into their ranks (Epstein 1981: 67–87). The American Female Moral Reform Society, the largest and most influential of the antebellum groups, had twenty thousand members from Maine to Alabama by the 1840s. These women acted to institutionalize the idea that their pious influence in the home could ultimately reform the world in their own interests as they crusaded against prostitution, alcohol, and seduction of young women. In the view of the historian Mary Ryan, the women engaged in Moral Reform resemble, sociologically, contemporary New Right activists. Not only did they come to prominence at a time when conventional familial arrangements seemed in disarray, but they reacted to this sense of crisis "by defending the domestic institutions which seem to offer them security along with inequality" (1979: 83).

According to Carol Smith-Rosenberg, women in the Society continually exhibited an "angry and emphatic insistence upon the lascivious and predatory nature of the American male" and the need for women to make men accountable for what was seen as irresponsible sexual behavior (1979: 204). Thus, it is not only the social context that is similar to the current situation, but activists' understanding of male and female gender attributes as the causes of the problems that need to be addressed.

Postbellum Temperance and Social Purity Movements

In the era after the Civil War, the antagonism toward men and "masculine values" that evangelical women expressed through piety was now translated into full-fledged campaigns for temperance and sexual restraint. In Colonial times, drinking had not been considered dangerous but was part of home and community life. By the early nineteenth century, however, alcohol increasingly was identified with saloons, a social space designated as a male world where wages were spent on liquor, gambling, and prostitution. Thus it was viewed as depriving the home of the emotional and material resources of men (Epstein 1981: 90–91, 108; Degler 1980: 316). To control alcohol consumption was to assert the values of the domestic domain in a male-defined arena. In the view of some historians, it was also expressive of middle-class women's fears not only of an oppositional "masculine culture" symbolized by saloons, but also of swelling immigrant and working-class populations in their communities (Epstein 1981: 110–14).[5]

In 1874, local temperance efforts coalesced in the founding of what would become the largest women's association in America, the Women's Christian Temperance Union (WCTU). The WCTU's particularly strong appeal in the growing industrial towns and cities of America suggests that the movement's positioning of temperance within a more general critique of an expanding state and economy spoke to those who were experiencing its effects most directly. In the following passage, WCTU president Frances Willard articulates a vision of the household invaded by commercial and state interests in terms that mobilized a broad cross-section of American women to social action.[6]

The home was once almost a world apart in which the state interfered but little. In that home woman was queen. Now that kingdom has been invaded, her crown despoiled, her very children taken possession of by the state. These changes were inevitable. With the progress of civilization the claims of society grew. . . . But woman, the dethroned queen, demands and has a right to demand that her position of equal authority in the home be recognized in the state. ("Annual Minutes," 19th Meeting, 1892, 113, cited in Epstein 1981: 129–30)

According to Willard, the impact of the crusades was not so much on the liquor business but in the mobilizing and politicizing of women activists to other issues (Epstein 1981: 100). Like most social purists, WCTU members believed the development of civilization to be stymied by the subjection of women to what was seen as men's excessive sexual desire. For example, the WCTU's Department of Social Purity inaugurated the Society for the White Cross for men and The Knights of the Silver Crown for boys. Members of these groups pledged to "treat all women with respect, to maintain the laws of purity as binding upon men and women and to fulfill the command, 'Keep Thyself Pure'" (Epstein 1981: 127). Moral reformers also agitated for greater educational and employment opportunities for women in order to reduce their dependence on marriage and prostitution as their only reliable means of support (Degler 1980: 289). Harmony and altruism—traits attributed to "women's sphere" and the vocation of motherhood—were being eclipsed, they maintained, by competition, greed, and the commercialization of human relations, qualities linked with the growth of industry and monopoly capital and directly, or indirectly, with male sexual behavior.

The Progressive Era Campaigns

The years bridging the nineteenth and twentieth centuries witnessed an unprecedented growth in public activism of women, covering a range of ideological groupings, from militant women's rights activists to antisuffragists to "social feminists."[7] Yet, in campaigns for and against women's sexual and political rights during this period, activists justified their actions as a defense not necessarily of motherhood per se, but of the cultural values attached to it. For example, feminists such as Charlotte Perkins Gilman and social purists like Frances Willard advanced ideas of "scientific motherhood," which promoted women's independent development without disengaging female identity from maternity. Influenced by the Progressive Era's critique of paternalism and its romance with science as the key to social welfare, their advocacy of a child's need for a well-trained mother fueled campaigns for sex education and women's education in general (Gordon 1977: 129–30).

Dissension over what actions would be in the best interests of women fragmented female action in the early twentieth century. Developments such as the conflict over female suffrage, for example, suggest parallels with contemporary debates over abortion and the ERA. The campaigns emerged during a time when women's legal and economic positions were generally improving. Like pro-choice and pro-life activists today, both sides argued that women had a unique role to play in society that men could or would not assume; that the position of women in the home needed to be recognized and improved; and that women were morally superior but socially vulnerable to men and needed greater protection. They differed in their views of how best to advance these causes.

Antisuffragists viewed suffrage as endangering the ideology of separate spheres on which the prevailing gender arrangements had been based. These activists argued that giving women the vote would shift the democratic base of government from families to individuals and that this would promote dissension in the family unit. This view rested on an understanding of gender in which men and women are different but not necessarily unequal by virtue of their biological and social differences (Camhi 1973, quoted in Degler 1980: 349–50).[8] The point was elaborated by one antisuffragist, Margaret Robinson:

That woman could develop better under masculine conditions of life is a totally unsupported theory. Woman cannot become man—she can only become a poor imitation. She develops best along the lines of her aptitudes and instincts. (Quoted in Degler 1980: 352)

The popular stereotype, that suffrage would undermine the family, was sustained despite the fact that most women activists of the

Progressive Era, including suffragists, also defended their position on the basis of a separate-sphere ideology.[9] They too, for the most part, considered nurturance as an essential condition of female identity and authority.

More generally, the challenge this generation of women faced was the translation of the traditional values of domesticity—benevolence and selfless nurturance—into terms appropriate to the transformation of America into a nation-state built on industrial and monopoly capitalism. The decades of the Progressive Era were marked by continual upheavals, contributing to the sense of crisis, conflict, and change that generated what one historian has called "the search for order" (Wiebe 1967). Positivism, technical rationality, utilitarianism, and scientific authority became the guiding principles for reform efforts designed as much to quell unrest as they were to improve conditions. Perhaps of greatest significance, it was a period of increasing centralization of governmental control and legislation during which the foundations of the regulatory welfare state were laid (Zaretsky 1982: 188). Female activists of this period turned increasingly to state authority to expand and to enforce male support of, or at least buttress, the domain and vocation of nurturance assigned to their gender.

For example, social feminist Jane Addams, through her work in the Settlement Movement,[10] advocated a view of governmental responsibility to the needy as a form of "enlarged housekeeping." She succeeded in articulating a transformation of the old doctrine of domesticity that not only permitted female activism in the public arena but required it.

The very multifariousness and complexity of a city government demands the help of minds accustomed to detail and variety of work, to a sense of obligation for the health and welfare of young children, and to a responsibility for the cleanliness and comfort of others.

Because all these things have traditionally been in the hands of women, if they take no part in them now, they are not only missing the education which the natural participation in civic life would bring to them, but they are losing what they have always had. From the beginning of tribal life women have been held responsible for the health of the community. (1973: 606)

Yet most "social feminists," almost all of whom were ardent supporters of suffrage, were opposed to the introduction of the Equal

Rights Amendment to Congress by Alice Paul and the National Women's Party in 1923. To leaders like Jane Addams and Frances Willard, women as a gender group required state protection and this amendment would undermine what they had achieved in this direction. To abandon the hard-won protection of women by the state would be to leave women at the mercy of men and the market. The formulation of their opposition was based on a particular understanding of gender and the culture in general—the protection of a locus of nurturance (female) against the self-interest of the market (male)—that suggests continuities with contemporary abortion activists.

The Contradictions of Nurturance in American Women's Movements

Since the eighteenth century, American female activists have attempted to defend, expand, and redefine their assigned domain of domesticity in contests over the rights and obligations of women. In casting female concerns as unified (regardless of actual differences) in opposition to those of men and the market, American women activists have used the moral authority of nurturance to establish their legitimacy as a basis for advocating change. The contradictory qualities of nurturance in American culture—as a source of female power, a counter-discourse to capitalist values, as well as a factor in women's subordination—are particularly apparent in moments of collective action by women engaged in changing the conditions of their lives. In their efforts to reshape the social order, activists involved in the contemporary abortion controversy, like women involved in prior moral reform movements in America, always face a dilemma: they must struggle within the terms of the culture's existing understandings of gender in order to mobilize the social power they need to transcend those limits.

Still, despite the contradictions and constraints, women activists *have* redefined historically prior understandings of male and female arenas. Such challenges by women to conventional understandings have often been interpreted as signs of cultural decay or disorder. Recurrent panics over the "breakdown" of society have occurred not only when women engage directly in social action that challenges existing conditions, but also when they do so by indirect means such as limiting their fertility, entering wage labor, or raising children on their own.

When such changes in the organization of everyday life pose alternatives to existing cultural ideals, there have been several different interpretations of this "disorder." The system might be considered in jeopardy, as occurred in the accusations of "race suicide" leveled against white women engaged in the Voluntary Motherhood movement in the late nineteenth century (Gordon 1977: 130).[11] Or, the system could be retained if people interpret their experiences to the contrary as aberrations; this happened when women supporting families in the Depression explained their labor force participation as a temporary response to crisis (Milkman 1979: 527).[12] Finally, the system might be increasingly open to contest, as people reformulate the characteristics defining it, in order to accommodate their own increasingly dissonant experiences. This occurred, for example, in the suffrage campaigns and in the second wave of feminism. In this tension between cultural structures and changing historical experience lies the potential for social transformation (Sahlins 1985: vii).[13] By looking at the abortion controversy in the context of this "longue durée," it can be seen as part of a pattern, a contemporary moment in the ongoing process of the reconstruction through social action of the organization of gender in America.

Chapter Twelve

Conclusion

Life in America has altered irreversibly in the last half century. The most recent shifts in the "sexual economy," part of a complex of general socioeconomic changes, have provoked a range of responses, from female activism to "panics" over impending social decay or rising conservatism, depending on one's point of view.

From World War II until the present, the definitions of female domesticity as established in the nineteenth century were reformulated to accommodate two central shifts in the sexual division of labor. These are the ever-increasing numbers and range of American women in the wage labor force,[1] and the erosion of the domestic sphere so that it is reduced more and more to procreation and childrearing.[2]

As a result of these changes, women have been confronting directly the contradictions in American culture between the domains of production (the creation of commodities for sale in a capitalized wage labor system) and reproduction (the "unpaid labor" that goes into the daily care and nurturance of people, and especially children). Despite the increasing availability of domestic goods and services in the marketplace and the movement of women into the wage labor system, the typical working female in the 1970s still spent an average of thirty hours or more each week on household labor (Vanek 1974); in 1986, women were still doing 84 percent of the housecleaning (Stark 1987).[3] In 1985, there were 1.4 million working women with newborn babies (O'Connell and Bloom 1987). A study of what scholars have come to call "the new home economics" by the Social Service Administration calculated that on average a mother in the work force who pays to replace her own domestic services would lose money at least until her children entered public school, at which point she might net an average of $1,078 per year (Berk and Berk 1983). Nonetheless, the income of women with children has been increasingly relied upon as a buffer against inflation, poverty, or as the sole support of a family. In terms of the experience of everyday life, maintaining the dual role of homemaker and wage earner is a constant strain, as expressed by a woman balancing two sets of responsibilities:

When I work, I feel like I want to be doing a real good job, and I want to be absolutely responsible. Then, if the little one gets a cold, I feel like I should be home with her. That causes complications because whatever you do isn't right. You're either at work feeling like you should be at home with your sick child, or you're at home feeling like you should be at work. (Interview in Rubin 1976: 172)

That these changes challenge a construction of female gender identity linked to motherhood, nurturance, and the work and ideals associated with domesticity is clear in the opposing positions held in the contemporary battle over abortion's legislation. At a historical locus when domesticity is increasingly defined by and reduced to reproduction, although women are spending fewer years of their lives engaged exclusively in childrearing,[4] the cultural meaning and social location of nurturance is particularly problematic.

For these reasons, I argue that both symbolically and experientially the definitions of female gender identity and the domestic domain have focused more and more on questions regarding reproduction and its relationship to nurturance. Their meaning and practice have emerged as important and intense concerns of female activists. Each position represents conflicting interpretations of the shifting social consequences of and connections between sexual activity, reproduction, and motherhood for women in American culture. Thus, control over the womb—the last unambiguous symbol of an exclusive female arena—is especially meaningful and threatening in the current American context and provides the central concern of abortion activists on either side. Conflicts over the applications of new reproductive technology—amniocentesis, surrogate motherhood, in-vitro fertilization—are further developments of this already established trend (e.g., Rapp, n.d.; Rothman 1986).

It is hardly surprising that players on both sides in the contempo-

rary abortion debate defend their positions with arguments about
the lack of social forms other than marriage that can ensure reliable
emotional and material support of women with children. Because
of a high divorce rate, increasing numbers of single-parent families,
and the delinquency of many men in making child support payments, women on both sides have increasing cause to worry. In
1985, 18 percent of white and 57 percent of black families were
headed by women. Of these only 15 percent were awarded and received child support. By 1987, half of women with children under
the age of three worked outside the home. The wages they and
other women receive are, at best average, seventy cents to every
dollar made by men.[5]

Statistics like these have caused more than one expert to specu-
late. Andrew Hacker, for example, suggests:

The main way women depreciate themselves in the market is by becoming mothers and allowing that condition to dominate their lives. (1983: 29)

The "trickle-down" effect of such thinking on the conditions most
American women face can be read in the conflicting positions of the
abortion activists in Fargo. They represent the situation in oppositional terms, although these conditions shape the social world of
pro-life and pro-choice women alike. To generalize: pro-choice
women would recognize Hacker's interpretation as integral to a
system that discriminates against women in the political, legal, and
economic spheres. From the right-to-life perspective, Hacker's
view represents the prevalence of "utilitarian" thinking and would
be taken as a sign of serious cultural decadence, accompanying the
devaluation of motherhood and nurturance in America.

The Right-to-Life Agenda: Domesticating the State

Right-to-life proponents see easy access to abortion as decreasing women's power by weakening social pressure on men to take
emotional and financial responsibility for the reproductive consequences of intercourse. In this sense, it undercuts a system in
which the linking of sex to pregnancy and marriage is the linchpin
for the material security of women with dependents. To work, this
system must be seen as inevitable, a "natural order." When a
woman can safely and legally terminate a pregnancy for whatever

reason, the insistent motivation to connect female sexuality to this cultural chain of events is undone. The links are exposed as social constructions—that is, not inevitable—and the imperative of motherhood as a condition beyond human control is dismantled. The desire of pro-life activists to prohibit abortions for all women is rooted in a desire to reverse the social causes and consequences of this unraveling, which they attribute to increasing materialism and selfishness. In their rhetoric, a collective obligation for nurturance is set against "heartless individualism." As Jean Garton, head of Lutherans for Life, writes,

It is realistic, accurate and humane to recognize that pregnancies exist which are distressful to the woman and her family. Unfortunately, because abortion on demand erodes a sense of collective responsibility for the woman in actual crisis, she is abandoned to heartless individualism. . . . In a society where programs, services and funding are geared toward abortion rather than toward addressing the causes which make a particular pregnancy a problem, the woman in stress is forsaken. Adjustment of health care plans could eliminate one form of coercion to abort. . . . Insurance policies to cover newborns from birth would relieve the economic pressures confronting those who discover that they are to be parents of a handicapped child. (1979: 74, 83)

The movement's political actions make clear that the pro-life agenda, like the visions of other American moral reform activists, is not simply a defense of a disappearing domain of domesticity. Prolife activists hope to claim alliances with—one might say domesticate—church and state to serve what they see as women's interests. For example, right-to-life leader and U.S. Representative Henry Hyde, who has sponsored amendments denying Medicaid payments for abortion, also promotes legislation to give federal health insurance to poor pregnant women. In this way, the right-to-life movement resembles other campaigns in American history to reconstruct culturally constituted female domains against what are seen as opposing forces.

Gender Disembodied

Although the pro-life defense of female nurturance against male self-interest resembles that of prior female moral reform movements, the construction of sexual antagonism has taken a significant new turn. It is directed not only at aspects of the economy and culture coded as male that in their view are antagonistic to female needs and values. It is also directed at women who, by seeking sexual pleasure for its own sake, pursuing material gain and self-aggrandizement at the expense of others, or eschewing motherhood, are acting in culturally male terms. This is clear in the following comments by a pro-life leader.

Men are using abortion as a way out of their problems. It is increasingly a way for the male sexual partner to avoid responsibility for his actions. . . .

Abortion also permits the woman to adopt the same sexual pattern as the male, although it is a pattern alien to her nature. Blessed by God with a much longer view of society and the world, the woman is normally the stabilizing force in the male-female relationship, insisting that the man subordinate his sexual passions to the need to provide for the family over the long run. (Jones 1983: 240)

For most right-to-life advocates, abortion is not simply the termination of an individual potential life, or even that act multiplied a millionfold. In the pro-life view of the world, abortion destroys the bases of gender difference critical to biological, cultural, and social reproduction. It subverts the fertile union of men and women, either by denying procreative sex or the differentiation of male and female sexuality. This prospect threatens the union of opposites on which the continuity of the social whole is presumed to rest.

For pro-life women, opposition to abortion, like other moral reform campaigns, is a gesture against what they see as the final triumph of self-interest, a principle that represents both men and the market.[6] At a time when wombs can be rented and sperm and zygotes are commodities, abortion is understood by right-to-life women as an emblematic symbol for the increasing commercialization and exploitation of human dependency. In their image of the unborn child ripped from the womb, they have symbolized the final penetration and destruction of the last arena of women's domain thought to be exempt from the truncated relations identified with both male sexuality and commercial exchange: reproduction and motherhood.

Abortion, then, represents an active denial by women of two essential conditions of female gender identity: pregnancy and the obligations of nurturance that should follow. Given this perspective, support for abortion is seen as a sign of women moving into structurally male roles. As a pro-life leader explained:

The Feminists are so thoroughly absorbed by the masculine ideal that they denigrate things that are biologically female. Pregnancy—all of a sudden, it's being seen as a high-risk occupation. . . .

It's funny. The pro-abortionists call themselves the women's movement, making all the rest of us nonwomen, when in actual fact, the pro-abortionist career women identify fully with the ideal of the bourgeois male and his individualistic, atomized, carefree sex and his no responsibility. (Juli Loesch, quoted in Paige 1983: 68-69)

The pro-life perception of their opponents' gender identity as culturally male—sexual pleasure and individual ambition separated from procreation and social bonds of caretaking—is set against their own identification of "true femininity" with the traits of nurturance that are, in American culture, conflated with motherhood. In the words of a pro-life activist:

Abortion is of crucial importance because it negates the one irrefutable difference between men and women. It symbolically destroys the precious essence of womanliness—nurturance. . . .

Pro-abortion feminists open themselves to charges of crass hypocrisy by indulging in the very same behavior for which they condemn men: the unethical use of power to usurp the rights of the less powerful.

Right-to-life women, then, consider "womanliness" not simply as the consequence of the somatic difference in reproductive capacities, but the *acceptance* of these biological features as a basis for a presumed female character. The emergence of this position was almost inevitable once abortion was legalized; when that option is both sanctioned and available, carrying a pregnancy to term becomes, simultaneously, a decision not to abort. Thus, the interpretation of gender that underpins pro-life arguments is based not on a woman's possession of, but in her *stance toward* her reproductive capacities as signifying her capacity for nurturance. That such nurturance is not a natural quality but is achieved through effort is illustrated in the pro-life procreation stories in which the point of the narrative is to show that pregnancy and motherhood are accepted *despite* the ambivalent feelings they produce. Thus, a woman who endorses abortion stresses the other side of the ambivalence and is "like a man" (though always ready for redemption) regardless of the shape of her body.

The right-to-life position rests, paradoxically, on a view of gender that is both essentialist and radically cultural: the category "woman" is produced by but also disconnected from the female body. The pro-life formulation of female identity as an achievement gained through the acceptance of pregnancy and nurturance, rather than a biologically based ascription, draws attention to a larger condition: the disembodiment of gender from the bodies that ultimately bear the consequences and contradictions entailed in its shifting cultural and social formulations.

A System at War with Itself

Like earlier American female reformers, grass-roots pro-life and pro-choice women alike envision their work as a full-scale social crusade to enhance rather than diminish women's position. Yet gender constructions in American culture cast women in dual, contradictory positions, exemplifying what Mary Douglas has called "a system at war with itself" (1966: 152). An ethic of egalitarianism stresses women as autonomous individuals who should have rights equal to men—the basis for libertarian or liberal arguments. This poses a danger to the long-standing emphasis on gender difference as the basis for the social and cultural organization of the polity, the economy, household, sexuality, and the very reproduction of society. Battles such as the one taking place over abortion are not only over that specific issue but over which interpretation of gender will prevail.

Are the two sides hopelessly at odds, destined to an interminable battle for cultural and political dominance? I went to Fargo to seek an answer from the perspective of those activists who provide the constituencies on which the opposed movements are based. In the end, the abstractions of the abortion debate and national policy take on shape and meaning in particular places, framed by local interpretations. Initially, the assertions of Fargo activists on both sides that they represented the real interests of all women gave the overt public controversy over abortion, played out over the Fargo clinic, the quality of irreconcilable conflict that characterizes the debate at the national level.

However, at the practical level of daily life—where an ethnographer's project must begin and return—the concerns shared by pro-life and pro-choice activists alike were apparent, on occasion, to both anthropologist and actors. The incidents around the clinic described in chapter 6, when opponents crossed each other's boundaries, voluntarily or involuntarily, revealed moments when activists acknowledged their common interest in helping women with unplanned pregnancies. Such recognition resulted in new, competitive developments over claims to authority through "nurturant" activity—such as the "problem pregnancy industry," as well as in very occasional cooperative action to help women in trouble. The latter occurred, for example, when the clinic director phoned the head of LIFE Coalition to get financial help for a pregnant indigent woman.

Another dimension of shared dilemmas that underscores the conflict was apparent in the prominence of experiential dissonance between motherhood and wage labor in activists' life stories. Both pro-life and pro-choice women, as narrators, were concerned with creating a sense of continuity between action and meaning in these two domains as they moved in and out of them over their life cycle at different historical moments. The plots that characterized the narratives of each group developed in particular ways that revealed how historical events entered into each side's interpretation of this contradiction faced by most American women. Abortion activism not only offered a framework for organizing such life transitions and extending a newly articulated sense of self in both space and time, it also provided narrators with a means of symbolically controlling interpretations different than their own.

Activists' verbal and political performances are created to fix irreversible meaning to events in the female life course that are inherently contingent, variable, and liminal. It is their own and other women's lives that are the evidence and substance activists draw on in personal and public testimony. The narratives, rhetoric, and action give shape and closure to the experiences of women that stress one side of a cultural contradiction between the domains of production and reproduction. It is not surprising that the contest arouses such passion. In their differing positions as to what desirable social change should be, both groups lay claim not only to moral authority, but to a particular view of the culture. The procreation stories told by women on each side—spun from the uneven threads of women's daily experience and woven into durable plots—offer two compelling yet incompatible interpretations for the place of women in America.

By casting two interpretations of female lives against each other, the abortion debate masks their common roots in the problematic conditions faced by women living in a system in which wage labor and individual achievement are placed in conflict with reproduction, motherhood, and nurturance. These dilemmas are faced by all parties to the debate but are played out on women's bodies in particular. In this sense, there is a tragic dimension to the polarization around the issue. Thus, abortion persists as a contested domain in which the struggle over the place and meaning of procreation in women's lives, and its relation to the place of women in reproducing the culture, are being reorganized in oppositional terms.

Viewed from an anthropological perspective, one can see in the abortion controversy of the 1980s the most recent manifestation of an ongoing cultural process in which struggles over the material, political, and symbolic definitions of gender are intertwined, dramatized, coded, and continually transformed. As the abortion debate has come increasingly to stand for opposing views of gender, the possibility of mutual recognition seems to decrease as each side claims to speak a truth regarding contemporary as well as past and future generations of women. As long as the American gender system is "at war with itself," it seems, "the truth" about women will continue to be in dispute.

Self-Definition and Social Action

Although this study has focused on grass-roots female activists in the abortion controversy, in the end it led me to consider the broader meaning of this type of activity in American culture. The ease with which activists constituted life stories in relation to the movement that engaged them suggests a dynamic relationship between the construction of self and social action in this society.

The American social system stresses the importance of individual identity, yet lacks or diminishes regular forms of person-defining ascription that characterize other cultures, such as a kin group or a caste. Even class is largely denied, seen, ideally, as mutable by individual effort. Consequently, a critical task for social actors over the life course is to constitute a social identity.

This ideology of the self is reflective of the American charter myth of "starting over" without the weight of origins, as noted by observers of American life, from the Colonial era to the present (e.g., Crèvecoeur 1904; Fitzgerald 1986). Hence, the metaphor of being "born again" (or its secular version of "free choice") is an especially powerful one that marks not only the prevalent forms of American Christian practice but many secular groups as well, from Alcoholics Anonymous to feminist consciousness-raising. What is important to note here is that the social forms that focus on making or remaking the self in new terms require association with like-minded others. In other words, the cultural system requires that the individual constitute himself or herself in order to achieve a social identity, and that the means available for achieving identity are through voluntary affiliations with others in a group that offers a comprehensive reframing of the place of the self in the social world.

In this model, "individual" and "community" are not oppositional givens in American culture, but indeterminate constructs that take on definition through each other. "Becoming American," then, might be understood as a process of "making oneself up." However, this can occur only in relationship with others; the problem of constituting the self in relation to changing historical experience is solved, frequently, through the creation of new social formations. This dynamic is most obvious in religious and political movements, but is visible as well in other forms, from professional associations to the human potential movement. It is this process of self-definition through social action, I am suggesting, that helps foster the proliferation of social experiments and voluntary associations—including female reform movements—that so impressed Alexis de Tocqueville in 1831 and many others since then. Viewed from this perspective, abortion activists are engaged in more than the particular issue at hand. As they redefine themselves through their efforts to reshape society, they are accomplishing a paradigmatically American task.

Pro-Dialogue

When I first began thinking about this research, I hoped to answer several related questions. Why was the abortion debate still able to arouse so much passion and set women against each other? Who were the grass-roots activists that national leaders claimed as their own? What catalyzed pro-life women and were they wholly different from their pro-choice counterparts? Is it possible that these women opposed on abortion might find common cause as well and even act on it together? The last was the naive hope of an ardent young feminist worried about the growing divisions in the women's movement in the 1980s.

Because of these motivations that I brought to my work, I distrusted any findings that suggested the kind of similarities between activists that I thought might exist. I recalled warnings of anthropologists against the temptation to discover one's own arguments in the mouths of natives, hoping that the latter have "something strikingly original and different to say in terms of substance than does intellectualist discourse" (Marcus 1986: 25). Nonetheless, despite their obvious differences, shared concerns in the social worlds, interests, and ideas of women activists on both sides continued to emerge, and so I wove the thread of their common discourse into my writing.

After I returned from the field and began to present my work in public, the reactions of colleagues raised new problems for me. It is one thing, I learned quickly, for an anthropologist to offer the natives' point of view when the subjects are hidden in the highlands of New Guinea and have little impact on the lives of the assembled audience. It is quite another to describe the world view of people from the same culture whom some people in my audiences considered to be "the enemy." I tried to think of the mission of Boas and Mead to break down cultural stereotypes when I found myself fielding occasionally hostile responses from colleagues. Some explained to me their concern that I had "gone native" and become a right-to-life advocate. One skeptic suggested that my data were simply not true. I started wondering if I had been overly optimistic, reading too much into the words of my interpreters, hoping that the commonalities I was seeing were evident to them in ways more significant than the tentative demonstrations and confessions of recognition that I had witnessed.

These doubts were prominent in my mind when I returned to Fargo in the summer of 1986 to put a copy of my dissertation in the public library. On my first day back, I quickly fell into the pace of things, catching up on local developments over a backyard barbecue. Something was going on, my hostess told me, that sounded like the kind of thing that would interest me. A new group had formed called Pro-Dialogue, she explained, that was trying to get pro-life and pro-choice women to talk together. She gave me the name and number of the woman organizing it and I called first thing the next day.

The woman who answered the phone recognized my name. I coughed nervously when she told me the group had used an article I had written as one of their readings. Reassuring me that she thought I had been accurate, she went on to relate Pro-Dialogue's history. She dated the group's origins to a meeting of the North Dakota Democratic Women's Caucus in March 1984, in preparation for that year's State Democratic Convention. The question was raised as to whether to have a plank on abortion for the state platform. A pro-choice plank was proposed and, after much debate, defeated. A woman who found she had friends arguing on both sides suggested a compromise position based on areas of agreement between the two groups. The result, presented at the State Convention, read:

The North Dakota Democratic party believes public policy on abortion should provide some positive alternatives which would stress effective sex education, continued research on safer means of contraception, improved adoption services, support for parents of exceptional children, and economic programs which make it possible for parents to both raise children with love and pursue a productive work life.

Not long after, at a local Women's Political Caucus, several women who had worked on the compromise plank had heard that Sister Marjorie Tuite, one of the "Vatican 24," would be speaking in the area.[1] They decided to ask her to serve as moderator for a dialogue between pro-life and pro-choice activists in the spring. As it turned out, Sister Tuite never arrived because she was called to the Vatican to defend her signature on a letter calling for a dialogue about abortion. The assembled local women decided that if Sister Tuite could confront the Pope at the Vatican, they could proceed with their agenda in Fargo, North Dakota. Participants described their initial feelings about the event as distrust and skepticism. Minutes from this meeting read:

We began by having each person tell their reasons for coming to the meeting. The most frequent reason given was "I just want to get to know people on the other side of the issue—I've never really talked about abortion with someone who's on the other side."

. . . Another said "We should be allies on most of women's issues—but our disagreement on one issue (abortion) has kept us from cooperating on all of the other issues that would insure a better life for all people."

As we talked and *listened* that night, we discovered some *very* important common ground. We wished that women would not be faced with pregnancies

—that they couldn't afford,
—that at times they weren't ready for
—by people they didn't love
—or for any of the many reasons women have abortions.

That common ground gave us something concrete . . . a goal we could work toward *together*.

"To direct our energies toward reducing as much as possible, the need for abortion."

Here we were in—as [ABC] called us—"The Community Ripped Apart by Abortion" and we were: talking, listening, discussing, agreeing, disagreeing, and reaching consensus. We were:

Picketers of Abortion Clinics
and
Patient Advocates who walked with women
through the picket lines to the clinics.

After that meeting in April 1985, the group continued to meet for a few hours every two weeks. Although there was considerable hesitation at first, the women involved gained confidence in their common goal to reduce the need for abortion by "fighting together to solve some of the problems women face." The group is devoted more to dialogue than to action, although it has set up projects such as putting together a directory of family planning services available in the area.

According to the minutes from a Pro-Dialogue meeting in the summer of 1986, the group asked itself the same questions I had: "Is it working, this dialogue process?" The answer was provided in part by testimonies:

One night a pro-life woman told us that she wasn't picketing at an abortion clinic anymore—she said, "I picketed the clinic because I wanted to help the women going there—but I can see that's not how they perceived me. I still care about the women and want to help them, but I know picketing isn't the answer for me."

A pro-choice woman told us that "Pro-Dialogue has helped me to focus again on problems I thought I had already solved—it's re-opened the abortion question for me."

and by claims:

People from both sides still believe firmly in their principals [*sic*] but we have gained an understanding of each others' positions. . . .

The stereotypes are disappearing as we work together toward a common goal.

We're still Radicals
But now we are Pro-Dialogue Radicals.

Despite the optimistic tone to these minutes, it is unclear if Pro-Dialogue will continue. To my knowledge, the 1986 meeting was the last; members who dropped out said that other commitments—family, work, politics—had priority. What, then, is the significance of this group, other than providing some reassurance to the anthropologist regarding some of her conclusions?

Pro-Dialogue offered visible, empirical evidence that the pro-life and pro-choice stances, like all genuine dialectical oppositions, have a number of elements in common. Both sides voice a critique of a society that increasingly stresses materialism and self-enhancement while denying the cultural value of dependents and those who care for them. Although their solutions differ, each group desires, in its own way, to alleviate the unequal conditions faced by women in American culture. Pro-Dialogue was a clear, if brief, demonstration of activists' awareness of these concerns.

The formation of Pro-Dialogue is an unusual event in the abortion controversy. Very likely, it could only happen in a setting like Fargo where moderation is highly valued and the "enemy" inevitably bears a familiar face. My "discovery" of a social phenomenon like Pro-Dialogue speaks for the value of an anthropological inquiry that investigates the local enactment of a national debate such as the abortion controversy. However ephemeral, it is the sort of moment that surveys and headlines rarely register, but that suggests a new perspective on a complex issue and, perhaps, unanticipated cultural possibilities.

Female Moral Reform
Movements in America

Introduction

The following section examines organized periodic activism by female reformers in America as an ongoing social form in order to see what larger
cultural processes are signified in the actions of these movements. The
cases I use demonstrate how a particular American gender construct is
continually renegotiated in social process. Speaking very generally, since
the late eighteenth century, the male arena has been marked as one of
competitive individual achievement in the "marketplace," whereas the
arena of "the home" assumes the "female" qualities of moral superiority,
self-sacrifice, and unconditional nurturance of others.

In surveying female reform movements over the past two hundred
years, I have tried to show the relationship of such formations to each
other, through time, and to changing cultural and material conditions.
I am particularly interested in understanding how these activists shape
and are shaped by shifts in the social organization of production and reproduction in America. In seeing both the recurrence and changing shape
of past contests over gender in American culture, one can see what role
they have played in creating transformations or reinforcing the status quo.
All of this is, of course, generated by my interest in understanding cultural continuities between past movements and the contemporary case of
abortion activism that is the larger subject of this book.

My review of historical materials is not based on primary research (since
I am not a historian). Rather, it relies on the ever-increasing scholarship in
women's and social history that has flowered since the 1970s, providing
both a wealth of material and instructive debates on the issues involved.
The connections drawn to my own material are, of course, my own.

Women's Role in the First and
Second Great Awakenings

The Protestant religious revivals known as the First and Second Great Awakenings spread initially through the socially homogeneous villages of New England in the 1740s and later, in the early nineteenth century, to western New York and the industrializing Connecticut River Valley (Epstein 1981: 13, 45). According to the historian Barbara Epstein, there were few differences between men and women in the number or substance of the conversion narratives in the first Great Awakening. She interprets this as an index of the relative equality of the sexes in Colonial New England (in contrast, say, to their position under English common law), which, in turn, she sees as a reflection of the common participation of both genders in the eighteenth-century household-based economy. Whether or not one agrees with this interpretation of women's position in the Colonial period, the fact is that women did not use the First Great Awakening—a moment of subversion of conventional lines of authority— to voice discontent against men. For Epstein and others, this indicates that "male domination was not widely experienced by women as an issue in their lives" (Epstein 1981: 24–29, 37; Berg 1978: chap. 1).

However, differences between men and women are prominent in conversion narratives from the Second Great Awakening of 1797 to 1840 (Epstein 1981: 1). Over one-half of the converts were young unmarried women from the middle economic strata (daughters of shopkeepers, artisans, and farmers) whose confessions were organized around internal torment over their sinful desire to rebel against God's authority. Male converts were, typically, of the same class, brought to conversion by social pressure from religious female kin. Their testimonies stressed the practical rewards of being saved (Epstein 1981: 45–47).

The appeal of the Second Great Awakening, then, was not merely the possibility it offered for playing a role in one's own salvation, a doctrine more suited to a climate of commercial capitalism and Jacksonian democracy than the determinism and pious self-denial of earlier Puritan forms of Protestantism.[1] Evangelical reform also offered a means of strengthening ideological and communal pressure on men who might be tempted to abandon dependent women and children as they began to feel the burdens of support brought about by the shift in the sexual division of labor in a burgeoning cash economy. Deprived of the identity and purpose that worldly occupations were providing for men, women turned to evangelical Christianity. Nancy Cott suggests that they found in it positive principles around which to organize their lives, the support of male clergy, and, perhaps most important, a female community of peers "that served them both as a resource and a resort outside the family" (1977: 159).

Antebellum Moral Reform: From
Benevolence Movements to Feminism

The threshold period between the eighteenth and nineteenth centuries was a time of intensive economic growth. The development of transportation systems promoted regional specialization and national markets, which in turn stimulated industrial production and ultimately the substitution of factory-produced goods for household manufacture. The growth of the internal market and specialized production for commercial exchange thus diminished the importance of women's work in the household economy at the same time that it increased the dependency of those households on cash for basic commodities. The effects on the social organization of gender were multiple. Increasingly, mothers and children were isolated in the home, separate from yet dependent on male wage labor. At the same time, single, childless, and poor women were becoming wage-laborers in textile factories, in teaching, or in domestic service. Despite the opportunities for women to participate in wage labor, most did so only for limited periods of their life cycle or out of economic necessity.

Whereas the scarcity of workers in Colonial towns had encouraged the entry of women into the labor market, the growing surplus of available labor in industrializing cities contributed to male opposition to female participation in the work force in all occupations (Berg 1978: 63). Such animosity toward women working outside the home was one of the many strands woven into the web that enmeshed women into the material and symbolic boundaries of the "cult of true womanhood" (Welter 1966).

From this context, female reform associations developed in the antebellum period. They were a bridge between the millennial concerns of eighteenth century evangelical women and the more overtly political temperance, suffrage, and social purity groups of the late nineteenth century that drew a large number and wide range of women into their ranks (Berg 1978: chap. 7).

The American Female Moral Reform Society was the largest of these groups. An examination of the Utica branch reveals how shifts in women's understanding of social power and gender relations were played out at the community level. As an example of an earlier manifestation of grass-roots female activism, the Utica case offers an instructive comparison to the dynamics of twentieth-century local abortion conflicts.

The Utica Female Moral Reform Society pledged itself to the control of seduction, prostitution, and vice, a crusade described in their First Annual Report as "warfare for life" (Ryan 1979: 70). The core organizers were veterans of evangelical reform; members ranged from well-to-do wives of professionals to "working girls." Most were married women with children whose concerns, as voiced in the Society's records, were "a repository of the anxieties of mothers" (Ryan 1979: 73). In Ryan's view, the Society and similar associations can be seen as responses to the circumstances that generated such anxiety over the loss of parental control. As production shifted increasingly to wage labor, young people were becoming more mobile in their search for work; family-, church-, and community-based means of controlling their behavior diminished. Uprooted youths—epitomized in Utica by the clerks, canal boys, servants, seamstresses, and prostitutes—represented for many of the women of the city the loss of their ability to exercise control over the next generation (Ryan 1979: 72–73).

Accordingly, the reformers turned their campaign toward their own ascribed vocation of motherhood. They specified methods of childrearing "designed to instill sexual control in the very personalities of the rising generation" (Ryan 1979: 77), making connections between the food and clothing permitted children and their later sexual behavior. In the line of maternal duty and the interests of delayed marriage, they hoped to purge "loose morals" from the next generation.

Ryan traces the decline of the Utica Moral Reform Society by 1845 to several sources. By mid-century, as Utica became an industrial center inundated by immigrant labor, it also became more closely integrated into the national economic and political system, so that "vital decisions were transferred from the neighborhood to a formidable city hall and then on to Washington and Wall St." Ryan argues that it was not simply the loss of local social power that caused the organization's demise, but the more widespread acceptance of the discourse of sexual continence (1979: 81).

Historian Barbara Berg offers a variant interpretation to Ryan's. The documents of the society she studied, in her view,

fail to disclose significant social-control motivation, but examples abound of women risking their person, property and reputation to assist less fortunate members of their sex. (1978: 149)

Benevolent societies were slowly creating change. Whereas the woman-belle ideal had insisted that all females had the same needs, abilities, and aspirations, voluntary organizations enabled their members to recognize that they were not alike. And rather than the isolation or alienation that often accompanies the realization of individual differences, a sense of community with other women developed. (1978: 165–66)

Ironically, while enacting their moral authority in the public sphere, they simultaneously elaborated an ideology that served increasingly to confine women to motherhood and the domestic sphere.

Yet the moral reformers learned to assert women's interests in the male-dominated world beyond the home. Although the society operated initially through networks of friendship, kin, and church and through the circulation of tracts, petitions, and publications, by 1841 the women reformers began to be more public. They would accuse young male clerks on the street of seducing women; publicize the clientele of brothels; and send committees into poor neighborhoods to report on conditions and minister aid. Occasionally they brought to trial men who had violated norms of domestic propriety—abusing wives, impregnating servants, abandoning children—while providing female victims with legal and personal assistance. By adapting "male-directed methods of moral surveillance . . . to their own interests," these moral reformers created not only politically effective networks of women, but also unprecedented models for female action (Ryan 1979: 75–78; Berg 1978: 166).

These movements had their greatest public presence at the historical moment when the future leaders of the first wave of feminism were just coming of age. The organizational abilities and political awareness of feminists such as Elizabeth Cady Stanton and Lucretia Mott were honed not only in abolition work (O'Neill 1971: 9–12) but in the moral reform movements as well. This experience enabled them to turn suffrage agitation into a full-fledged women's movement separate from the abolition wing of the Republican party. By the time of the 1848 Women's Rights Convention in Seneca Falls, the Moral Reform Society had succeeded in making seduction a crime in New York State and had taken on the need for equitable employment of women as their own cause, urging women to join unions and insisting on female staffing of the organization, from typesetters to executive officers. Nonetheless, Sarah Grimké's article in *The Advocate of Moral Reform* attacking masculine interpretations of the Bible drew angry responses from readers, indicating that much of the membership would not go so far as to question the authority of men in families or Christian doctrine (Smith-Rosenberg 1979: 209-15).

Postbellum Movements:
Temperance and Social Purity

Women may not have wanted to tamper overtly with an ideology on which their daily life depended for recognition and material support. However, the temperance and social purity movements in the postbellum era emerged as an arena in which concern over sexual inequality was "expressed in a new and more socially effective way" (Epstein 1981: 89).

The unprecedented and rapid growth of the WCTU over the last decades of the nineteenth century and first few decades of the twentieth provides an index of its continuing significance as an expression of women's interests. The Ohio Women's Crusade catalyzed the movement. In this mass female assault during 1873–74, one hundred middle-class and upper-class women prayed before the saloons of Hillsboro, urging the owners to shut down their businesses. Within six months, the "sit-ins" spread to other towns in Ohio and four other states. They were particularly effective in small communities. In less than two years, these campaigns succeeded in closing—usually temporarily—over three thousand saloons through persuasion, harassment, or legal technicalities. Federal revenues from excise taxes in Ohio and Indiana reportedly fell by $350,000 in two months; temperance bills made their way to Congress (Epstein 1981: 90–100; Degler 1980: 315–19). By 1911, the national membership had grown to 245,000. Under the leadership of Frances Willard, the WCTU president for nineteen years, the scope of the organization broadened. She linked the temperance cause of defense of the home to a whole range of issues. By 1889, Willard had created thirty-nine departments within the union, addressing causes as diverse as health, labor, social purity, peace, and arbitration (Degler 1980: 317–18).

Women in the WCTU were distinguished by their view that women were nurturant by nature, and therefore morally superior to men. More generally, this view was the basis of a movement for social purity that manifested itself in a variety of forms over the nineteenth century. Women's active campaigns to enforce a single sexual standard—their own—on men began with the antebellum moral reformers' efforts to curb prostitution. They succeeded in getting police and medical associations to regulate such business by confining it to "red-light zones" and requiring medical surveillance to control the spread of disease (Degler 1980: 280–85). To defend the interests of women, the social purists worked to raise the age of female consent to engage in sexual activity so that by 1900, only two states had limits below age fourteen. The historian Linda Gordon sees in the social purity movements the consolidation of a more general cultural critique, "intent upon transforming the consciousness, changing the basic 'needs,' to use a twentieth-century term, of society" (Gordon 1977: 119). Casting sexuality as a culturally determined product allowed women to demand the control and regulation of men's sexual behavior.

Some analysts of the late nineteenth century view the preoccupation with sexual continence and control of male lust as sexual metaphors expressing the conservation required in the early stages of a capitalist economy when accumulation of capital was of primary concern (Cominus 1963; Marcus 1966). This interpretation is problematic on two counts. First, as Degler and others have noted, it does not accurately reflect the development of the American postbellum economy. By 1860, American industries were producing goods in large quantities; further development of capital required consumption, not accumulation (Neale 1972: 127). Second, it ignores the significance of gender interests indicated by the prominence of women in the shaping of the social purity movements, and the relationship of that activism to the changing sexual division of labor. The increasing substitution of commodities for household-based domestic production was further eroding the status and economic necessity of the domain assigned to women in American life. The arguments of activists themselves suggest that the concern with control of male sexuality had less to do with capital accumulation and more to do with the defense of the domestic domain against an expanding market.

The effects of these shifts did not pass unnoticed by the female activists of the Gilded Age. As Mary Jo Buhle points out, these women, most of whom were born between 1819 and 1832, had

an understanding that the vaunted women's sphere of their youth had been blown to the winds. . . . Indeed, the advancement of women from private to public life became the premise of the entire Woman Question. . . . They believed that industrialism had substantially changed American society and necessarily created a new conception of womanhood. (1980: 40)

Writing in 1898, Charlotte Perkins Gilman addressed the issue of the declining "bargaining power" of women in marriage in her widely read book, *Women and Economics.* In it she argued that because housekeeping, cooking, and domestic production were all services that could be purchased by men outside marriage, the fundamental reciprocity between husband and wife was reduced to an exchange of a woman's sexuality and maternity for the financial support of her spouse. Gilman advocated several solutions for this situation: that women be able to support themselves with wage labor; that domestic labor be collectivized; and that wives increase their value in the marriage exchange by "making their resources scarce"—that is, by controlling their husbands' sexual access and limiting pregnancies. Historian Linda Gordon underscores the necessity of placing such ideas and behavior in their context with regard to the social meaning of sex and reproduction experienced by nearly all women of that era.

In the 19th century women needed marriage far more than men. Lacking economic independence, women needed husbands to support them, or at least free them from a usually more humiliating economic dependence on fathers. . . . The belief that motherhood was women's fulfillment had a material basis: parenthood was often the only creative and challenging activity in a woman's life, a key part of her self-esteem. (1977: 110)

The Voluntary Motherhood Movement

Not surprisingly, pregnancy and motherhood—the last arenas in women's domain that were not yet monetized or legally available outside of marriage—became key rallying points for female activists of the late nineteenth and early twentieth centuries. The principle that women had the right to determine the timing and frequency of intercourse and pregnancy took shape in the discourse of what was called the Voluntary Motherhood

movement beginning in the 1870s. The degree to which these ideas spoke
to the needs of women of that period is indicated by the variety of groups
that advocated voluntary motherhood ideas. They ranged from "free-
love" activists who eschewed marriage and monogamy, to suffragists, to
the most conservative of moral reformers (Gordon 1977: 95).

While the Voluntary Motherhood movement promoted various natural
forms of pregnancy prevention, including coitus interruptus, "karezza"
(coitus reservatus), abstinence, and especially a woman's right to refuse
her husband sexual access, it condemned contraceptive devices and abortion. Such forms of birth control were seen as unnatural and unsafe and,
more significantly, as vehicles that would encourage the independence of
women and the promiscuity of men (Gordon 1977: 98). Contraceptives
were associated with prostitution and, more generally, with the separation of sexuality from reproduction. Thus, they also presented the possibility of women as active sexual subjects, an idea at odds with Victorian
understandings of female sexuality as dictated by a self-sacrificing maternal instinct. As the birth rate dropped and more women were entering
the paid labor force, nurturance as a critical feature of female identity,
paradoxically, became more entrenched ideologically in the notion of maternal instinct (Gordon 1977: 115).

This prevailing view of women as selfless and generous, by nature im-
mune to the dehumanizing effects of capitalism, was used by voluntary
motherhood advocates to promote acceptance of their efforts for fertility
control. Gordon argues that these ideas, along with those of the eugenics
movement that were gaining popularity at the turn of the century, produced a sort of Lamarckian theory in which children conceived in emotionally fraught circumstances were considered prone to mental or physical
disabilities. Voluntary motherhood activists claimed that the conditions of
intercourse itself could affect the child's character. Sexual intercourse during pregnancy, under the influence of alcohol, or in circumstances in
which women were unwilling was viewed as a cause of inherited damage.
Thus, the right of a woman to refuse her husband sexually became "biolo-
gized" and the drive to curb men's sexual demands on women was now
justified in terms of evolutionary progress. By extension, many voluntary
motherhood advocates argued that the emancipation of women would
have immediate beneficial eugenic effects (Gordon 1977: 120–27).

Initially, such thinking drew on women's selfless nurturance as the
source of female moral and genetic superiority, but by the late 1890s,
groups such as the National Purity Association were issuing pamphlets that
declared self-sacrifice in women to be a violation of duty to unborn children
(Gordon 1977: 129). Similarly, the nineteenth-century advocates of higher
learning for women argued that education would improve women's abilities to perform their traditional roles as wives and mothers (Beecher

1872). The arguments were apparently successful. American colleges excluded women until 1837; by 1870, 11,000 women were enrolled in 582 institutions of higher education (O'Neill 1971: 13).

However, the publication of statistics that showed that a quarter to half of college-educated women never married (approximately double the number of noncollege women) and that they generally had fewer children and harder pregnancies than poor or working-class women were used by opponents of higher education for women to undercut support, despite the fact that less than 10 percent of American women had actually abandoned motherhood in favor of a professional career (Degler 1980: 314; O'Neill 1971: 80, 148). By the early 1900s, such ideas were used to oppose the Voluntary Motherhood movement as well. The arguments of "race suicide" condemned white middle-class women who voluntarily lowered their fertility for allowing other "races" to outbreed them. These ideas have been popularly identified with Theodore Roosevelt, yet they had broad appeal at the time, even among women (Gordon 1977: 130–35).

The Suffrage and Antisuffrage Campaigns

Much like feminism in the 1970s, turn-of-the-century campaigns for women's sexual and political rights provoked opposition and divisions among women. Although Frances Willard supported female suffrage, the WCTU never openly embraced the suffrage cause; its members were considered much more conservative than their contemporaries in the National Women's Suffrage Association (NWSA). Yet there are some striking similarities (as well as differences) between the two groups that offer an instructive parallel to the contemporary abortion controversy. A study by Janet Giele (1961) comparing leaders of the WCTU and the NWSA shows that both movements had a high proportion of educated women whose philosophies converged on several points. Both argued that women had a unique social role, distinct from that of men; that the position of women in the home deserved recognition and support; and that women were morally superior but socially vulnerable to men and needed greater protection. They differed in their strategies for action. Suffrage activists tended to favor structural reforms in labor, education, and government, stressing the civic and intellectual equality of women as individuals. The WCTU members worked in "other-serving" causes—charity, childcare, or social purity movements.

The Alliance of Domesticity with the State: Social Feminism

During the years bridging the nineteenth and twentieth centuries, America witnessed the greatest industrial depression in its history, dramatizing the deleterious impact that increasing corporate control of American manufacturing was having on the lives of most people. Farmers' revolts and the populist uprisings, the Spanish-American War, violent strikes such as those at Homestead and Pullman, and massive immigration from southern and eastern Europe all contributed to the sense of crisis, conflict, and change that generated what one historian has called "the search for order" (Wiebe 1967). Technical rationality and scientific authority became the guiding principles for reform efforts designed as much to quell unrest as they were to improve conditions. Wiebe and other interpreters of the period consider this new "romance with science" as the basis for the cognitive style that shaped mass liberal culture in which the growth of corporations, elite institutions, and professions played a central role. Perhaps of greatest significance, the foundations of the regulatory welfare state were laid. Orphanages, prisons, and mental asylums and the personnel to staff them were justified as institutions involved in caretaking that families could not or would not do (Zaretsky 1982: 188).

The intertwining of these themes, the rational management of human dependency with the concerns of female activists for social reform, took its paradigmatic form in the Settlement House Movement, initiated in the United States with the founding of Hull House in Chicago. Its director, Jane Addams, criticized the paternalistic social Darwinism of the late nineteenth century and its corollary idea of "scientific charity," which blamed the poor for their poverty. Instead, she advocated "maternalism," an idea first articulated by Lester Ward in the 1880s. Under Addams, the Settlement Movement succeeded in transforming female domesticity into an essential "civilizing" element of public life. The rapid spread of the Settlement houses by 1900 was a sign of their usefulness in helping immigrants and poor people cope with life in American cities. In addition, as organizations staffed and run almost entirely by women, Settlement houses were quickly accepted as an extension of women's sphere, thus providing a purposeful career outside the home to the increasing numbers of educated American women.

The most representative, at least in numbers, of women's organizations of the Progressive Era was the General Federation of Women's Clubs (GFWC), a network of thousands of grass-roots groups, composed mainly of middle-class wives and mothers across the country "whose homes were cleaned by servants and supplied commercially with all manner of goods and services" (O'Neill 1971: 86). The clubs they formed initially stressed female education and companionship. By 1898, the GFWC had 160,000 members devoted increasingly to civic reform—from building kindergartens and public laundries to investigating the harassment of immigrants in New York City (Degler 1980: 325).

In the early 1900s, the GFWC pressured Congress to investigate what other reformers had been urging for years without success: the conditions of female and child labor. Their goal of securing protective legislation for this segment of the labor force was shared by almost every women's organization of the time. The six-hundred-page brief they and the National Consumers' League provided was critical in eventually winning the Supreme Court ruling upholding the constitutionality of protective legislation for women workers, the *Muller* v. *Oregon* appeal argued by Louis Brandeis in 1908 (O'Neill 1971: 152; Degler 1980: 358). The court's justification of maximum hour limits for female laborers illustrates the persistence of the identification of the female gender with maternity, nurturance, and dependency, opposed to male lust and irresponsibility. They wrote, for example, that

woman has always been dependent upon man. He established his control at the outset by superior physical strength. . . . Even though all restrictions on political, personal, and contractual rights were taken away . . . her physical structure and a proper discharge of her maternal functions . . . justify legislation to protect her from the greed as well as the passion of man. (Quoted in O'Neill 1971: 289)

The decision, which ultimately enabled the passage of a host of protective statutes throughout the country, was considered a great triumph by groups such as the GFWC and the Settlement Movement. In their view, the state had secured the collective interests of women both as workers and mothers. Despite the growing female labor force, it was the concern for protecting women's position in the domestic sphere around which female activists rallied. Ironically, the reforms they won also helped underwrite gender segregation in the sexual division of labor in America so that, over the course of the twentieth century, female labor at home and in wage work were cast increasingly in opposition.

At the time, however, diverse female reform groups joined together around the principle of protecting women's role as nurturers from men and the market through the authority of the state. They formed the women's Joint Congressional Union to lobby Congress for further protective reforms such as child-labor laws and maternal-infant health programs (Ryan 1983: 218). The Married Women's Property Acts, for example, which gave wives the right to earn and spend their own wages, were interpreted not so much as granting women greater autonomy but as protecting them from negligent husbands (Basch 1979). Similarly, in the early twentieth century, the enactment in several states of "mother's pensions"—public cash grants for widows with children—was not intended to replace the family but to provide the means to extend to the poor and disadvantaged the familial ideal in which women and children depended on male support (Zaretsky 1982: 213).

What all this indicates is the increasing acceptance of the ideal of a "family wage" as the mediating principle on which the negotiation of male and female spheres should rest. The idea that a male worker should be paid a salary sufficient to support a wife and children had, by World War I, become the basis for pay scales in all war production industries and the critical issue in most labor negotiations in general (Zaretsky 1982: 217).

Despite the support for these developments by nearly every progressive movement at the time, many contemporary scholars have been critical of the family wage, protective legislation, and the range of government policies and institutions that entrenched a social arrangement that assigned men to the role of breadwinner and women to motherhood and unpaid domestic labor. Christopher Lasch, for example, considers the expansion of the government's role in caring for whole categories of dependent people as "an invasion of the private realm," the "proletarianization of parents by the state" by self-interested middle-class professionals (1977). Heidi Hartmann—in analyzing how the family wage and protective legislation for women succeeded in establishing a gender-based occupational hierarchy that has excluded women from equal participation in wage labor—attributes the reforms she criticizes to a collusion of "capitalism" and "patriarchy" against women (1979). There is no question that trade union men opposed the movement for a minimum wage for women; and that the organization of family life around a male wage and unpaid female domestic labor served both the interests of a capitalist class and an increasingly centralized state that proclaimed children a crucial national resource. However, this assignment of blame to abstract forces dismisses the motivations of whole categories of people—for example "women" or "working-class families"—who were essential, interested parties in the material and ideological transformations in question.

The 1920s and the Emergence of "Commercial Culture"

The split over the National Women's Party proposal of the equal rights amendment—and its implicit ideology of the fundamental equality of men and women—was only one index of the growing divisions and dissension among female social activists, despite the official gains they had made in the political arena by the 1920s. In assessing the causes of the disintegration of female reform efforts, leaders of the Progressive Era movements attributed the decline to the growing emphases on individual consumerism and sexuality. The new social milieu was seen as eroding the issues and cultural concerns that had shaped female activists born in the 1870s and 1880s. Jane Addams, writing in 1930, observed that women had become willing to "dovetail into the political themes of men [rather] than release the innate concerns of women which might be equivalent to a revolutionary force," a change she saw as "associated in some way with the breaking down of sex taboos and the establishment of new standards of marriage" (1930: 110, 120). The very successes of Addams and other social feminists who came of age in the 1890s may have contributed to the obsolescence of their ideals; the work they championed also appropriated and bureaucratized their activism.

Although the growth of state institutions was critical to the cultural transformations of the early twentieth century, these developments were tied equally to the expansion of corporate capitalism requiring ever-greater levels of mass consumption. The doubling of industrial manufacture that resulted was based on the increasing production, consumption, and marketing of nondurable goods—food, apparel, and personal hygiene items; products such as automobiles and sewing and washing machines; and the energy to run such equipment. By 1929, consumer goods and services almost completely replaced most domestic manufacture in households of all classes (Matthaei 1982: 238; Ryan 1983: 221).

Rayna Rapp and Ellen Ross point out how this massive social change affected female activism in the early twentieth century.

A dramatic transformation of American culture—fusing sex, love and consumerism—made the all-female organizations of the feminists seem stodgy and outmoded. The new commercial culture of the 1920s was not so much directly anti-feminist as it was cooptive of feminist issues and concerns. (Rapp and Ross 1983: 55)

Not only did arguments for sexual restraint gradually lose efficacy. The small-town Protestant base for social purity campaigns was eclipsed by the growth of urban, culturally diverse populations and a new generation of geographically and socially mobile young people (Fass 1977: chap. 3).

If the conservative sexual attitudes of social purity advocates seemed atavistic, the nascent birth control movement did not gain widespread appeal, in part because of its association, initially, with anarchism and socialism. Early advocates of dissemination of birth control knowledge such as Emma Goldman promoted contraception in the hope that ending sexual repression based on fear of pregnancy would expedite a socialist revolution (Epstein 1983). Organized conservative and right-wing groups such as the Sentinels of the Republic and the Ku Klux Klan that emerged following World War I played on existing tensions during a period of rising conservatism. Similarly, initial support among women's groups for the Sheppard-Towner Bill, which funded child and maternal welfare programs, was eventually split by charges that it was a program designed for "female celibates," part of a socialist conspiracy to undermine the family. The program was defeated in Congress in 1929 (Ryan 1983: 220).

Nonetheless, a significant increase in the use of contraception was taking place.[2] These changes were due in part to the development of relatively safe, effective, and inexpensive devices, especially the Mensinga diaphragm. However, the shift in attitudes and practice was not simply due to technology. If sex manuals, popular women's magazines, or movies of the 1920s are any indication (e.g., Lynd and Lynd 1937: 241–48), the end of World War I signaled a clear shift from the campaigns against sexual excess of the nineteenth century. Contraception had become acceptable for the middle class, as had heterosexual eroticism, especially women's, as a central ingredient of marriage.[3]

Given these developments, it is not surprising that the birth rate dropped from 3.56 in 1900 to 2.45 by 1930 (Degler 1980: 181, 414; Ryan 1983: 245). At the same time, children were spending more time in schools and nurseries (Uhlenberg 1974) while household labor became increasingly a matter of consumption with the development of domestic technology. It was not only the work of housework and childrearing that was being reorganized. After 1920, both birth and birth control were increasingly under the control of the medical establishment. By 1930, the use of midwives had declined significantly; 75 percent of all births occurred in hospitals, and the price increased tenfold. Contraception became more expensive as well so that "even women's basic reproduction function had become imbricated in the marketplace and converted into something more, and less, than domestic labor" (Ryan 1983: 246). Thus, the productive base of the domestic domain was being transformed by changes in sexual practice and by the expansion of both consumer markets and the state.

The Depression: Domesticity Revived

During the Depression, women played a crucial role in providing a buffer for families and households against the effects of the economic crisis that followed the 1929 stock market crash. A revival of domesticity occurred both in the renewed material involvement of women in household manufacture and in a cultural shift away from the stress on female freedom and sexuality of the preceding decade. This reversal of trends of the 1920s occurred despite the fact that the number of women working increased by 25.1 percent between 1930 and 1940, a rate greater than that of any prior decade in the twentieth century (Degler 1980: 415; Milkman 1979: 518). Yet, because this shift in the traditional sexual division of labor took place under duress, it apparently was experienced negatively by many involved. Unlike working women in the 1920s who spoke of jobs as a vehicle for independence and identity, the Depression cohort viewed their behavior as a temporary response to emergency. Consequently, according to the sociologist Ruth Milkman, "the impact of the crisis was to define women in terms of the traditional roles even more rigidly than before" (Milkman 1979: 527). Thus, despite the growing number of female workers during the Depression, the separate-sphere ideology—supported by the state and accommodating the participation of women in wage labor—endured nonetheless. What this shows more generally is how changes in American gender constructs have a complex and often unexpected relationship to shifts in the sexual division of labor.

World War II and the Postwar Era

From World War II until the present, the definitions of female domesticity as established in the nineteenth century were reformulated to accommodate the increasing numbers of women in wage labor and the decline of productive activity in the household. The huge demand for female workers created by war-related industrial production broke the gender boundary between the world of paid labor and the domestic domain assigned to wives and mothers. Whereas typical female wage earners during the first half of the twentieth century were single and in their twenties, 60 percent of the new workers were thirty-five or older; over half of them were married, widowed, or divorced (Milkman 1979: 529). Many had had prior work experience as "working girls" in the 1920s, left the paid labor force upon marriage, and were ready to reenter it once their children were in school or grown.

Although female workers were laid off in large numbers immediately following the war, many were eventually reabsorbed into the jobs created by the postwar conversion of the economy from war-related to consumer-oriented production. While employment in manufacturing went up by only 16 percent between 1941 and 1963, the tertiary sector of the economy—government, trade, finance, health, transport, recreation, research, and education—grew by 53 percent (Oppenheimer 1970: 70–75). Given that the clerical and service jobs this expanding sector provided were identified as female labor, it is not surprising that during the same period male labor force participation declined while the participation of women increased (Milkman 1979: 533). Yet labor force participation cannot be attributed simply to the needs of capital. As Mary Ryan notes:

Joining the labor force for these women was something more than an obliging response to the prodding of the War Manpower Commission. . . . It was not the dictates of international affairs nor supply and demand that drove women to seek employment after 1940, but their own priorities as they evolved over the life cycle. (1983: 279–80)

At the peak of the baby boom in 1955—a period identified with female domesticity—over 30 percent of adult women were in the labor force (Oppenheimer 1970: table 1.2).

While a larger proportion (94 percent) of the female population of childbearing age was having children during the 1940s and 1950s than at any other time in American history, for most women the phase of their life following family completion was becoming the longest stretch of their life cycle (Uhlenberg 1974: 51–53; Milkman 1979: 535). Nevertheless, by the 1950s, reproduction was coming to occupy an increasingly prominent place as the key feature defining and giving meaning to the domestic domain.

Consuming Motherhood

The revived identification of reproduction and female identity was tied to the postwar growth of commodity production and services. This process reestablished the shift of domestic production to the marketplace and public sector after the hiatus of the Depression and World War II. The result, in addition to an expansion of opportunity in occupational groups sex typed as female, was the growing availability for purchase of services and commodities previously provided by unpaid labor in the household. As new products were linked more and more to domesticity, women were targeted by American business interests as the key to expanding the consumer market. A 1957 cover of *Life* magazine captioned a photograph of a mass of toddlers, "KIDS—Built-in Recession Cure—How 4 Million a Year Make Millions in Business." Market research conducted by *Fortune* magazine in the 1950s projected that young wives and mothers would provide the impetus for $10 billion worth of home construction, $60 billion worth of food purchases, $30 billion spent on family recreation, and $12 billion on home furnishings and appliances (Ryan 1983: 269).

Although the actual amount of time required for maternity had decreased in relation to a woman's total life cycle, time spent in housework actually increased from an average of fifty-two to fifty-four hours a week between 1920 and 1960. This was due in part to the reintroduction of tasks such as laundry into households, shorter spacings between births, and the promotion of new standards of cleanliness and childcare (Vanek 1974). Intensive mothering was also buttressed by new childrearing theories. Gesell, Spock, and others counseled the constant presence of the mother for children to develop properly. The centrality of maternity was further elaborated in popular versions of Freudian psychology. The theories of Helene Deutsch managed to update the Victorian conflation of female sexual pleasure with the idea of innate maternal instinct, infusing it with contemporary scientific authority: "In the normal, healthy woman, coitus psychologically represents the first act of motherhood" (Deutsch 1945: 107, 258).

Such ideas reached people and especially women in a variety of ways: by the 1950s the majority of psychotherapy clients and the most likely patients to be assigned to mental institutions were female. In the course of treatment, working women especially were encouraged to return to domestic duties to "recapture their femininity and have more babies" (Deutsch 1945: 331). The tenets of the new female psychology also reached mass audiences through popular magazines and paperbacks. The widely read popularization of Deutsch's work, *Modern Woman: The Lost Sex* by Marynia Farnham and Ferdinand Lundberg, held that women who worked and sought a life independent from the family were unrealized and trying to become men (Ryan 1983: 264–65).

The reformulation of female domesticity and consuming motherhood was evident in social theory as well. In 1955, Talcott Parsons was defining the family as a narrow isolated unit, an emotional refuge against the impersonal institutions of modern society. As a private subsystem, the ideal home would function through the "instrumental" work of men in the public world, and the "expressive" labors of women at home who were to provide a haven of intimacy and emotional support for children and husbands (Parsons and Bales 1955). Through this lens, "the family" was viewed as a unit that had been stripped of its productive functions as the result of industrialization. All that remained was the expressive natural "core," the very center of which was the mother and child, the ultimate symbol of nurturance and affect in American society. Like the psychological theories already described, the Parsonian view also managed to interpret anew and with scientific authority a separate-sphere ideology for a mid-twentieth-century context. However, as these experts' condemnations of women who chose to move beyond the domain of domesticity were increasingly dissonant with the experiences of large numbers of women, the "conventional schemes" began to be challenged.

The Revival of Female Activism: The Second Wave of Feminism

The three-decade quiescence of female activism and public debate over "women's proper place" ended in the 1960s. Historians of this period attribute this resurgence to a number of causes. Many view President Kennedy's appointment in 1961 of a Presidential Commission on the Status of Women as critical to the emergence of the second wave of feminism (e.g., Freeman 1973; Degler 1980: 441–42). At the time, it was considered a "kind of consolation prize to the women of the Democratic party" (Ryan 1983: 308). The Commission, chaired by Eleanor Roosevelt and Esther Peterson of the Women's Bureau, issued a report in 1963, *American*

Women, that took a stand against the ERA and recommended training of young women for marriage and motherhood. Nonetheless, the report also brought attention to the discrimination encountered by the many women, and wives and mothers especially, who had been entering the work force since 1940 (Ryan 1983: 308). Furthermore, the Commission provided women activists an alliance with the federal government and an institutional base as well. By 1967, all fifty states had established commissions on the status of women, providing a national network that brought together female political activists (Freeman 1973: 36). Thus, both ideologically and organizationally, they offered a legitimate alternative to existing definitions of female domesticity. Confronted with the evidence of their unequal status, these women began to address what role they would play in alleviating these discriminatory conditions in the terms of liberal democracy.

The growing recognition of the contradictions between official policy and women's lives, and more generally the transitions women faced as they moved into the labor force, were articulated by Betty Friedan in *The Feminine Mystique*. Published in 1963, this work became a watershed document in the emerging women's movement, taking what had been experienced as dissonance by large numbers of women and reframing it as a social problem. The book gave voice to the conflicts encountered by a whole cohort of middle-class women coming into a critical moment in their life cycles after spending a decade or more of their lives at home rearing children. Friedan managed not only to describe this "problem that had no name." She also was instrumental in turning this dissatisfaction into organized political activity.

In 1966 Friedan, along with thirty other women and men, founded NOW. The organization's aim—"to take actions needed to bring women into full participation in the mainstream of American society now, assuming all the privileges and responsibilities thereof in truly equal partnership with men"—shaped a new style of liberal feminism that, unlike prior incarnations, rejected the "women's sphere" altogether in both tactics and ideology. Reflecting the concerns of the educated, relatively affluent professional woman who composed its initial constituency, NOW concentrated on structural reform of the legal and economic system. Its agenda addressed a range of issues affecting women, from divorce to the ERA. Working through the traditional political process and embracing a formal, top-down style, NOW had expanded to over fifty-five thousand members in eight hundred chapters across the country by the mid-1970s (Ryan 1983: 309).

Whereas women in NOW—many in their thirties and forties—used mainstream political tactics to redress discrimination experienced by women making the shift from the home to the labor force, the women in their twenties—40 percent of the college student population by 1968—were the vanguard of a new style of female activism in both form and substance.[4] Work in radical politics provided these younger women with a network, a style of political action, and a framework for analysis that took shape in the numerous "consciousness-raising" groups that emerged around the country during the late 1960s. In addition, the experience of New Left and Civil Rights organizing brought these young women, like female abolitionists a century earlier, face to face with the contradiction of being treated unequally as women while working for freedom and equality of others. Thus, both branches of the movement, despite their differences, mobilized against what they saw as the unwillingness of their male colleagues to extend these principles to women.

By the late 1960s, the younger women activists were agitating on issues that were more radical challenges to the definition of female identity in prevailing gender arrangements: lesbian rights, subsidized daycare, and abortion rights.[5] These women challenged the ranks of NOW and formed their own more radical political groupings. For example, the radical feminist women who eventually formed Redstockings invaded the New York State legislature hearings on abortion and then held their own counter-hearings, which used women's testimony about illegal abortion to demand that it be redefined as legal (Willis 1971: 117–18). This confrontational style was used in other parts of the country as well, including a nationwide "strike day" on August 26, 1970, in which dramatic demonstrations were held in a number of American cities (Hole and Levine 1971: 295–99).[6] Their reinterpretation of abortion as an unconditional right for women succeeded in bringing that perspective into the debate. In the view of both participants and observers to the abortion repeal campaign, the radical feminists, although few in number, helped create effective pressure to break through legal barriers to abortion repeal, culminating in the passage of *Roe* v. *Wade* in 1973.

In her analysis of the second wave of feminism, Jo Freeman stresses the importance of generational differences (1973: 35). She rejects the more frequently used categories of "reform" versus "radical" (e.g., Hole and Levine 1971) as a misguided effort to fit feminists into an inappropriate left-right spectrum. Freeman designates NOW and other "reform" groups such as the Women's Equity Action League and Human Rights for Women as the "older branch of the movement," partly because these groups had an older constituency than and formed before the "younger" more radical organizations that came to be known as the Women's Liberation Movement (WLM) (1973: 33). Mary Ryan attributes even more substantial explanatory weight to generational and life-cycle factors in the resurgence of female activism in the 1960s and 1970s. Perhaps of equal importance to political history, she writes, "were more basic causal factors intrinsic to the gender system itself" (Ryan 1983: 312). Demographic, economic, and social changes coincided to create unprecedented gaps— what might be termed new liminal periods—between what previously had been continuous phases of the conventional female life cycle. Between 1960 and 1974, the number of single women between the ages of twenty and twenty-four rose from 28 to 40 percent. The younger female activists came from this expanding group, "suspended between the families of their birth and the family of marriage" (Ryan 1983: 313). Thus, they were—in addition to being primarily white, middle-class, and college-educated—structurally parallel to the older cohort that was making the transition from motherhood to wage labor; each generation was, in its own way, "enjoying a reprieve from domesticity" (Ryan 1983: 313).

Revising Domesticity

The International Women's Year Congress (IWY) held in Houston, Texas, in 1977 seemed to substantiate the claims of the second wave of feminism to represent the interests of all women, regardless of the preeminence of white, educated, middle-class women as activists. Funded by the U.S. Congress, the IWY Congress also dramatized the degree to which the movement had gained strength through its alliance with the state. The concerns addressed at the Congress in the twenty-five resolutions passed there reflected the diverse interests of the gathered constituency: homemakers and lesbians, mothers and career women, urban blacks and rural whites. Not surprisingly, the two thousand women present did not agree on all the issues. Nearly 25 percent of the representatives were opposed to at least portions of the feminist agenda and its broader claim to speak for all women.

Significant in its absence from their complaints was the question of equal pay for equal work, a principle that had, by 1977, been accepted by the majority of Americans who might not otherwise identify themselves as "feminist" (Giele and Smock 1977: 316). As Mary Ryan documents it:

Even more conservative women's magazines, such as *Family Circle,* greeted housewives at supermarket checkout counters with explicit attacks on the "sex discrimination" to which housewives and working women were equally susceptible. The working woman, not the feminist per se, was given the largest and most respected treatment in these popular journals. Whole new magazines were devoted to her, *The Working Woman, The New Woman,* and *Savvy,* for the females of the executive suite. (1983: 316)

Broad support for pay equity is not surprising. By 1978, over 50 percent of adult women were in the labor force. Although the mass media portrayed the female workers as carrying Gucci briefcases, most working women were less concerned with the label on their portfolio than with the size of the paycheck they put into it. Their wages hovered at an average of fifty-nine cents to every dollar made by men, a fact that was an affront to nearly universal American ideals of equality and fair play. Despite increasing female participation in the professions, most continued to work in the low-wage "pink-collar" ghettos of the clerical, retail, and service industries.

Between 1973 and 1980, 70 percent of all new jobs in the private economy were in retail trade and services, especially health care and eating and drinking places (Rothschild 1981: 12). By 1980, one out of every two dollars Americans paid for food was spent in restaurants. Even child-care—long considered the one aspect of domestic labor (besides reproduction itself) that could not be rationalized—has been targeted as a vast unexploited market. The Kindercare franchised child care centers in shopping malls across the country offer a graphic example of the penetration of capital into this aspect of domestic work (Bellm 1987). Between 1980 and 1986, a commercial home cleaning company, "Maids—America's Maid Service," expanded from three franchises and a $180,000 income to two hundred offices in thirty-nine states and a gross income of over $11 million (Stark 1987). This steady transformation of unpaid domestic labor into a waged service economy is the root and flower of the transformation, from the household out, of the sexual division of labor and the productive and reproductive activities associated with gender.

The sexual division of labor that constituted the cultural construction of separate spheres in the eighteenth century has changed irreversibly. It is my argument that as the material base of domesticity has been subsumed into the market economy, female identity is increasingly defined by and reduced to reproduction. Women activists have focused increasingly on redefining the terms of reproduction, because it is the critical feature, at this historical moment, in the domain assigned them in the social construction of gender in America. Female activists from the Great Awakening to the WCTU to the suffrage movement, have been reformulating available understandings of gender identity as they defended, expanded, and redefined the domestic domain. In contests over the rights and obligations of women in American culture that have taken place in America since the late eighteenth century, one can see how a particular gender opposition has been sustained and transformed through dynamics similar to those at play in the contemporary struggles over abortion.

Notes

Chapter 1. Introduction

1. Statistics on abortion rates in the area support research that shows that geographic availability of abortion services is a critical factor influencing a woman's ability to obtain a safe, legal abortion (Borders and Cutright 1979). In the first year of the clinic's existence, abortions performed in the state rose from 3,140 to 3,350 (Henshaw, Forrest, Sullivan, and Tietze 1982: table 2; Henshaw, Forrest, and Van Vort 1987: table 3).

According to the Fargo Women's Health Organization, the staff is committed to providing care that includes careful counseling and screening of patients as well as postabortion checkups.

2. According to the latest periodic survey of U.S. abortion services by the Alan Guttmacher Institute, in 1984–85 the approximately 399 abortion clinics (i.e., clinics in which 50 percent or more of patients' visits are for abortions) provided 60 percent of all abortions; 438 clinics with smaller proportions of abortion caseloads accounted for 23 percent of all abortions. In 1985, only 18 percent of all U.S. counties had abortion providers. For a full analysis of the 1984–85 statistics, see Henshaw, Forrest, and Van Vort (1987).

3. Information for this section is drawn from the following sources: Ron Abrahamson, *Fifteen Minutes in Fargo* (Fargo, N.D.: Fargo Chamber of Commerce, Fargo–Moorhead Centennial Corporation, 1981); *A History of Fargo North Dakota and Moorhead Minnesota* (Fargo, N.D.: Knight Printing, 1975); *Fargo, N.D. Community and Downtown Business Information* (Fargo, N.D.: Downtown Business Association, September 1982); *Fargo Economic Indicators* (Fargo, N.D.: Fargo Chamber of Commerce and Fargo/Cass County Industrial Development Corporation, June 1982); *Fargo: The Largest City in North Dakota* (Fargo, N.D.: The Fargo Cham-

ber of Commerce, June 1981); *Moorhead Minnesota Community Profile* (St. Paul, Minn.: Minnesota Dept. of Economic Development, March 1981); Office of the North Dakota Conference of Churches, Bismarck, N.D.; Office of Statistical Services, North Dakota Department of Health; Jerome Tweton and Theodore B. Jelliff, *North Dakota: The Heritage of a People* (Fargo, N.D.: North Dakota Institute for Regional Studies, 1983); *General Social and Economic Characteristics of North Dakota* (U.S. Department of Commerce, Bureau of the Census, 1970), table 85; *Supplementary Report: Advance Estimate of Social, Economic and Housing Characteristics, North Dakota* (U.S. Dept. of Commerce, Bureau of the Census, 1980), table P-3.

4. The two industries projected to generate the largest numbers of new wage and salary jobs between the years 1986 and 2000 are eating and drinking places and offices of health practitioners (U.S. Bureau of Labor Statistics, reported in *New York Times*, October 11, 1987).

5. I worked as associate producer for an hour-long documentary on the conflict over the clinic in Fargo. The show, "Prairie Storm," produced for the Public Affairs Unit of WCCO-TV, Minneapolis (CBS), and broadcast in April 1982, was well received by pro-choice and pro-life activists alike.

6. Rebecca Klatch's comments on women and class are useful here:

Recent feminist scholarship has pointed out the difficulty of delineating women's class position. While clearly women cannot simply be reduced to the class position of their husband or father, on the other hand all women do not occupy the same class position. Most studies of anti-feminist women measure class by father's background or husband's employment. Even so, the findings are discrepant. (1987: 223, n. 34)

7. In her study, *Women of the New Right*, Rebecca Klatch makes a similar point. She argues that while both feminists and antifeminists are concerned about the vulnerability of women, the former see women's economic independence as the solution, whereas the latter are concerned that men support women in marriage.

It is not, then, that social conservative women suffer from "false consciousness" in not recognizing their own self-interest as women, as some feminists charge. In fact, social conservative women are well aware of their interests as women and act in defense of these interests. The difference between social conservative women and feminists, rather, is rooted in the fundamentally different meanings each attaches to being female. (1987: 139)

8. While this was certainly the view promoted by both Right and Left at the time of Reagan's election, some offer revisionist understandings eight years later. For example, conservative analyst Kevin Phillips who predicted the rise of the New Right, now argues that the Reagan administration was the finale of a coalition built by Goldwater, Nixon, and Wal-

lace in the 1960s rather than the debut of a new conservativism. See E. J. Dionne, Jr., "High Tide for Conservatives, But Some Fear What Follows," *New York Times,* October, 13, 1987.

9. This distinction is a central point made by Rebecca Klatch in her book *Women of the New Right.*

> Where one looks through a religious lens, and sees the family at the center of the vision, the other views the world through the lens of liberty, with the individual standing firmly in the foreground. Where one sees a hierarchy of men and women, the other sees the sexes standing equal and alone. (1987: 54)

While there is some overlap between "social conservatives" and right-to-life activists, from my own research, the position of many pro-life women on gender, while advocating differences between men and women, is not so accepting of hierarchy. In fact, their view of women as nurturant is used as an argument for the authority of "female values" and their importance as a corrective to the materialism and individualism of American life.

10. There is no single definition or social group that defines feminism. In general usage, feminism is used as a gloss for a variety of contemporary and historical social movements and ideologies that view a given society as sexist and propose action for improving the position of women in it. Proponents of different analyses and strategies for accomplishing that goal are not always in agreement, despite the common claim to the name feminist. Properly, then, the term should be not feminism but feminisms.

In this book, unless otherwise noted, I use the term in reference to "social facts"—that is, when people or groups *claim* some connection to feminism, whether or not I regard this claim as accurate. So, for example, Noonan's subtext, connecting opposition to abortion to feminist roots, is unexpected but not uncommon in the' pro-life movement, but does not make the position feminist. Similarly, in her pro-life dissent from the Rockefeller Commission on Population, Gracie Olivarez wrote that abortion was "anti-women's liberation," because it subverted the equality of men and women. Equality, she observed, meant "an equal sharing of responsibilities *by* and *as* men and women." Abortion on demand confirmed "the existing irresponsible attitude some men have toward their relationship to women and their offspring" (1972: 160–61, quoted in Noonan 1979: 48). In my view, such rhetorical incorporation by each side of the opponent's "high ground" is part of the dialectical nature of this conflict, a phenomenon I analyze in some detail in chapters 6 through 10.

11. In *Sexual Meanings,* a cross-cultural collection on gender and sexual symbolism, anthropologists Sherry Ortner and Harriet Whitehead write that:

> Women are seen as tending toward more involvement with (often divisive) private and particularistic concerns, benefiting themselves, and perhaps their chil-

dren, without regard for larger social consequences, whereas men are seen as having a more universalistic orientation, as being concerned with the welfare of the social whole. (1981: 7)

12. See for example Marshall Sahlins, *Islands of History* (Chicago: University of Chicago Press, 1985); Eric Wolf, *Europe and the People without History* (Berkeley: University of California Press, 1982); Marc Augé, *The Anthropological Circle* (New York: Cambridge University Press, 1979).

13. French social historian Ferdinand Braudel's notion of "the structures of la longue durée" examines historical material to discover continuities of cultural categories that structure meaning and action through time (1958). My approach borrows from this idea as well as the work of Sahlins (1981; 1985) and Giddens (1979) who are concerned with how structures are changed, by the intended or unintended consequences of social action.

14. By life crisis, I simply mean a period in the life cycle experienced as a stressful interruption, marked as a shift from one culturally defined stage of life to another.

15. In a recent article based on surveys of abortion providers, Jacqueline Forrest and Stanley Henshaw estimate that 83 percent of patients obtaining abortions were harassed in 1985 (Forrest and Henshaw 1987).

16. In addition to the sort of conflicts I describe in this book, abortion services have been affected through changes in government policy that were created in response to pro-life pressure. Initially, these were implemented in overseas population programs. The Reagan administration's effort to deny funds to family planning services that offer patients abortion information or services was dubbed the Mexico City Policy because it was first announced in August 1984 at the U.N. Conference on Population in Mexico City. The primary impact of that policy was the elimination of the $15-million annual payment that the Agency for International Development had been giving to the International Planned Parenthood Federation. Plans also to end funding for the overseas programs of the Planned Parenthood Federation of America mobilized that group to bring a federal suit and launch a publicity campaign against the government for violation of free speech rights (Lewis 1987).

Until 1987, right-to-life political efforts were more successful on the overseas than the domestic front. In May of that year, the Senate Foreign Relations Committee approved overturning the Mexico City policy and voted to end curbs on U.S. funds for the U.N. Fund for Population Activities. In September 1987, the Department of Health and Human Services proposed rulings to deny federal funding to family planning agencies that counsel for abortion, and allow federal support for pro-life "problem pregnancy clinics." The proposal was suspended in March 1988, after a federal district judge in Boston, Walter Skinner, issued a nationwide injunction permanently prohibiting enforcement of the restriction. However, a July 1, 1988, ruling by Federal District Judge Louis Stanton upheld the regulations, increasing the likelihood that this issue will come before the Supreme Court. See also chapter 3, n. 7.

17. Struggles over local delivery of abortion services have dominated the conflict in the 1980s; legislative right-to-life efforts have been relatively unsuccessful. The judiciary is another arena for action, since the possibility remains that the *Roe* v. *Wade* decision might be reversed by the Supreme Court, particularly with the appointment of more conservative Justices. In June 1986, Chief Justice Burger announced his retirement from the Supreme Court. President Reagan nominated Justice Rehnquist to take his place as Chief Justice, and Judge Antonin Scalia, a conservative, to replace Rehnquist. The Republican-controlled Congress confirmed these choices. On July 1, 1987, when Justice Lewis Powell, considered the swing vote between conservatives and liberals on the Court, decided to retire, Reagan nominated Judge Robert Bork to replace him. The Bork nomination mobilized abortion activists on both sides. NARAL's three-day national convention in July 1987 was transformed from an organizational to an activist session to stop his confirmation. In response, the National Right-to-Life Committee urged its members to write their senators in support of Bork and "use telephone trees, church bulletins, letters to newspaper editors, and so forth to get the word out to like-minded citizens" (*National Right to Life News*, August 16, 1987). The Bork nomination was ultimately defeated by Congress, as was the subsequent Reagan nomination of Douglas Ginsburg. It is unclear whether the nominee who *was* confirmed, Anthony Kennedy, will join antiabortion colleagues on the Court—Rehnquist, O'Connor, Scalia, and White— to constitute a new working majority that might overturn or modify the current laws.

The significance of this new Justice for the abortion issue was underscored on December 14, 1987, when the Supreme Court deadlocked on a decision regarding a 1983 Illinois state law (struck down by federal district and appeals courts) that would require parental notification or the permission of a judge for minors seeking abortions. The December deadlock postponed a ruling on this matter. A number of challenges to state restrictions on minors' abortion rights are now pending in federal lower courts.

18. Since the early 1980s pro-life "problem pregnancy centers" have mushroomed from almost none to over two thousand. Since 1981, such centers have been receiving support from the Department of Health and Human Services under the Adolescent Family Life Act, designed to promote teenage chastity and care for pregnant teenagers. More than a

dozen centers have been the subject of litigation, including the one in Fargo. Women seeking abortion services contend the centers misled them through false advertising. For example, in October 1986, the founder of a "pregnancy center" in Fort Worth, Texas, was convicted of falsely advertising as an abortion clinic and fined $39,000. In December 1986, the Subcommittee on Civil and Constitutional Rights, part of the House Judiciary Committee, held hearings on these centers. See "Anti-Abortion Clinics Focus of Hearing in House Today," *New York Times*, December 17, 1986.

19. I draw this definition from ideas expressed in an article on new anthropological views of the family by Collier, Rosaldo, and Yanagisako:

> One of the central notions in the modern American construct of The Family is that of nurturance . . . a relationship that entails affection and love, that is based on cooperation as opposed to competition, that is enduring rather than temporary, that is noncontingent rather than contingent upon performance, and that is governed by feeling and morality instead of law and contract. . . . What gives shape to much of our conception of The Family is its symbolic opposition to . . . the market relations of capitalism. (1982: 34)

20. I take this phrase from the collection, *Hidden in the Household: Women's Domestic Labour under Capitalism*, ed. Bonnie Fox (Toronto, Ontario: The Women's Press, 1980).

Chapter 2. From the Physicians' Campaign to *Roe* v. *Wade*

1. The most comprehensive overview of the nineteenth-century abortion battles is James Mohr's *Abortion in America* (1978). In this chapter, I rely primarily on Mohr, as well as Luker (1984a), Petchesky (1984), and Tatalovich and Daynes (1981).

2. Luker points out that the *Roe* v. *Wade* decision's classification of abortion by trimesters resembles the "quickening" distinctions used in nineteenth-century common law. In a sense, then, the Supreme Court's 1973 ruling represents a modern revision of the legal understandings that were in place prior to the criminalization of abortion (1984a: 14).

3. James Mohr considers that the physicians succeeded in part because of their access to advances in science (Mohr 1978: 204). Others question whether such training actually resulted in greater survival rates for patients of regular physicians, at least until the 1880s when the antiabortion battle had virtually been won. Luker suggests, for example, that it was because physicians could *not* demonstrate greater healing ability that abortion was so critical for them as a social issue. She points out that physicians were conspicuously absent from other social reform issues of the

time such as temperance, abolition, women's rights, and social purity. None of these issues, Luker argues, would have given physicians the special status that abortion provided (1984a: 31).

4. Sources include works by Edwin M. Hale (1860; 1866), a leading spokesman for the field of homeopathy, which was in competition with the allopathic-style medicine practiced by the regular physicians. Until 1867, Hale was not intolerant of and, in fact, performed abortions. On the basis of his experience in the Chicago area, Hale concluded that approximately 20 percent of all pregnancies were aborted (Mohr 1978: 76–77). Antiabortion crusader Horatio M. Storer estimated on the basis of officially recorded figures that 25 percent of pregnancies resulted in abortion (1868) (Mohr 1978: 79). It should be noted that these figures generally combined spontaneous and induced abortions.

Other medical reports from cities, such as Boston, Philadelphia, and Amherst, as well as from rural areas in Iowa, Maine, Michigan, Illinois, Minnesota, and Wisconsin, gave similar figures, estimating that anywhere from one-fifth to one-third of all pregnancies were terminated (Mohr 1978: 79–82).

5. Given that many of the physicians who published in medical journals at the time were central in the antiabortion campaign, one might question the reliability of their accounts. However, as Mohr notes, the evidence is overwhelming and, in any case, no other data are available.

6. The physicians' stress on the decline in "native" birth rates presaged the "race suicide arguments" brought against white middle-class women who promoted fertility control through abstinence in the Voluntary Motherhood movement of the 1870s. Consider the following passage from J. J. Mulheron, "Foeticide," *Peninsular Journal of Medicine* 10 (September 1874): 390–91, cited in Mohr 1978: 167:

> The annual destruction of foetuses [had become so] truly appalling [that] the Puritanic blood of '76 will be but sparingly represented in the approaching centenary. [There was] more sense than nonsense in the remark of one of our humorists that it would be a paying investment to some showman to catch and preserve a pure American for fifty years hence, he would be a phenomenon. America is fast losing her national characteristics.

7. The fertility rate is the average number of children born to women between puberty and menopause. Nineteenth-century rates are based on the fertility of white women between the ages of fourteen and forty-five. There are no reliable data in the nineteenth century for black or other nonwhite populations.

8. While this coincided with the years of apparent increasing abortion practice, one cannot determine whether the fall was the result of abstinence, abortion, or contraception. Angus MacLaren argues that in the ini-

tial stages of increased contraception usage, there is a high rate of un-wanted conceptions, for which abortion provides a backup form of birth control (1978).

9. In fact, average household size was actually greater in urban and small-town settlements than in rural regions between 1850 and 1880 (Degler 1980: 182). Some attribute this finding to the delay of marriage as second and third generations engaged in agricultural production have less access to resources (Yasuba 1961; Forster and Tucker 1972). A 1976 study by Easterlin shows that not only is the formation of new farm households delayed; members of these households also stopped having children ear-lier, indicating the decline is also due to some intentional use of con-traception or abortion (1976: 600–12).

10. The demographic transition describes a gradual process associated with industrial development in which there is a shift first from high to low mortality rates, resulting in population expansion, followed by a similar decline in the birth rate, presumably through the introduction or in-creased use of new contraceptive techniques. There is a voluminous literature on the topic ranging across many fields and encompassing a number of critiques. Some scholars associate the demographic transition with the spread of urbanization, industrialization, the loss of arable land, and other extrinsic socioeconomic conditions. These explanations have been called into question in the last two decades. For a representative view of this critique within history, see Tilly (1978) and Himes (1970).

Critiques based on studies of preindustrial societies, both contempo-rary and historical, demonstrate that such groups possess(ed) and use(d) fertility control methods. These might include "unconscious methods" such as delayed marriage or prohibitions on sexual intercourse during lac-tation—methods that might not be intended to control conception but nonetheless have that effect—as well as more deliberate practices such as abstinence, coitus interruptus, or abortion (Polgar 1972).

11. Perhaps the simplest refutation of the technological innovation ar-gument is simply that from ancient times until the twentieth century, techniques of birth control essentially remained unchanged. For a sum-mation of the debate, see Etienne Van de Walle (1980).

Among those who regard human intentionality as a significant causal factor, there are a range of hypotheses. Two representative examples are provided by Wells (1975) and Ariés (1960). Both assume that the desire to control fertility is more or less a human universal. However, they argue that its practice became more prevalent and acceptable with the develop-ment of capitalism, and the increasing emphasis on rational control and calculation of not only production but human life in general—what some have called "a new fertility ethic." For a thorough discussion of these issues, see Petchesky (1984: 27–34).

12. From Elizabeth Cady Stanton, "Infanticide and Prostitution," *Revolution I* 5 (February 5, 1868): 65, and Matilda Gage in *Revolution I* 14 (April 9, 1869): 215–16, quoted in Mohr 1978: 111–12.

13. Despite systematic attempts on the part of the AMA to persuade clergy to support their campaign, most remained more or less uninvolved, apart from a few relatively powerless groups such as the Congregationalists and Old School Presbyterians. The Roman Catholic Church issued a pastoral and then a papal condemnation of abortion in 1869 (Mohr 1978: 182–96). However, at the time, with Catholics constituting less than 10 percent of the population and representing primarily working-class and immigrant populations, they had little influence. As Luker (1984a: 60) notes on this topic:

Nineteenth-century abortion laws were by no means passed in response to Catholic concerns. If anything, they were passed in response to feelings *against* Catholics, in particular, their high fertility rates.

She goes on to explain:

Although nineteenth-century anti-abortionists admired the unwillingness of a largely Catholic immigrant population to use abortion, it was feared that they would "possess New England," as Brevard Sinclair put it in 1892, because native-born Protestant women were using abortion so frequently (*Crowning Sin of the Age,* p. 17).

14. Anthony Comstock spearheaded a successful antiobscenity movement in the 1870s and was instrumental in getting Congress to pass an act for the Suppression of Trade in the Circulation of Obscene Literature and Articles of Immoral Use; it was signed into law by President Grant in 1873 (Pivar 1974: 78–130).

15. Kristin Luker cites the following abortion studies for the early twentieth century (1984a: 49). One of the first comprehensive statistical surveys, published in 1936, estimated, from a sample of 1,241 pregnancies, 1 abortion for every 3.28 births (Taussig 1936: 185). A Kinsey Institute study estimated that 90 percent of premarital conceptions and 20 to 25 percent of conceptions within marriage were terminated (Gebhard et al. 1958: 93–94, 55).

16. Luker quotes (1984a: 53) a telling passage from Dr. Frederick Taussig. Writing in the 1930s, he commented:

We are amazed at the frankness with which decent women discuss this matter among themselves or with their physician. Every physician will testify that it is without any feeling of guilt that most women speak of induced abortions in the consultation room. The most striking evidence of the attitude for the public is the fact that, even when positive evidence of guilt is brought in the trial of an abortionist, he is rarely punished by the jury before whom the case is tried. (1936: 49)

17. Abortion committees were to:

1) serve as deterrents to the indiscriminate use of therapeutic abortion;
2) act in the best interests of the patient;
3) be a medicolegal safeguard for the physician; and
4) serve as repositories for the accumulation of data concerning the utilization and outcome of cases submitted for the therapeutic interruption of pregnancy. (Russell 1964: 349–55)

18. Finkbine had read a report by Dr. Frances Kelsey of the FDA, who had refused to allow sales of the drug in the United States. In West Germany, four thousand to six thousand deformed infants had been born to mothers who had taken thalidomide. When taken early in pregnancy, the drug induced phocomelia, a malformation in which children usually had flaps instead of arms, shortened thigh bones, and twisted legs (Tatalovich and Daynes 1981: 44–45).

19. In a Gallup poll taken at the time, 52 percent said she was right, 32 percent said she was wrong, and 16 percent had no opinion (Matthews 1987).

20. Notable among these referral agencies were The Parent's Aid Society in New York (1965) formed by Bill Baird; the Association to Repeal Abortion Laws (1966) established by Pat Maginnis in California; and the Reverend Howard Moody's Clergy Consultation Service (1967) operating out of Judson Memorial Church in New York City (Hole and Levine 1971: 253).

21. The states that passed reform laws between 1967 and 1972 were Arkansas, California, Colorado, Delaware, Florida, Georgia, Kansas, Maryland, Mississippi, North Carolina, New Mexico, Oregon, South Carolina, and Virginia. Alaska, Hawaii, and New York repealed their laws in 1970 (Tatalovich and Daynes 1981: 24).

22. Nearly one hundred national organizations endorsed abortion repeal or reform prior to 1973, from the Moravian Church to the American Jewish Committee to the Sierra Club. For a nearly complete list of these groups see table 2.2 in Tatalovich and Daynes (1981: 66–67).

23. One radical feminist described her sense of the division at the time:

"Reform" and "repeal" are actually fundamentally incompatible ideas. . . . Proposals for "reform" are based on the notion that abortions must be regulated, meted out to deserving women under an elaborate set of rules designed to provide a "safeguard against abuse." . . . "Repeal" is based on the quaint idea of *justice:* that abortion is a woman's right and that no one can veto her decision and compel her to bear a child against her will. (Cisler 1970: 283)

24. For overviews of feminist organizing on abortion prior to 1973, see Hole and Levine (1971: 299–301); Petchesky (1984: 125–32); and Luker (1984a: 95–125).

25. The Association to Repeal Abortion Laws founded in July 1966 by medical technologist Pat Maginnis was the first total repeal organization,

maintaining that abortion is the only surgical procedure considered to be a criminal offense. ARAL's political activities included civil disobedience through direct action, referral services, and classes in self-abortion, as well as more conventional forms of political actions such as lobbying (Hole and Levine 1971: 295–96).

26. This is clear, for example in the following statement by one of NARAL's founders.

If we could make a national association and succeed in overthrowing the tyranny of abortion laws, it could offer a vision of action and accomplishment at the most fundamental democratic level. It seemed to me the country needed this desperately: that if the present social order, or any order was to survive, the individual had to prove to himself once again that a revolution was still possible. The whole abortion movement was, in effect, an act of faith. (Lader 1973: 88)

27. For a summary of these battles, see Tatalovich and Daynes (1981: 70–74). For more complete accounts, see Fujita and Wagner (1973); Guttmacher (1973); Lader (1973); Nathanson (1979); and Steinhoff and Diamond (1977).

28. The *Roe* v. *Wade* case involved a challenge to an 1854 Texas law that barred abortion except when the woman's life was in danger. *Doe* v. *Bolton* challenged a Georgia reform statute that allowed abortions to be performed, with the approval of a hospital committee, to save the mother's life, or in cases of rape or fetal abnormality.

The court ruled that a state could not intervene in the abortion decision between a woman and her physician in the first three months of pregnancy. During the second trimester when (according to medical practice in 1973) abortion is possibly hazardous, the decision is still essentially between a woman and her physician. However, the state's interest in the health of the mother permits regulations to protect maternal health—for example, by permitting regulations that require abortions from the fourth month on be performed in hospitals. When the fetus is potentially viable, during the third trimester, the state may prohibit abortion except when it is necessary to preserve the life of the mother.

These rulings were based on the doctrine of "the right to privacy," a broad interpretation of the 14th Amendment's protection of personal liberty: that the state shall not deprive any person of life, liberty, or due process of law. It was *not* based on the position argued by attorneys Sarah Weddington and Margie Pitts that women have an unconditional right to abortion. Regarding the fetus, the Court ruled that the unborn are not recognized in the law as persons in the whole sense. See U.S. Supreme Court, *Roe* v. *Wade*, 410 U.S. 113 (1973), and *Doe* v. *Bolton*, 410 U.S. 179 (1973).

29. "The [*Roe* v. *Wade*] decision vindicated the right of the physician

to administer medical treatment, according to his professional judgment, up to the points where important state interests provide compelling justifications for intervention [maternal health and the viability of the fetus]. *Up to these points, the abortion decision in all its aspects is inherently, and primarily, a medical decision, and basic responsibility for it must rest with the physician"* (*Roe* v. *Wade,* 410 U.S. 113 [1973]: 166) (emphasis added).

In the companion *Doe* v. *Bolton* decision, the Court ruled that abortions did not require the approval of hospital abortion committees. Although this had the effect of increasing women's access to abortion, it was intended to support the physician's right to make and carry out medical judgments (*Doe* v. *Bolton,* 410 U.S. 179 [1973]: 189).

Chapter 3. The Rise of the Right-to-Life Movement

1. For a useful summary of these developments, see Petchesky (1984: 252–54); and Paige (1983: chaps. 3 and 4).

2. The amendment strategy has had two foci. One, introduced at almost every Congressional session by Senator Jesse Helms, would add to the Constitution that life begins at conception. It became known as either the Helms or the human life amendment (HLA). The other strategy, sponsored by Senator Orrin Hatch, is to return the abortion legislation to the states; it is commonly referred to as the Hatch or states' rights amendment.

The HLA has been favored by "purists" because it represents the key philosophical base in the right-to-life position. However, because it poses a direct challenge to a decision of the Supreme Court, it is considered difficult to pass and is not favored as a strategy by much of the movement. The Hatch amendment is endorsed by the more moderate right-to-life forces, including most of the Catholic pro-life leadership. It is considered more likely to pass because it constitutes less direct a threat to the judiciary. It also has the support of those who object to the expanding "judiciary activism" of the Supreme Court.

In any case, passing a Constitutional amendment is extremely difficult. It must receive the backing of a two-thirds majority in the House and the Senate, and then be ratified by three-fourths of the states. Even when it is clear that the required votes are not there, right-to-life groups have pushed these proposals through Congress and state legislatures to obtain a public record on where representatives stand on the issue. These voting records played a significant role in the mobilization of abortion activists to defeat or elect particular candidates on this "single issue." For a detailed account of the growing role of abortion activists in elections, see Paige (1983: chap. 8).

3. In addition to efforts to ban the procedure, the bills and ordinances raised questions regarding requirements for:

—parental or spousal consent;

—hospitalization for second- and third-trimester abortions;

—disposal of fetal remains;

—informing a woman of the "human-like" characteristics of the fetus;

—a twenty-four-hour waiting period between the scheduling and carrying out of an abortion;

—municipal zoning and regulation of abortion clinics;

—the presence of a second physician for late abortions when the fetus could be viable.

4. In July 1976, the Court ruled, in *Planned Parenthood of Central Missouri* v. *Danforth*, that it was unconstitutional for a husband or for parents to have veto power in a contested abortion. In 1979, in *Belotti* v. *Baird*, the Court ruled that states could require parental notification in the case of an abortion for a minor, provided that alternative means of obtaining consent were available—that is, the approval of a judge if just cause were shown as to why parents should not be informed. At least twenty-three states have created laws requiring parental consent or notification for minors seeking abortions.

Regarding the last issue, in December 1987, the Supreme Court, with only eight justices sitting pending the approval of Justice Powell's replacement, deadlocked on an Illinois case requiring parental notification. The effect of the tie is to postpone a definitive ruling until some future case.

5. The Hyde amendment, named for its sponsor Henry Hyde of Illinois, is attached to annual appropriations for the Department of Health and Human Services (DHHS). Currently, only the District of Columbia and fourteen states provide Medicaid funding for abortions. As of 1987, the states are Alaska, California, Connecticut, Hawaii, Maryland, Massachusetts, Michigan, New Jersey, New York, North Carolina, Oregon, Vermont, Washington, and West Virginia.

6. When the Hyde amendment first passed in 1976, it was immediately challenged by Planned Parenthood and ruled unconstitutional by Judge John Dooling of the Brooklyn Federal District Court. This decision was overruled in 1977, when the Supreme Court ruled, in *Maher* v. *Roe*, that states are not obligated to pay for nontherapeutic abortions, thus allowing the enactment of the Hyde amendment. In 1980, in *Harris* v. *McRae*, the

court again upheld the constitutionality of withholding federal funds for abortion.

Most analysts see *Harris* v. *McRae* as inconsistent with *Roe* v. *Wade*. Petchesky, for example, notes that "it attacks the idea that women's right to abortion is so fundamental that *no* woman would be denied it . . . and that decent health care is a basic human need. It is impossible to reconcile the position the court took in 1980 with its opinion in 1973" (1984: 299).

Radical feminist lawyer Catharine MacKinnon argues that the Hyde amendment and the attendant Supreme Court rulings are consistent with *Roe* v. *Wade* in that the "privacy doctrine" assumes the liberal view that "private life" is a realm of autonomous, freely contracting individuals, rather than a realm of pervasive inequality that requires public remedy (1983).

7. Abortion funds have been cut off for government employees, Peace Corps volunteers, members of the military and their dependents, and working women dependent on employment-related pregnancy disability benefits.

On September 1, 1987, DHHS, under orders from the Reagan administration, proposed new Title X regulations that would have reversed seventeen years of U.S. legislation and practice by denying federal funding to any organization that presents abortion as an option. In the past, Title X programs served primarily low-income women and children. These changes would have undercut support for those groups most in need. The proposal was suspended in March 1988 (see chapter 1, n. 16). Also see "Compromise Clears the Way for Reagan Abortion Curbs," *New York Times,* December 17, 1987.

8. In her recent book *Women of the New Right,* Rebecca Klatch writes:

No consensus exists on the exact boundaries of the New Right. Generally, when people use the term "New Right" they refer to a network of people that came into prominence in the mid-1970s, including conservative politicians such as Jesse Helms, Orrin Hatch, and Jack Kemp, conservative think-tanks such as the Heritage Foundation, general-purpose organizations such as the Conservative Caucus, the National Conservative Political Action Committee, and the Committee for the Survival of a Free Congress, as well as the religious sector, including prime-time preachers, the Moral Majority, and groups working against such issues as abortion, gay rights, and pornography. (1987: 13)

For further discussion of the origins of the term "New Right," see Klatch (1987: 218, n. 18).

9. There was little pretense as to the goals behind the New Right's "pro-family" agenda. As New Right political strategist Paul Weyrich commented in a special report on his movement in a 1979 issue of *Conservative Digest,* "The New Right is looking for issues that fit the bill . . . gun

control, abortion, taxes and crime. Yes, they're emotional issues but they're better than talking about capital formation."

10. This may be an oversimplification of the New Right as well, or at least not a reflection of current trends. At the end of 1987, the Free Congress Research and Education Foundation, a group closely aligned with the New Right, published a 146-page document called "Cultural Conservatism: Toward a New National Agenda" that reflects some convergences between right and left. At a press conference announcing the report, Free Congress president Paul Weyrich commented:

> Conservatives make a mistake in identifying with a politics that says it really doesn't matter what happens to the community as long as those who can survive get theirs.

Defining themselves as cultural conservatives, the report distinguishes that position from free-market conservatives.

> In their view, if the free economy leaves some people destitute—so be it. The cultural conservative view is different. We accept the obligation to the less fortunate that welfare represents. (E. J. Dionne, Jr. "A Conservative Call for Compassion," *New York Times*, November 30, 1987)

For further discussion of these issues, also see chapter 1, n. 8.

11. Nonetheless, in the popular media, the antiabortion movement was increasingly associated with both the religious right and the New Right, which, judging by the responses, was making the moderate right-to-life leadership uneasy. The NRLC made a point of publicizing the liberal and democratic races that they supported that were anathema to the conservative program (Paige 1983: 223). The liberal evangelical Christian magazine *Sojourners* warned against an alliance between the antiabortion movement and the right-wing (Wallis 1980). The U.S. Conference of Catholic Bishops, by clearly linking its "human life" position to support of a nuclear freeze and increases in social welfare, has further distanced a large part of the pro-life movement from other conservative interests.

12. According to journalist Connie Paige, in 1979 NRLC staff person Judie Brown left that organization and began working with New Right leader Paul Weyrich to set up the American Life Lobby (ALL), while her husband Paul set up the Life Amendment Political Action Committee (LAPAC). With aid from New Right fund-raiser and strategist Richard Viguerie, and with a mandate to organize fundamentalist Christians, ALL claimed sixty-eight thousand names on its mailing lists by 1981. According to Paige, these New Right right-to-life groups have been in competition with NRLC since their inception. Fights over membership, political strategy, and ideology are frequent, as is oblique slander between the leaders of each group (Paige 1983: 148–50, 169).

Although they never formally joined the New Right's "winning coalition," the NRLC was, nonetheless, among the principal beneficiaries of the 1980 conservative political victories. These campaigns yielded ten new "pro-life" seats in the Senate and twenty-five in the House (*National Right to Life News,* November 10, 1980).

13. By the mid-term elections in 1982, it was not only the popular press that saw the right-to-life movement as losing its political effectiveness. New Right leader Terry Dolan, while predicting exponential growth for his own movement, declared that the right-to-life advocates had made clear to Congress that they were a "paper tiger" (quoted in Paige 1983: 239).

14. The cases ruled on were City Council ordinances that created extensive local restrictions on abortion, passed and challenged in Ohio (*City of Akron* v. *Akron Center for Reproductive Health Inc.*), Missouri (*Planned Parenthood, Kansas City, Mo.* v. *Ashcroft*), and Virginia (*Simopoulos* v. *Virginia*). The vote was six to three. The dissenters were Associate Justices O'Connor, Rehnquist, and White. In brief, the court struck down as unconstitutional the following restrictions:

—abortions after twelve weeks of pregnancy must be done in hospitals only;

—physicians must inform patients of dangers of and alternatives to abortion;

—physicians must enforce a twenty-four-hour waiting period on patients;

—physicians must dispose of fetal remains in a "humane and sanitary" manner.

The following were declared constitutional by votes of five to four:

—abortions after twelve weeks of pregnancy must be done in hospitals or clinics;

—a second physician must be present during abortions that occur when the fetus might be able to live outside the womb (currently at about twenty-four-weeks' gestation);

—minors seeking abortions must obtain consent from a parent or a judge.

The most substantial dissent to the rulings came from Justice Sandra Day O'Connor, who was concerned with problems raised by fetal viability.

15. Unless the American public suddenly switches its decade of steady support for legal abortion, right-to-life forces are unlikely to reverse these defeats through national antiabortion legislation. On the basis of analyses by the National Opinion Research Center and Gallup polls between 1973

and 1985, it appears that the level of approval for legalized abortion has remained stable since 1973. Approximately 23 percent believe that abortion should be legal in all cases, while 19 to 22 percent believe it should be illegal. The remainder believe it should be legal for some cases such as rape, incest, or endangerment to the woman's life. For further analyses of these data, see Granberg (1987).

16. According to the National Abortion Federation, "acts of violence" include invasions, vandalism, death threats, bomb threats, assaults, burglaries, kidnapping, arson and arson attempts, and bombings. The figures cited are from National Abortion Federation (1985).

17. For example, in August 1983, Scheidler led a demonstration in front of a Catholic hospital to protest the appointment of Dr. Hector Zevallos, the abortion clinic owner who had been kidnapped and held at gunpoint for a week in 1982 by two pro-lifers who called themselves "The Army of God." Scheidler told the media that en route to the protest he stopped to visit the wife of the man convicted of that kidnapping and of bombing two clinics (Roeser 1983).

18. The bases of their disagreements were made clear in a 1985 review of Scheidler's book in the NRLC's newsletter. James Bopp, Jr., NRLC's general counsel, wrote:

[Scheidler's] alternate strategy represents a radical departure from the focus of traditional right-to-life activity in two important ways. First, right-to-life educational activities have primarily focused on informing and motivating the great number of uncommitted persons to a pro-life philosophy and action. By contrast, Mr. Scheidler's focus is on battling those most committed to the pro-abortion philosophy.

Secondly, the right-to-life movement has focused on increasing the respect for all human life in society and restoring the protection of human life through our laws . . . with the law changed, the power of the state turns against the abortionist. . . . Only in America, pro-life in its heart and mind, will babies ultimately be safe. (1905: 6)

19. In 1986, the Supreme Court ruled on two cases that more or less paralleled the 1983 cases (see n. 11)—requiring "informed consent" and the use of certain abortion techniques to maximize chances of fetal survival, even if maternal health were endangered—that the Court had declared unconstitutional. For that reason, it was and remains unclear why the Court chose to accept these cases, other than "as vehicles for firming up the law, for clarifying the 'bright line' between permissible and impermissible statutes" (Rubin 1987: 146).

On April 30, 1986, the Supreme Court dismissed *Diamond* v. *Charles*, an appeal by an antiabortion group, Americans United for Life, for a pro-life pediatrician, on the grounds that the appellant had no standing to defend the law in court. Six weeks later, the court ruled on Pennsylvania's

Abortion Control Act of 1982 in the case of *Thornburgh* v. *American College of Obstetricians and Gynecologists;* they overturned, by a five to four vote, six sections of the act as endangering the woman's health and safety and invasive of physician-patient confidentiality (Rubin 1987: 145–49). Despite an *amicus curiae* brief filed by the Justice Department urging the overruling of *Roe* v. *Wade,* the Court essentially confirmed its prior decisions, although the close vote indicated some differences regarding the permissible limits of state regulation of abortion, and what abortion procedures can be used in late pregnancies.

By 1986, it was clear that one of the few paths left for undermining the *Roe* v. *Wade* decision was to alter the composition of the court (see chapter 1, n. 17).

20. Various legal tactics have been used to stop clinic harassment, from criminal complaints to the use of statutes against racketeering. In June 1986, NOW filed a civil suit at the Federal District Court in Wilmington, Delaware, through the Southern Poverty Law Center against Joseph Scheidler and his Pro-Life Action League, and John Ryan's related group, the Pro-Life Direct Action League. The suit, based on a successful 1982 court action against the Ku Klux Klan, asked for a nationwide injunction against disruptive activities by antiabortion leaders on the grounds that their actions are a restraint of trade, intended to drive away business (Herbers 1986).

21. While the adoption of new services by hospitals generally spreads in a wave from large teaching hospitals to smaller institutions (Moch and Morse 1977), the case of abortion is apparently atypical. According to at least one study, the range in hospital policies is accounted for primarily by the personal attitudes of medical personnel, hospital officials, or the governing body (Nathanson and Becker 1980: 126).

The lack of hospital response to community needs for abortion is consistent with the actions of hospital committees between 1945 and 1973. This transfer of authority for abortion decisions from doctors to senior medical staff had the opposite effect of the stated intent, to make abortions more equitably available, because committees made arbitrary decisions based on personal views (Sarvis and Rodman 1974: 36–45). In addition, hospital administrators and boards, concerned more with the hospital's image than women's health care needs, feared that too high an abortion rate would brand them as a "mill." The effect of these policies was that between 1945 and the mid 1960s, reported hospital abortions dropped from thirty thousand to eight thousand annually (Lader 1966: 24).

22. I have combined the authors' figures for freestanding clinics and physicians' offices in which 50 percent or more of the visits were for abortions, and for clinics that offer abortions as one of a range of services.

In addition, the authors cite 714 medical offices where abortions are performed but are less than 50 percent of the caseload. Together, these nonhospital services account for 82 percent of abortions (Henshaw, Forrest, and Blaine 1984: table 6).

23. Abortion clinics are distinguished from hospitals in other ways as well. For example, 86 percent are open on Saturdays or have late hours to accommodate patients' schedules. Unlike hospitals, almost all clinics have specially trained abortion counselors. Such counseling, often available for "significant others" as well as patients, generally includes a review of the medical risks, a description of the procedure, birth control information, and often a discussion of possible alternatives to abortion. Eighty percent of clinics encourage parental involvement in the decision. Most require in-house pregnancy tests, perform the abortion within a week of that test, and provide optional postabortion checkups (Henshaw 1982; Landy and Lewit 1982).

For an ethnographic account and analysis of the operation of a family planning and abortion clinic that stresses the complex role counselors play in these settings, see Joffe (1987).

24. Henshaw, Forrest, and Blaine, in their 1984 overview of abortion in the United States, note the following obstacles imposed by the need to travel to obtain an abortion: increased expenses due to transportation and lodging costs, loss of work time, and the possibility—due to increased delay—of aborting at a later stage of pregnancy when abortion is not only more expensive but more dangerous to the woman's health.

These problems are particular burdens for poor and teenage women who are often those in greatest need and with the least resources. For example, a study for the Centers for Disease Control based on 1974 data from Georgia showed that for every ten miles that a woman lived outside of Atlanta, where abortion services are located, abortion rates for teens dropped by eleven per one thousand live births (Shelton et al. 1976).

25. In an analysis of abortion services in the United States, authors Henshaw, Forrest, and Van Vort write:

> States with relatively high average costs (over $240) [for abortions] are Idaho, Iowa, North Dakota, Oklahoma, Utah, and Wyoming. Most of these are less-urbanized states, where community pressures may make it difficult for facilities to offer abortion services and where there are few providers to stimulate competition. (1987: 69)

Chapter 4. The First Phase of Conflict

1. The National Women's Health Organization (NWHO) is an independent business. Its owner, Sharon, established NWHO in 1976 after having worked in abortion clinics that she felt did not respond to the needs of

female patients, either in their location or services. Her commitment, as she expresses it, is "to meet health needs of women outside of large metropolitan areas by setting up clinics in underserved regions and working with them to be sure they are integrated into the community." The Fargo clinic, established in 1981, is the tenth. The others are located in Jacksonville, Florida; Fort Wayne, Indiana; Fairfield, New Jersey; Raleigh, North Carolina; Orlando, Florida; Columbus, Ohio; Wilmington, Delaware; White Plains, New York; and Milwaukee, Wisconsin.

The national office pinpoints areas of the country that are underserved, looks for local people interested in working with it, and provides capital and medical and legal expertise for starting the new clinic. Once established, they provide day-to-day management, staying in close touch with staff, all of whom are NWHO employees, although the clinic administrator takes charge of those working in her clinic. Accounting and overall administration are centralized in the main office. Otherwise, the daily running of the clinic is left to local administrators and staff, most of whom are trained health care workers or abortion rights activists. Clinics are under pressure to be cost-effective. Should protests create a need for lawsuits or extra security help (as occurred in Fargo), those costs are underwritten by NWHO. Sharon makes regular visits to each of the clinics and takes a strong personal and professional interest in seeing that they are well run and that medical staff are performing well, and in establishing good relations with community leaders in the area.

According to Sharon, she chose to make NWHO a for-profit organization so that it would not be dependent on a board or funding from government or local sources; these factors, she feels, explain why nonprofit clinics have a hard time surviving far from major urban areas. Fargo is a good example of her claim. It is doubtful that without resources from the outside the clinic would have been established. A nonprofit facility, subject to local support, would have had difficulty raising the capital needed and been much more vulnerable to right-to-life pressure tactics. In addition, the clinic has access to medical and legal expertise that it might not have had at its disposal if it were dependent on local resources. In this sense, the clinic represents outside forces, and this is cause for some criticism from both LIFE and CRC activists. Having made that clear, however, it seems to me that in its daily operations and in the activism that has emerged around it, the clinic operates as a local institution, and much of that has to do with Kay's strong presence as a Fargo activist.

2. When first developed, this model reconceptualized conflict as indicative of rather than a deviant form of social structure, and helped encompass a temporal dimension in social analysis. In Turner's view, the social drama is of particular interest because "disturbances of the normal

and regular often give us greater insight into the normal than does direct study" (1974: 34).

3. Turner describes these phases as:

1. *breach* . . . a symbolic trigger of confrontation or encounter (1974: 38);

2. *crisis* . . . a tendency for the breach to widen and extend until it becomes coextensive with some dominant cleavage in the widest set of relevant social relations to which the conflicting or antagonistic parties belong . . . a threshold between more or less stable phases of the social process (1974: 38–39);

3. *redressive action.* In order to limit the spread of crisis, certain adjustive and redressive "mechanisms," . . . informal or formal, institutional or ad hoc, are swiftly brought into operation by leading or structurally representative members of the disturbed social system (1974: 39);

4. *reintegration* of the disturbed social group or of the social recognition and legitimization of irreparable schism between the contesting parties (1974: 41).

4. For example, the *Reader's Guide to Periodical Literature* lists only a single article on abortion before 1930. In the next decade, there were twenty-five and in the 1940s, twenty-six (Plant 1971, cited in Sarvis and Rodman 1974: 7).

5. In an informal study conducted by students at the University of North Dakota at Grand Forks, women born at the turn of the century reported that they used few methods of birth control, but had a range of "home remedies" (i.e., abortion methods) for terminating unwanted pregnancies (Sherry O'Donnell, personal communication).

6. D. and C. refers to dilation and curettage, the most popular abortion technique in the United States until recent years, and still the most widely used procedure for early termination of pregnancy. The cervix is dilated to allow the insertion of a curette, a scraping instrument, into the uterus, in order to scrape the pregnancy from the uterine wall (Sarvis and Rodman 1974: 89).

7. According to Luker's account, the experiences of assemblymen John Knox and Anthony Beilenson in California, who introduced the first abortion reform measures into that state's legislature in 1961 and 1963 respectively, were almost identical to those of their counterpart in North Dakota. They had no prior experience on the issue, and were moved by their initial exposure to the sufferings caused by illegal abortions. As young

politicians, they wanted to "make a name for themselves by supporting causes that were new but not dangerously controversial," indicating how differently abortion was perceived as a political issue at that time. For more detail and interviews with Knox and Beilenson, see Luker (1984a: 66–72).

8. According to participants at the 1971 hearings, the bill was done in by testimony from the Mecklenbergs, who were among the earliest prominent leaders of the Right-to-Life movement. Founders of the well-respected, moderate Minnesota Citizens Concerned for Life (MCCL), they were also instrumental in the break of the NRLC from the Catholic Church (they are Methodists). Fred Mecklenberg is a physician specializing in obstetrics and gynecology. Marjorie Mecklenberg is a former home economics teacher, mother of four, a key figure in setting up support services for pregnant teens in Minnesota, and later for the Reagan administration.

9. In Fargo, as in most parts of the country, the League of Women Voters is identified as a liberal, upper-middle-class organization devoted to increasing public awareness on civil matters.

10. In Luker's view, because of their professional identities, early abortion activists

faced a number of pressures not to appear "fanatic" on the pro-life issue but to be "dignified" or "professional" in pursuit of pro-life goals. For example, virtually all of the early pro-life activists had some friends who disagreed with them on abortion. (1984a: 146)

11. Birthright, established in 1968 in Canada by Louise Summerhill, now has about 510 centers in the United States and 85 in Canada. They are nondenominational, nonprofit, local operations run by volunteers, with small annual budgets from local donations. The national office provides each chapter with a small portion of its $80,000 per year income to establish a telephone "hotline." By the national organization's own estimates, they see about half a million women a year (Summerhill 1968; Ridgeway 1985: 29).

In Fargo, until recently, the group operated out of volunteers' homes, on an annual budget of $2,000 to $3,000. It offered pregnancy tests, medical help from sympathetic professionals, and "shelter homes" to approximately five to seven pregnant teens per year. In 1982, under pressure from LIFE Coalition to be more active, the group became more professional. They opened an office, hired a director, began to advertise and aimed for a budget of $20,000 per year. They receive about sixty phone calls and provide about fifteen pregnancy tests a month, and place about seven unwed mothers in homes in a year. Recently they have started a "Parent's Support Network" for the families of pregnant teens. Although the group is officially nondenominational, most of its board, volunteers, and support come from Catholic clergy and laity.

Chapter 5. The Clinic Conflict

1. For an articulation of some of the arguments made by feminists who are pro-life, see Callahan et al. (1986) and McDonnell (1984).

2. Women Aglow is an international, interdenominational charismatic Christian organization. (The male counterpart to Aglow is the Full Gospel Businessmen's Fellowship.) Founded in Seattle in 1967, the group's headquarters are now in Edmonds, Washington. There are now 1,300 chapters worldwide. Each chapter is run by a board, and has four advisors, usually men. North Dakota has chapters in practically every town and city, and two area boards to oversee them. Members pay ten dollars to join; these funds go to serve the 122 chapters outside the United States. The group emphasizes the two central "gifts of the spirit" that are central to the Pentecostal Christian experience of speaking in tongues: one is receiving and speaking a "prayer language"; the second is the gift of speaking prophecy in public—that is, interpreting the content of charismatic speech. This behavior, as well as singing and "joyous prayer," indicates being "alive to God and aglow in the spirit."

Aglow meetings are held once a month and are not a substitute for church. Members are expected to be active in their own denominations. Meetings begin with "praise and worship," which includes time for "prophesying" when people interpret the meaning of people's testimony while speaking in tongues. There is usually a scheduled speaker, during which interruptions are not allowed. At the end of a meeting, anyone is allowed to talk privately with Aglow board members, counselors, and advisors.

3. In this way they have an ironic resemblance to the secular "human potential," movement, although there is undoubtedly a greater stress on keeping family units intact in the Christian groups. A similar paradox is the way their concerns also mirror, in many ways, those of feminist groups. Both stress consensus in their meetings; the substance of much discussion is concerned with reducing violence and competition in the culture. Each group encourages women to turn to other women for pleasure, inspiration, and help with personal troubles through the strength and companionship of "sisters." When I noted this resemblance to a pro-life woman active in such groups, she nodded her head and said, "Oh yes, people don't understand the church has an underground women's movement."

4. During the time I was in Fargo, the First Assemblies of God church regularly drew several hundred people for their three weekly worship

services, many of them "visitors" from other churches. The church had also started a campaign of sending out buses to poor neighborhoods to bring children and adolescents to the services. Their "music ministry," led by a handsome young pastor who had been a rock-and-roll musician before he received Jesus, was particularly successful in reaching teenagers. The church's ability to engage this age group was cited by a number of recent adult converts as one of the important reasons they had joined the church. They wanted to counteract the "drugs, sex, and rock-and-roll" subculture at the high schools; the mainline congregations they had formerly belonged to seemed to hold very little appeal for teens. At the end of 1983, First Assemblies was building a new complex on the outskirts of Fargo that reportedly could hold over two thousand people for a single worship service. The funds for the building project were raised entirely from congregation membership.

5. Through the late 1970s and early 1980s, *Assignment: Life* was one of the main films used by the pro-life movement to recruit new members. It is advertised in *The National Right to Life News* by its distributor, American Portrait Films, as an "uncompromising 52-minute documentary on abortion in which journalist Ann Summers makes a personal odyssey into life and death. Shows actual abortions and a live birth."

Chapter 6. Interpretive Battleground

1. Since 1983, such centers have grown from a handful to as many as 2,000 to 3,000. The Christian Action Council, for example, had 11 "crisis pregnancy centers" in 1981 and reported over 240 in 1986. A pro-life group, Intercessors for America, estimated 2,100 such centers were in existence by the end of 1984 (cited in Bolotin 1986: 482, 541).

2. In addition to the focus on problem pregnancies after they have occurred, there is also a growing concern with providing better and earlier sex education for young people. For example, I regularly attended a series of Junior League meetings being run by a high school home economics teacher that brought almost all the social service counselors in the area together to discuss what would be the most effective way to deal with teenage sexuality on three fronts:

—helping teen mothers raising children on their own through education (a special program to help them finish high school) and assistance (support groups and "parenting" classes);

—reaching pregnant teens and assisting them regardless of their decision;

—developing a "preventative sexuality program" in order to diminish what was seen as a local epidemic in teen pregnancy.

Regardless of one's position on abortion or politics, almost all adults who spoke on this topic felt that teenage girls were under enormous pressure to have sex, and that they needed to be told that "It's OK to say 'no.'"

Contrary to popular stereotype, many pro-life women and men I spoke with were very committed to bringing responsible sex education into both their homes and schools. (See the life stories for Karen and Peggy in chapter 10.) Predictably, those most interested in pursuing this angle were parents of adolescents. Although they were not in favor of premarital intercourse, especially for teenagers, they recognized it as "a fact of life" and hoped to be able to communicate with young people realistically and effectively. Their worries seemed to be very similar in substance to those of most pro-choice activists of the same age. Although I did not inquire systematically into this issue, it is my impression that pro-life and pro-choice women are similar in their willingness to discuss sex with their children, although pro-life activists are unlikely to suggest or help an adolescent obtain access to birth control.

3. As the political scientist Rosalind Petchesky points out:

These facts create a reality that helps to construct the social meanings of sexuality in contemporary American culture and politics. Abortion—organized legal abortion—is associated with sex because it is seen to reveal sex; it is a signifier that helps make sex *visible* and therefore subject to scrutiny and an inevitable defining of limits between the licit and the illicit. Above all, it helps identify and categorize a new sexual subject: the "promiscuous" white teenage girl. (1984: 209)

4. Giddens developed this term as part of an effort to create language in social theory that comprehends the various modes through which social actors use knowledge about the society of which they are members to enter into practical social conduct. He distinguishes between

practical consciousness, as tacit stocks of knowledge which actors draw upon in the constitution of social activity, and . . . 'discursive consciousness,' involving knowledge which actors are able to express on the level of discourse. (1979: 5)

5. According to the Problem Pregnancy Center's Report in its February 1987 Newsletter, in 1986 an average of 15 clients per month came into the office and "1,200 contacts were made by phone." The center's report in the December 1986 Newsletter is instructive as to how to understand these figures.

Each girl who comes into the Center . . . views our educational presentation and receives individual counseling. Six of the fifteen girls had positive tests. Four girls decided to carry their babies; one girl, though still not certain, is leaning toward carrying her baby; and one was lost to abortion. . . . Five of the six girls came into the Center considering abortion, and changed their minds.

The center advertises in the newspaper and Yellow Pages under "Pregnancy Counseling," and through public service announcements on local television and radio, posters at area colleges, and an installation of a large street sign outside the center bearing its name.

6. For further analysis of recent developments in right-to-life visual imagery using techniques from new reproductive technology, see Petchesky (1987).

7. The saline injection or "salting out" method is rare, generally used for late abortions (i.e., after the fourth month). A hypodermic needle is inserted through the abdomen and uterine wall into the amniotic sac containing the fetus. Two hundred milliliters of amniotic fluid are removed and replaced by the same amount of a 20 percent saline solution, which kills the fetus and induces labor anywhere from twelve to thirty-six hours later (Sarvis and Rodman 1974: 90).

Right-to-life proponents find this method particularly objectionable because it is assumed to "burn the skin" of the fetus and therefore cause great pain. Also, since it is used for late abortions when the fetus might be viable (i.e., capable of surviving outside of the womb), it is condemned because it directly kills the fetus, thus excluding the possibility that it could be saved. Hysterotomies, for example, which can also be used at this stage, are more dangerous for the mother but increase the likelihood that the fetus will survive.

Chapter 7. Angles of Incidence, Angles of Reflection

1. The developments analyzed in this section began to take place in July 1983 and peaked over the following year. Since I left the field in September 1983 (except for a brief visit in the summer of 1986), I have relied heavily on written and telephone communication with Fargo activists for much of the information described here.

2. For background on Partners in Vision, see chapter 5.

3. Jerry Falwell's Save-A-Baby program, introduced in 1984, is working to establish one thousand centers, with a goal of setting up ten thousand across the country. It operates a twenty-four-hour-a-day hotline and claims to have counseled eighteen thousand women.

In 1986, the leaders of the Fargo group who originally went by the Save-A-Baby name received the Good Citizenship Award of the *Liberty Report*, the publication of The Liberty Federation, a semiautonomous arm of the Moral Majority.

4. In June 1986, NOW filed charges against Scheidler and his colleague Joseph Ryan under antitrust laws. The case, prepared by the Southern Poverty Law Center, asks for a nationwide injunction against these antiabortion leaders, contending that they have been traveling

throughout the country organizing efforts to harass and intimidate people who run and use abortion clinics. Speaking at a press conference, Eleanor Smeal (NOW's president at the time) said,

This is clearly a nationwide criminal conspiracy, which the Federal Government has refused to treat as such.

Mr. Scheidler was quoted in the press as agreeing that his aim is to close clinics, but claimed that he operated within the law, creating through demonstrations and other actions a community climate that made it difficult for the clinics to operate (Herbers 1986).

5. A recent study (Forrest and Henshaw 1987) documents the steady increase in this kind of activity across the country. According to their analysis, 88 percent of 501 nonhospital facilities reported antiabortion harassment in 1985. There were significant increases between 1984 and 1985 in more violent activities such as vandalism (53 percent increase); invasions of facility (60 percent increase); death threats (63 percent increase), and bomb threats (58 percent increase).

Characteristics significantly associated with harassment were type of facility (freestanding clinic), region of the country (Midwest and South), and those whose caseload primarily involved abortion patients.

6. This is consistent with findings across the country. While harassment might make abortions more difficult or costly due to increased security, legal and insurance expenses, and problems with staff, it seems not to have affected the number of abortions performed (Forrest and Henshaw 1987: 9).

7. Given these effects, one might ask what the goals of the producers were. My impression from speaking to the researchers on the show is that they were convinced that the right-to-life movement was largely made up of radical fringe types. Thus, there may have been some motivation to show images that conformed to that idea. From the point of view of these particular activists, publicity of any sort was desirable; they cultivate an image of being zealots and therefore are not concerned, as the more moderate activists are, if they are seen as extremists. The final show was not obviously biased to the average viewer; it attempted to present a "balanced point of view," showing both the extreme right-to-life protesters on the one hand, and confronting the pro-choice mayor with a fetus in a bottle on the other.

From my own experience in a commercial television documentary unit, producers are under pressure to get the most dramatic footage possible without overtly manipulating a situation. In my analysis of this particular show, I am not arguing that they set out to create certain effects as a result of systematic misrepresentation in their show. Rather, I use this case to illustrate how the intervention of outside media, operating under certain pressures, creates distortions in its portrayal of the local scene that increase a sense of alienation at that level. This was true even for those, such as the CRC leader, whose cause was helped by the show. In addition, while I think the "20/20" piece influenced legal action against the Save-A-Baby group, I doubt that events would have unfolded in a significantly different manner, except that activity might have been less violent during the period when filming took place.

8. These are consistent with other recent court actions, such as the June 1986 action taken by NOW (see n. 4). In October 1986, the Problem Pregnancy Center of Fort Worth, Texas, founded in 1984, was convicted of violating the Texas Deceptive Trade Practices Act because it falsely advertised itself as an abortion clinic. The jury recommended that it pay the state $108,000 in penalties and legal fees.

In December 1986, the House Subcommittee on Civil and Constitutional Rights held hearings on antiabortion centers. In a statement to the *New York Times* (December 17, 1986), Robert Pearson, founder of the Pearson Foundation in St. Louis, which has created the model for and materials used by many of these centers, explained,

We need our centers to look like the abortion clinics to reach people. There's no crime in that. It's like a Wendy's locating next to a McDonalds.

In May 1987, the first suit against antiabortion violence using racketeering laws was settled in favor of the abortion clinic, The Northeast Women's Center of Philadelphia. Twenty-five protesters were found guilty of intimidating patients and staff and were fined $91,000 in damages.

9. In Turner's model, a social drama ends either with this sort of schism or the reintegration of the disturbed social group (1974: 41).

10. As Turner points out, as a conflict moves through phases of breach, crisis, redress, regression, and reintegration,

the nature and intensity of the relations between parts, and the structure of the total field will have changed. Some components of the field will have less support, others more, still others will have fresh support, and some will have none. The distribution of the factors of legitimacy will have changed, as also the techniques used by leaders to gain compliance. (1974: 42)

11. Later in 1986, the Fargo Women's Health Organization brought charges against both the Women's Clinic of Fargo and the AAA Problem Pregnancy Center for deceptive advertisements in the Yellow Pages. The former group's advertisement read:

Free Pregnancy Test/Confidential/Abortion Information/Registered Nurse.

The Problem Pregnancy Center's advertisement read:

Confidential Counseling About: Abortion and Alternatives/Medical and Financial Assistance/Free Pregnancy Test.

12. By comparison, the membership of the National Right to Life Committee is 70 percent Catholic and 20 percent Protestant, with Lutherans and Baptists comprising the predominant Protestant affiliations. In the United States in general, approximately 28 percent of the population is Catholic and 60 percent is Protestant (Granberg 1981: 159).

Regarding local statistics, it is difficult to get a clear picture of religious affiliation in Fargo. Statistics are taken infrequently and reflect people who were baptized or confirmed in the denomination, not actual attendance or belief. From 1971 estimates of the North Dakota's Conference of Churches, of those who belong to a church in the area, about 30 to 35 percent are Catholic, 40 percent are Lutheran, and the remainder are divided between a variety of Protestant churches—Baptist, Presbyterian, Methodist, Episcopalian, Congregationalist, Assemblies of God—and a very small Jewish congregation. By 1983, it was clear that the Assemblies of God was drawing people away from other denominations in large numbers. Several ministers in town estimated they had as much as 20 percent of the church-going population at their weekly services. The picture is further complicated by the fact that people may nominally remain Lutheran while attending Pentecostal services or participating in informal charismatic prayer groups.

13. The Granberg study was conducted in June 1980 with the cooperation of the NRLC and NARAL, and funding from the Graduate Research Council of the University of Missouri. The mailing included letters from the author and a leader of the prospective respondent's organization and a postage-paid return envelope. While the NARAL names were selected at random by computer, NRLC preferred that the names be provided by the state affiliates that make up the NRLC coalition. This meant that each state organization had to be contacted and an attempt made to secure its cooperation in the study. Thirty-one states chose to cooperate, and nineteen either declined or did not send the requested lists. According to the authors, there seemed to be no regional or state bias from the NRLC names they received. The results are based on data from 426 (57 percent) of 750 dues-paying members of the NRLC who responded to questionnaires they received in the mail (Granberg 1981).

14. This representation is problematic for social theory as well. It reinforces the misleading Parsonian notion that industrialization stripped familial arrangements of their instrumental functions, leaving only an expressive "natural" core, the very center of which is the ultimate symbol of nurturance and affective relations in Western society, the mother-child dyad.

15. In an insightful article on abortion activists, authors Callahan and Callahan write:

There are, we think, two abortion debates now taking place, one of them tense, open and familiar, the other more relaxed, less public and in some ways surprising. At one level then, there is the fairly primitive monochromatic struggle that takes place between the most public and vociferous activists on both sides. At that level, the debate admits no accommodation.

But the relationship of abortion to deeper values such as feminism, the family, childrearing and the political culture is open to more flexible and interesting possibilities than have been apparent in much of the public debate. (1984: 220)

16. An interesting perspective on this situation is offered by Kristin Luker in a study of women who have repeated abortions. The women who aborted repeatedly apparently did so when pregnancy failed to transform an uncommitted lover into a husband. Luker argues that the subjects in her study, like many American women, feel themselves "bargaining with deflated currency," caught in an "option squeeze" between motherhood and wage labor (1978: 121).

Chapter 8. Interpreting Life Stories

1. Regarding "worldview," Redfield writes

Every worldview is a stage set. On that stage myself is an important character; in every worldview there is an "I" from which the view is taken. On the stage are other people, toward whom the view is directed. And man, as a collective character, is upon the stage; he may speak his lines very loudly or he may be seen as having but a minor part among other parts. (1953: 86)

2. In a 1984 review article on life histories, Daniel Bertaux and Martin Kohli use the term "life story" in this way. I find it a useful way to distinguish such narratives from more comprehensive, fully developed narrative texts that would more properly be called life histories, such as Crapanzano's *Tuhami* (1980b), Mintz's *Worker in the Cane* (1981), or Shostak's *Nisa* (1981).

3. Although I framed these questions in ways that seemed to "make sense" to the people I was interviewing in terms of the structure of the narratives they generated, queries were intended to produce answers to the following questions:

1. How are experiences of work and family, social and religious activity, and a sense of one's place in the culture framed in relation to abortion in the narrative of the life course?

2. Is the consciousness that led to abortion activism considered consistent with or a repudiation of prior beliefs and experiences? How is

the past negotiated in relation to current attitudes on the abortion controversy, gender arrangements, sexuality, and reproduction?

3. What aspects of contemporary life are seen as undesirable, how are these connected to abortion, and what is their real or imagined impact on individual lives?

4. What sorts of political, religious, or cultural activities are seen as appropriate correctives to these problems? How are these concerns enacted in the social organization of daily life?

4. In Van Gennep's model, ritual passage was studied as a means for describing, rather than explaining, a particular social formation. The following passage is exemplary of his approach:

The life of an individual in any society is a series of passages from one age to another and from one occupation to another. . . . Transitions from group to group and from one social situation to the next are looked on as implicit in the very fact of existence, so that a man's life comes to be made up of a succession of stages with similar ends and beginnings: birth, social puberty, marriage, fatherhood, advancement to a higher class, occupational specialization and death. For every one of these events there are ceremonies whose essential purpose is to enable the individual to pass from one defined position to another which is equally well-defined. (1960: 2–3)

5. See, for example, Anderson (1985); Rossi (1980); Hareven (1978).

6. I use the term along the lines established by Terdiman (1985) in his illuminating elaborations of Michel Foucault's (1971) discourse theory. Terdiman defines the terms as follows:

Put simply, discourses are the complexes of signs and practices which organize social existence and social reproduction. In their structured, material persistence, discourses are what give differential substance to membership in a social group or class or formation, which mediate an internal sense of belonging, an outward sense of otherness.

But we need to be careful about *defining* a concept like the discourse. Such a notion must be referred to the problematic from which it emerges, for this determines its operational sense. (1985: 54)

. . . Situated as other, counter-discourses have the capacity to *situate*: to relativize the authority and stability of a dominant system of utterances which cannot even countenance their existence. (1985: 16)

. . . We might argue that counter-discourses tend, in their relation to the dominant, to homology with the body's reaction to disease: either they seek to surround their antagonist and neutralize or explode it; or they strive to exclude it totally, to expunge it. . . . Between these theoretical extremes, like an unpredictable series of guerilla skirmishes, the multiform violations of the norms of the dominant constitute the realm of functionality of the counter-discourse. (1985: 69)

7. In my use of this idea of "counter-discourse" as well as the "plot/story" distinction, I am indebted to George Marcus for his insights re-

garding the use of literary criticism in the analysis of "elicited fieldwork dialogue" that embodies a cultural critique. In a paper prepared for a talk delivered at the "Constructing America Seminar" at the New York Institute for the Humanities in March 1986, Marcus writes:

I believe the hope of probing for counter-discourses in the field is indeed to find a fellowship between the criticism of everyday life and that of the intellectual. . . . But this hope is most often disappointed. Rather, the originality and depth of the ethnographically derived counter-discourses of subjects are in the form of such discourses.

8. In assessing the way that abortion opponents view the world in relation to their ideology, authors Callahan and Callahan write:

Both sides are prepared to argue that abortion is undesirable, a crude solution to problems that would better be solved by other means. The crucial difference, however, is that those on the pro-choice side believe that the world must be acknowledged as it is and not just as it ought to be.

By contrast, the pro-life group believes that a better future cannot be achieved . . . unless we are prepared to make present sacrifices toward future goals and unless aggression toward the fetus is denied, however high the individual cost of denying it. The dichotomies are experienced in our ordinary language when "idealists" are contrasted with "realists." (1984: 221)

Chapter 10. The Pro-Life Narrative

1. Giddens' working definition for ideology as "any system of belief which proclaims the need for radical change, reactionary or progressive, in the existing order of things" is useful for the purposes of this study (1979: 197).

Althusser's definition of ideology as representing "the imaginary relationship of individuals to their real conditions of existence" is also useful, but problematic in its assumption that one can establish with certainty what the "real conditions of existence" are (1971).

2. In an article entitled "Metaphor and Self: Symbolic Processes in Everyday Life," anthropologists Dan Merten and Gary Schwartz write:

Metaphor as conveyed by figurative speech and action transforms a ritual participant's sense of self. . . . Metaphorical movement operates both on the speaker's perception of the world . . . and how he or she affectively experiences himself or herself in that situation.

While the mechanisms that account for the affectively transformative powers of metaphor are not clear, it is clear that metaphor is one of the symbolic devices that can shift, reverse, intensify or otherwise change how the self is represented and how the speaker feels about the representation. (1982: 799)

3. In an article addressing that topic, authors Callahan and Callahan note:

Both sides tend to share a distrust of that form of libertarianism that would wholly sunder the individual from the community, setting up the private self as an isolated agent bound by no moral standards other than those perceived or devised by the agent. In this, they not only share some of the traditional conservative and neoconservative critiques of liberalism, but share as well a kind of questioning that has become part of the liberal tradition itself. . . . They want to be able to use the past selectively, preserving what remains valuable and rejecting what has either been harmful or wholly overtaken by time, and, in general, they see the past as a resource, requiring constant adjustment and adaptation for life in the present. (1984: 220–21)

Chapter 11. La Longue Durée

1. I draw, in part, on the ideas of French social historian Ferdinand Braudel. His notion of the structures of "la longue durée" is a method of examining historical material to discover continuities of cultural categories that structure meaning and action through time.

My approach also follows the work of Sahlins (1981; 1985) and Giddens (1979) in looking not simply for the endurance of categories, but to see how structures are changed, by the intended or unintended consequences of social action.

2. Whereas the scarcity of workers in colonial towns had encouraged the entry of women into the growing wage labor market, the growing surplus of available labor in industrializing cities in the nineteenth century eventually bred male opposition to female work-force participation in all occupations (Berg 1978: 63).

3. This ideology, according to historian Gerda Lerner,

extolled woman's predominance in the domestic sphere, while it tried to justify women's exclusion from the public domain, from equal education and from participation in the political process by claims to tradition, universality and a history dating back to antiquity, or at least to the "Mayflower." In a century of modernization and industrialization, women alone were to remain unchanging, embodying in their behavior and attitudes the longing of men and women caught in rapid social change for a mythical archaic past of agrarian family self-sufficiency. (1979: 192–93)

4. This is in no way meant to perpetuate the myth of the self-sufficient American yeoman, but to call attention to the fact that the processes that initially segregated the home worked eventually to erode its original material base.

5. In Epstein's analysis, women's campaigns to destroy saloons were charged by class as well as sex antagonisms. In demanding public recognition and action on the part of the state in defense of values to which they were culturally assigned, women were also helping to complete the cultural transformation begun largely by men in the early part of the century.

They were creating a definition of "respectable" middle-class behavior far removed from the preindustrial culture of the previous two centuries.

6. In its initial stages, the temperance movement was largely white, middle-class, and Protestant; and its members took their mission, in part, to be the conversion of the "lower classes" to proper ideas of family life and responsible behavior (Degler 1980: 316). However, by 1885, 30 percent of local WCTU organizers had husbands who were skilled or unskilled workers (Gusfield 1955: 230). What this suggests is that the movement was not only middle class but was gaining support of women across classes.

Between 1890 and 1911, national membership expanded from 176,000 to 245,000. Under the leadership of Frances Willard, the WCTU president for nineteen years, the temperance cause of defense of the home was linked to issues as diverse as health, labor, social purity, peace, and arbitration (Degler 1980: 317–18).

7. "Social feminist" was coined by historian William O'Neill for those who "while believing in women's rights, generally subordinated them to broad social reforms" (1971: x).

8. Material is drawn from Camhi (1973), as summarized and cited in Degler (1980).

9. In the end, the passage of the 19th Amendment in 1920 giving women the vote created few of the dire changes, such as the breakdown of the family and the polity, predicted by the antisuffragists.

10. Modeled on British prototypes, the Settlement House Movement was a response to the visibly disturbing effects of industrialization and social stratification in rapidly expanding urban centers. Socially conscious, college-educated, middle-class women moved into poor immigrant and working-class districts of large cities "in order to bring understanding, practical help, entertainment, and some intellectual experience to its inhabitants" (Degler 1980: 320).

11. The arguments of "race suicide" condemned white middle-class women who voluntarily lowered their fertility for allowing other "races" to outbreed them.

12. During the Depression, women played a crucial role in providing a buffer for families and households against the effects of the economic crisis that followed the 1929 stock market crash. Unlike working women in the 1920s who spoke of jobs as a vehicle for independence and identity, the Depression cohort viewed their behavior as a temporary response to family emergency. Consequently, according to the sociologist Ruth Milkman, "the impact of the crisis was to define women in terms of the traditional roles even more rigidly than before" (1979: 527). Thus, despite the growing number of female workers during the Depression, the separate sphere

ideology—supported by the state and accommodating the participation of women in wage labor—endured nonetheless.

13. Regarding such dynamics, Marshall Sahlins writes:

As the contingent circumstances of action need not conform to the significance some group might assign them, people are known to creatively reconsider their conventional schemes. And to that extent, the culture is historically altered in action. We can speak even of "structural transformation" since the alteration of some meanings changes the positional relations among the cultural categories, thus a "systems-change." (1985: vii)

Conclusion

1. Between 1940 and 1944, the female labor force not only doubled; its composition began to shift. As opposed to 1900 when 70 percent of women working were under thirty-five, the female labor force gradually began to reflect the adult female population as a whole (see Appendix). The percentage of women in the work force rose to 55.8 percent in 1985. For women ages 25 to 34, the percentage is 71 percent. According to a March 1987 survey by the Labor Department, the number of working women who have children under three years old jumped from 31.6 percent in 1977 to 43.2 in 1982 and 51.9 as of March 1987. For interesting discussion of the overall meaning of these figures, see Bianchi and Spain (1986); O'Connell and Bloom (1987); and Uchitelle (1987).

2. Work such as food preparation, laundry, sewing, and care for dependents that had been carried out by unpaid female labor in households, "a bulwark against the cold calculations of cash," was and is increasingly provided for by wage workers in the arena of commercial exchange (Ryan 1983: 342). See Appendix.

3. This figure comes from a 1986 survey, sponsored by Johnson Wax, of 1,409 households, reported in an article in the *New York Times*. The piece summarizes current research on housework and women's labor. The results of a nationwide study show that time spent in housework for the individual aged twenty-five to forty-four has declined 40 percent from the mid-1960s (from 11.3 to 6.8 hours a week). Although that same study showed a slight increase, from 1.3 to 2.4 hours a week during the same period, in men's contribution to housework (cooking and cleaning), another study conducted with 210 families in Virginia found that men were spending an average of 1.6 minutes a day on housecleaning in 1986, down from 6.3 minutes in 1978.

4. By the 1950s, the period of time devoted to maternity and child-rearing in relation to female life expectancy was steadily decreasing, taking up less than one-seventh of the average female life span (Sullerot

1971). The sociologist Ruth Milkman points out that the significance of the changes in the female life cycle cannot be understood without looking at the transformations in women's activity in the American economy as well.

As women's role in the paid labor force has come to take up a longer period of their lives, their family role has yielded more and more of its direct productive functions to the sphere of commodity production, while the reproduction of children, the one commodity which this society still inevitably depends on women to produce, now takes up a much shorter period of their lives. (1979: 536)

5. These figures are based on the U.S. Department of Commerce, Bureau of the Census, reports (1986a; 1986b); O'Connell and Bloom (1987); Pear (1987); and Weitzman (1985).

6. Rebecca Klatch notes a similar ideological framing in her research on women and the New Right. "Like feminists," she writes,

the social conservative woman protests male values, but she does so on totally different grounds. The social conservative woman fears that a gender-free society will mean a world enveloped in self-interest, devoid of qualities such as nurturance, altruism, and self-sacrifice associated with the female role. If women become more like men, she reasons, there will be no one left to instill moral values in the young, to ensure that passions are controlled, to guard against a world besieged by self-interest. (1987: 206)

Epilogue: Pro-Dialogue

1. Vatican 24 refers to twenty-four American nuns who, along with four priests, signed an advertisement, supporting the right to dissent from the Church's teaching on abortion.

Appendix: Female Moral Reform Movements in America

1. The Second Great Awakening was particularly strong among Methodist and Baptist preachers, who stressed faith over theology and personal salvation as the means of escaping eternal damnation. By pulling believers into their fold, they undercut the authority of the Congregational and Episcopal clergy, the two dominant denominations of the Colonial period (Berg 1978: 34).

2. By 1929, studies among middle-class women born around 1900 indicated that 75 to 90 percent of them advocated or used contraception in marriage; among men of the same age and class, reported sex with prostitutes decreased by 50 percent from the prior generation while their report of premarital sex, generally with fiancées, increased commensurately (Fass 1977: 76–77).

3. Barbara Epstein calls the increasing acceptance of sexual expression within marriage as the "New Deal of family politics" (1983: 118). Commenting on the same period, Mary Ryan notes:

Young women who had been instructed in the new ideology of the family looked to marriage for a "fuller richer life" . . . or simply "companionship." The newlyweds took up residence in an intimate social space whose function was to produce neither social service nor material goods, but an elusive commodity called "happiness." (1983: 244)

4. In Jo Freeman's estimation:

No single "youth movement" activity or organization was responsible for the younger branch of the WLM [Women's Liberation Movement]; . . . The women in it thought of themselves as "movement people" and had incorporated the adjective "radical" into their personal identities. (1973: 26–27)

5. The dispute over adoption of an abortion repeal statement at the Second Annual Convention of NOW in November 1967 is instructive. According to some analysts, few members disagreed with the principle of repeal. The split was over tactics. Some felt that support for abortion repeal was too radical and would discourage support for the rest of NOW's agenda by more conventional groups, such as the YWCA, the Girl Scouts, and the League of Women Voters, which were beginning to incorporate feminist concerns such as women's health and child and spouse abuse into their programs (Hole and Levine 1971; Ryan 1983: 315). The position finally passed and the fears that had been articulated were temporarily assuaged as the abortion rights movement picked up momentum.

6. For overviews of feminist organizing on abortion prior to 1973, see Hole and Levine (1971: 299–301); Petchesky (1984: 125–32); and Luker (1984: 95–125).

Bibliography

Addams, Jane
>   1930   *The Second Twenty Years at Hull House.* New York:
>   Macmillan.
>   1973 (1907) Utilization of Women in City Government. Excerpted in
>   *The Feminist Papers*, ed. A. Rossi, 604–12. New York:
>   Bantam.
Althusser, Louis
>   1971   Ideology and Ideological State Apparatuses. In *Lenin and
>   Philosophy and Other Essays*, 121–73. New York: New
>   Left Books.
American Law Institute
>   1962   *Model Penal Code.* Philadelphia: American Law Institute.
Anderson, Michael
>   1985   The Emergence of the Modern Life Cycle in Britain. *Jour-
>   nal of Social History* 10(1): 69–87.
Andrusko, Dave
>   1983   Zealots, Zanies, and Assorted Kooks: How the Major Media
>   Interprets the Pro-Life Movement. In *To Rescue the Future:
>   The Pro-Life Movement in the 1980's.* ed. D. Andrusko,
>   183–200. Harrison, N.Y.: Life Cycle Press.
Arendt, Hannah
>   1969   *On Violence.* New York: Harcourt Brace and World.
Ariés, Philippe
>   1960   Interpretation pour une histoire des mentalités. In *La pre-
>   vention des naissances dans la famille*, ed. Helen Bergues,
>   314–18. Paris: Institut National d'Etudes Demographiques.
Augé, Marc
>   1979   *The Anthropological Circle.* New York: Cambridge Univer-
>   sity Press.

Austin, J. L.
  1962   *How to Do Things with Words.* New York: Oxford University Press.
Bartlett, Frederic C.
  1932   *Remembering.* Cambridge: Cambridge University Press.
Basch, Norma
  1979   Invisible Women: The Legal Fiction of Marital Unity in Nineteenth Century America. *Feminist Studies* 5(2): 346–66.
Beecher, Catharine
  1872   *Women's Profession as Mother and Educator, with Views in Opposition to Suffrage.* Boston: G. Maclean.
Bellm, Dan
  1987   The McChild-Care Empire. *Ms. Magazine.* April: 32–38.
Bellotti v. *Baird*
  1979   443 U.S. 622.
Bennett, Tony
  1979   *Formalism and Marxism.* New York: Methuen.
Bennetts, Leslie
  1981   Anti-Abortion Movement in Disarray less than a Year after Elections. *New York Times.* September 22.
Berg, Barbara
  1978   *The Remembered Gate: Origins of American Feminism, The Woman and the City 1800–1860.* New York: Oxford University Press.
Berk, Sarah, and J. Berk
  1983   Supply Side Sociology of the Family: The Challenge of the New Home Economics. *Annual Review of Sociology* 9: 175–90.
Bertaux, Daniel, and Martin Kohli
  1984   The Life Story Approach: A Continental View. *Annual Review of Sociology* 10: 215–37.
Bianchi, Suzanne, and Daphne Spain
  1986   *American Women in Transition.* New York: Russell Sage.
Blake, Judith, and Jorge del Pinal
  1980   Predicting Polar Attitudes toward Abortion in the U.S. In *Abortion Parley,* ed. J. Burthchaell, 27–56. New York: Andrews and McMeel.
Bolotin, Susan
  1986   Selling Chastity. *Vogue.* March.
Bonaparte, Marie
  1945   *Female Sexuality.* New York: Macmillan.

Bopp, James
    1985   Review of *Closed: 99 Ways to Stop Abortion* by Joseph Scheidler. In *The National Right to Life News*. August 26.

Borders, C., and P. Cutright
    1979   Community Determinants of U.S. Legal Abortion Rates. *Family Planning Perspectives* 11: 117–33.

Bourdieu, Pierre
    1977   *Outline of a Theory of Practice*. New York: Cambridge University Press.

Braudel, Ferdinand
    1958   Histoire et sciences sociales: La longue durée. *Annales: Economies, societies, civilisations* 13: 725–53.

Briggs, Kenneth
    1982   Majority of Bishops Said to Back Arms Letter. *New York Times*. November 17.

Buhle, Mary Jo
    1980   Politics and Culture in Women's History. *Feminist Studies* 6(1): 37–42.

Callahan, Daniel, and Sidney Callahan
    1984   Abortion: Understanding Differences. *Family Planning Perspectives* 16(5): 219–21.

Callahan, Sidney, et al.
    1986   Is Abortion the Issue? *Harper's Magazine* 273 (July): 35–44.

Camhi, Jane Jerome
    1973   "Women Against Women: American Antisuffragism, 1880–1920." Ph.D. dissertation, Tufts University.

Carpenter, Teresa
    1985   Four Who Bombed in God's Name. *The Village Voice*. August 27: 19–26.

Cates, W., Jr., K. F. Schultz, D. A. Grimes, and C. W. Tyler, Jr.
    1977   The Effect of Delay and Method Choice on the Risk of Abortion Morbidity. *Family Planning Perspectives* 9: 266–72.

Centers for Disease Control
    1960–1984   *Abortion Surveillance Annual Summaries*. Atlanta, Ga.: Centers for Disease Control.

Cisler, Lucinda
    1970   Abortion Reform: The New Tokenism. *Ramparts* 9: 19–21.

City of Akron v. *Akron Center for Reproductive Health Inc.*
    1983   462 U.S. 416.

Coale, Awsley J., and Melvin Zelnick
    1963   *New Estimates of Fertility and Population in the United States*. Princeton, N.J.: Princeton University Press.

Collier, Jane, Michelle Rosaldo, and Sylvia Yanagisako
  1982   Is There a Family? New Anthropological Views. In *Re-thinking the Family*, ed. B. Thorne and M. Yalom, 25–39. New York: Longman.
Cominus, Peter
  1963   Late Victorian Sexual Respectability and the Social System. *International Review of Social History* 8: 18–48.
Conover, Pamela J., and Virginia Gray
  1983   *Feminism and The New Right*. New York: Praeger.
Conservative Digest
  1979   The New Right: A Special Report. *Conservative Digest*. June.
Cott, Nancy
  1977   *The Bonds of Womanhood: "Woman's Sphere" in New England, 1780–1835*. New Haven, Conn.: Yale University Press.
Cott, Nancy, and Elizabeth Pleck
  1979   Introduction to *A Heritage of Her Own*, 9–24. New York: Simon and Schuster.
Crapanzano, Vincent
  1980a   Rite of Return: Circumcision in Morocco. In *The Psycho-analytic Study of Society*, ed. W. Muensterberger and L. Bryce Boyer, 9: 15–36. New York: Library of Psychological Anthropology.
  1980b   *Tuhami*. Chicago: University of Chicago Press.
Crawford, Alan
  1980   *Thunder on the Right: The New Right and the Politics of Resentment*. New York: Pantheon.
Crèvecoeur, Michel Guillaume St. Jean de
  1904 (1782) *Letters from an American Farmer*. New York: Fox, Duffield.
Dawson, Debra, Denise Meny, and Jeanne Ridley
  1980   Fertility Control in the U.S. before the Contraceptive Revolution. *Family Planning Perspectives* 12 (2): 76–86.
Degler, Carl
  1980   *At Odds: Women and the Family in America from the Revolution to the Present*. New York: Oxford University Press.
Deutsch, Helene
  1945   *The Psychology of Women: A Psychoanalytic Interpretation*. New York: Macmillan.
Diamond v. *Charles*
  1986   106 U.S. 1697.

Dionne, E. J., Jr.
1987a   High Tide for Conservatives, But Some Fear What Fol-
          lows. *New York Times.* October 31.
1987b   A Conservative Call for Compassion. *New York Times.* No-
          vember 30.
Doe v. *Bolton*
1973   410 U.S. 179.
Douglas, Mary
1966   *Purity and Danger.* London: Ark Paperbooks.
Easterlin, Richard
1976   Factors in the Decline of Farm Family Fertility in the U.S.:
          Some Preliminary Research Results. *Journal of American
          History* 63: 600–12.
Edelman, Murray
1971   *Politics as Symbolic Action: Mass Arousal and Quiescence.*
          Chicago: Markham Publishing.
Ehrenreich, Barbara
1983   *The Hearts of Men.* Garden City, N.Y.: Anchor Press.
Eisenstein, Zillah
1984   *Feminism and Sexual Equality: Crisis in Liberal America.*
          New York: Monthly Review Press.
English, Deirdre
1981   The War against Choice. *Mother Jones* 6(11): 567–88.
Epstein, Barbara
1981   *The Politics of Domesticity.* Middletown, Conn.: Wesleyan
          University Press.
1983   Family, Sexual Morality, and Popular Movements in Turn-
          of-the-Century America. In *The Powers of Desire,* ed. Ann
          Snitow, C. Stansell, and S. Thompson, 117–30. New York:
          Monthly Review Press.
Erikson, Erik
1958   *Young Man Luther.* New York: Norton.
1969   *Gandhi's Truth.* New York: Norton
Farnham, Marinya, and Ferdinand Lundberg
1947   *Modern Woman: The Lost Sex.* New York: Free Press.
Fass, Paula
1977   *The Damned and the Beautiful.* New York: Oxford Univer-
          sity Press.
Faucher, Sandra
1983   The Best Kept Secret. In *To Rescue the Future,* ed. D. An-
          drusko, 59–66. Harrison, N.Y.: Life Cycle Books.

Finkbine, Sherry
    1967   The Lesser of Two Evils. In *The Case for Legalized Abortion Now*, ed. Alan Guttmacher, 12–25. Berkeley: Diablo Press.

Fitzgerald, Frances
    1981a   The Triumphs of the New Right. *New York Review of Books* 28: 19–26.
    1981b   A Reporter at Large: A Disciplined and Charging Army. *The New Yorker.* May 18: 53–141.
    1986   *Cities on a Hill.* New York: Simon and Schuster.

Flandrin, Jean-Louis
    1976   *Families in Former Times: Kinship, Household, and Sexuality.* Trans. R. Southern. Cambridge: Cambridge University Press.

Fletcher, John, and Mark Evans
    1983   Maternal Bonding in Early Fetal Ultrasound Examinations. *New England Journal of Medicine* 308: 392–93.

Forrest, Jacqueline D., and Stanley Henshaw
    1987   The Harassment of U.S. Abortion Providers. *Family Planning Perspectives* 19(1): 9–13.

Forster, Colin, and G. S. C. Tucker
    1972   *Economic Opportunity and White American Fertility Ratios, 1800–1860.* New Haven, Conn.: Yale University Press.

Foucault, Michel
    1971   *L'ordre du discours.* Paris: Gallimard.
    1978   *History of Sexuality.* volume I. New York: Pantheon.

Fox, Bonnie, ed.
    1980   *Hidden in the Household: Women's Domestic Labour Under Capitalism.* Toronto, Ontario: The Women's Press.

Freedman, Samuel
    1987   Abortion Bombings Suspect: A Portrait of Piety and Rage. *New York Times.* May 7.

Freeman, Jo
    1973   The Origins of the Women's Liberation Movement. *American Journal of Sociology* 78(4): 30–49.
    1975   *The Politics of Women's Liberation.* New York: McKay.

Friedan, Betty
    1963   *The Feminine Mystique.* New York: Dell.
    1968   Our Revolution Is Unique. In *President's Report to the National Conference of NOW.* Atlanta, December 6.

Fujita, N., and Nathaniel M. Wagner
    1973   Referendum 20: Abortion Reform in Washington State. In *The Abortion Experience*, ed. H. Osofsky and Joy D. Osofsky, 232–61. New York: Harper and Row.

Gage, Matilda
    1868   Child Murder. *Revolution* 1(14): 215–16.
Garton, Jean
    1979   *Who Broke the Baby?* Minneapolis: Bethany Fellowship.
Gebhard, Paul, W. B. Pomeroy, C. E. Martin, and C. V. Christianson
    1958   *Pregnancy, Birth and Abortion.* New York: Harper.
Giddens, Anthony
    1979   *Central Problems in Social Theory.* Berkeley: University of
              California Press.
Giele, Janet Z.
    1961   Social Change in the Feminine Role: A Comparison of Wom-
              en's Suffrage and Women's Temperance, 1870–1920. Ph.D.
              dissertation, Radcliffe College.
Giele, Janet Z., and Audrey C. Smock
    1977   *Women's Role and Status in Eight Countries.* New York:
              Macmillan.
Gilder, George
    1981   *Wealth and Poverty.* New York: Basic Books.
Gilman, Charlotte Perkins
    1898   *Women and Economics.* Boston: Small, Maynard and
              Company.
Glenn, Kristin Booth
    1978   Abortion in the Courts: A Laywoman's Guide to the New
              Disaster Area. *Feminist Studies* 4: 1–26.
Gluckman, Max
    1967   Introduction to *The Craft of Social Anthropology.* London:
              Tavistock.
Gordon, Linda
    1977   *Woman's Body, Woman's Right: A Social History of Birth
              Control in America.* New York: Penguin.
    1982   Why Nineteenth-Century Feminists Did Not Support
              "Birth Control" and Twentieth-Century Feminists Do:
              Feminism, Reproduction, and the Family. In *Rethinking
              the Family,* ed. B. Thorne and M. Yalom, 40–53. New
              York: Longman.
Gordon, Linda, and Allen Hunter
    1977–78 Sex, Family, and the New Right: Anti-Feminism as a Politi-
              cal Force. *Radical America* 11–12: 9–25.
Granberg, Daniel
    1981   The Abortion Activists. *Family Planning Perspectives* 13(4):
              158–61.
    1987   The Abortion Issue in the 1984 Elections. *Family Planning
              Perspectives* 19(2): 59–62.

Greenhouse, Linda
    1985   Justices Widen Review of State Abortion Curbs. *New York Times*. May 21.

Griswold v. *Connecticut*
    1965   381 U.S. 471.

Gusfield, Joseph
    1955   Social Structure and Moral Reform: A Study of the WCTU. *American Journal of Sociology* 61: 221–32.
    1966   *Symbolic Crusade*. Urbana: University of Illinois Press.

Guttmacher, Alan
    1967a   Introduction to *The Case For Legalized Abortion Now*, 1–17. Berkeley, Calif.: Diablo Press.
    1967b   The Legal Status of Therapeutic Abortions. In *Abortion in America*, ed. Harold Rosen, 175–86. Boston: Beacon.
    1973   The Genesis of Liberalized Abortion in New York. In *Abortion, Society and the Law*, ed. D. Wolbert and J. Douglas, 60–75. Cleveland: Case Western Reserve Press.

Hacker, Andrew
    1983   Where Have All the Jobs Gone? *New York Review of Books*. June 30: 27–32.

Hale, Edwin
    1860   *On the Homeopathic Treatment of Abortion*. Chicago: C. S. Halsey.
    1866   *A Systematic Treatise on Abortion*. Chicago: C. S. Halsey.
    1867   *The Great Crime of the Nineteenth Century*. Chicago: C. S. Halsey.

Hammond, Howard
    1964   Therapeutic Abortion: Ten Years Experience with Hospital Committee Control. *Journal of Obstetrics and Gynecology* 89: 349–55.

Harding, Susan F.
    1981   Family Reform Movements: Recent Feminism and Its Opposition. *Feminist Studies* 7(1): 57–75.
    1987   Convicted by the Holy Spirit: The Rhetoric of Fundamental Baptist Conversion. *American Ethnologist* 14(1): 167–81.

Hareven, Tamara, ed.
    1978   *Transitions: The Family and the Life Course in Historical Perspective*. New York: Academic Press.

Harris v. *McRae*
    1980   100 U.S. 2671.

Hartmann, Heidi
    1979   The Family as the Locus of Gender, Class and Political Struggle: The Example of Housework. *Signs* 6(3): 366–94.

Henley, Nancy
    1982   Women as a Social Problem. Unpublished speech to the American Psychological Association.

Henshaw, Stanley
    1982   Free-Standing Abortion Clinics: Services, Structures, Fees. *Family Planning Perspectives* 14(5): 248–56.
    1987   Characteristics of U.S. Women Having Abortions, 1982-1983. *Family Planning Perspectives* 19(1): 5–4.

Henshaw, Stanley, Jacqueline Forrest, and C. Blaine
    1984   Abortion Services in the U.S., 1981 and 1982. *Family Planning Perspectives* 16(3): 118–23.

Henshaw, Stanley, J. D. Forrest, E. Sullivan, and C. Tietze
    1982   Abortion Services in the United States: 1979–1980. *Family Planning Perspectives* 14(1): 5–15.

Henshaw, Stanley, Jacqueline D. Forrest, and J. Van Vort
    1987   Abortion Services in the United States, 1984 and 1985. *Family Planning Perspectives* 19(2): 63–70.

Henshaw, Stanley, and Kevin O'Reilly
    1983   Characteristics of Abortion Patients in the United States, 1979–80. *Family Planning Perspectives* 15(1): 5–16.

Herbers, John
    1984   Abortion Issue Threatens to Become Profoundly Divisive. *New York Times*. October 14.
    1986   NOW Seeks to Curb Anti-Abortionists. *New York Times*. June 11.

Hern, Warren M.
    1984   The Anti-Abortion Vigilantes. *New York Times*. December 21.

Himes, Norman
    1970   *Medical History of Contraception*. New York: Schocken.

Himmelstein, Jerome
    1983   The New Right. In *The New Christian Right*, ed. Robert Liebman and Robert Wuthnow, 15–31. Chicago: Aldine.
    1986   The Social Basis of Antifeminism: Religious Networks and Culture. *The Journal for the Scientific Study of Religion* 25(1): 1–15.

Hole, Judith, and Ellen Levine
    1971   *The Rebirth of Feminism*. New York: Quadrangle Books.

Hunter, Allen
    1981   In the Wings: New Right Ideology and Organization. In *Radical America* 15: 113–38.

Jaffe, Frederic, Barbara Lindheim, and Philip R. Lee
    1981   *Abortion Politics: Private Morality and Public Policy*. New York: McGraw-Hill.

Jepsen, Dee
    1984   *Beyond Equal Rights*. Waco, Tex.: Word Press.
Joffe, Carol
    1987   *Regulating Sexuality*. Philadelphia: University of Pennsyl-
                vania Press.
Johnson, Douglas
    1984   Why Is the National Right-to-Life Committee a "Single Is-
                sue" Organization? *National Right to Life News*. June 1:
                5–6.
Jones, Gordon S.
    1983   Abortion's Muddy Feet. In *To Rescue the Future: The Pro-
                Life Movement in the 1980's*, ed. D. Andrusko, 235–46.
                Harrison, N.Y.: Life Cycle Books.
Kelly, Joan
    1977   Did Women Have a Renaissance? In *Becoming Visible:
                Women in European History*, ed. R. Bridenthal and C.
                Koonz, 137–64. New York: Houghton Mifflin.
    1984   *Women, History and Theory*. Chicago: University of Chi-
                cago Press.
Klatch, Rebecca
    1987   *Women of the New Right*. Philadelphia: Temple University
                Press.
Knodel, John, and Etienne Van de Walle
    1979   Lessons from the Past: Policy Implications for Historical
                Fertility Studies. *Population and Development Review* 5:
                217–45.
Lader, Lawrence
    1966   *Abortion*. Boston: Beacon Press.
    1973   *Abortion II*. Boston: Beacon Press.
Landy, Uta, and Sarah Lewit
    1982   Administrative, Counseling and Medical Practices in Na-
                tional Abortion Federation Facilities. *Family Planning Per-
                spectives* 14(5): 257–62.
Lasch, Christopher
    1977   *Haven in a Heartless World: The Family Besieged*. New
                York: Basic Books.
    1980   Life in the Therapeutic State. *New York Review of Books*.
                June 12: 24–32.
Leach, Edmund
    1977   *Custom, Law and Terrorist Violence*. Edinburgh: Univer-
                sity Press.
Leahy, Peter
    1975   The Anti-Abortion Movement: Testing a Theory of the Rise

and Fall of Social Movements. Ph.D. dissertation, Syracuse University.

Lerner, Gerda
1979 (1969)   The Lady and the Mill Girl. Reprinted in *A Heritage of Her Own*, ed. N. Cott and E. Pleck, 182–96. New York: Simon and Schuster.

Lewis, Neil A.
1987   Abortions Abroad Are a New Focus of Widening Battle over Reagan's Policy. *New York Times*. June 1.

Lichter, S. Robert, and Stanley Rothman
1981   The Media Elite. *Public Opinion* 96: 117–25.

Lucas, Roy
1968   Constitutional Limitations on the Enforcement and Administration of State Abortion Statutes. *North Carolina Law Review* 46: 730–78.

Luker, Kristin
1978   *Taking Chances: Abortion and the Decision Not to Contracept*. Berkeley, University of California Press.

1984a   *Abortion and the Politics of Motherhood*. Berkeley: University of California Press.

1984b   The War between the Women. *Family Planning Perspectives* 16(3): 105–10.

Lynd, Robert S., and Helen Merrell Lynd
1929   *Middletown: A Study of Contemporary American Culture*. New York: Harcourt Brace and Jovanovich.

1937   *Middletown in Transition: A Study in Cultural Conflicts*. New York: Harcourt Brace and Jovanovich.

MacKinnon, Catharine
1983   The Male Ideology of Privacy: A Feminist Perspective on the Right to Abortion. *Radical America* 17(4): 23–35.

MacLaren, Angus
1978   *Birth Control in Nineteenth Century England*. London: Croom and Hale.

Maher vs. *Roe*
1977   432 U.S. 464.

Mandelbaum, David
1973   The Study of Life History: Gandhi. *Current Anthropology* 14(3): 177–206.

Mannheim, Karl
1970 (1952)   The Problem of Generations. *The Psychoanalytic Review* 57(3): 378–404. Reprinted from *Essays on the Sociology of Knowledge*, by K. Mannheim, 378–404. New York: Oxford University Press, 1952.

Marcus, George
    1986   The Finding and Fashioning of Counter-Discourses in Eth-
                nography. Talk delivered at the New York Institute for the
                Humanities. March.
Marcus, Steven
    1966   *The Other Victorians: A Study of Sexuality and Pornogra-
                phy in Mid-Nineteenth Century England.* New York: Ox-
                ford University Press.
Matthaei, Julie
    1982   *An Economic History of Women in America.* New York:
                Schocken.
Matthews, Jay
    1987   History's Most Public Abortion. *This World.* May 24: 8–9.
                Reprinted from *Washington Post.*
Mawyer, Martin
    1985   Bombing Clinics Causes Conflict within Pro-Life Move-
                ment. *Fundamentalist Journal.* March: 59–60.
McDonnell, Kathleen
    1984   *Not an Easy Choice.* Boston: South End Press.
Merten, Dan, and Gary Schwartz
    1982   Metaphor and Self: Symbolic Processes in Everyday Life.
                American Anthropologist 84: 796–809.
Merton, Andrew
    1981   *Enemies of Choice: The Right-to-Life Movement and Its
                Threat to Abortion.* Boston: Beacon Press.
Milkman, Ruth
    1979   Women's Work and the Economic Crisis: Some Lessons
                from the Great Depression. In *A Heritage of Her Own,*
                ed. N. Cott and E. Pleck, 507–41. New York: Simon and
                Schuster.
Minor, Diane
    1982   Burdick Poll Reveals Less Opposition to Abortion. *Fargo
                Forum.* January 21.
Mintz, Sidney
    1981   *Worker in the Cane,* 2nd ed. New York: Norton.
Mitchell, Clyde
    1983   Case and Situational Analysis. *The Sociological Review*
                31(2): 187–211.
Moch, M. K., and E. V. Morse
    1977   Size, Centralization, and Adoption of Innovations. *Ameri-
                can Sociological Review* 42: 716–26.
Mohr, James
    1978   *Abortion in America: The Origins and Evolution of Na-
                tional Policy.* New York: Oxford University Press.

Myerhoff, Barbara
1974   *Peyote Hunt*. Ithaca, N.Y.: Cornell University Press.
1978   *Number Our Days*. New York: Touchstone Books.
Nathanson, Bernard
1972   Ambulatory Abortion: Experiences with 26,000 Cases (July
            1, 1970–August 1, 1971). *New England Journal of Medi-
            cine* 286: 403.
1979   *Aborting America*. New York: Pinnacle Books.
Nathanson, C. A., and M. H. Becker
1980   Obstetricians' Attitudes and Hospital Abortion Services.
            Family Planning Perspectives 12: 26–30.
National Abortion Federation
1984a   *Reported Incidents of Arson and Bombing, 1984*. October
            1. Washington, D.C.: National Abortion Federation.
1984b   *Summary of Clinic Violence: 1977–1984*. October 9. Wash-
            ington, D.C.: National Abortion Federation.
1985   *Summary of Clinic Violence*. March 1985. Washington,
            D.C.: National Abortion Federation.
National Opinion Research Center
1984   Views on Abortion: 1972–1984. *New York Times*. Oc-
            tober 14.
Neale, R. S.
1972   *Class and Ideology in the Nineteenth Century*. London:
            Tavistock.
Nisbet, Robert
1969   *Social Change in History: Aspects of the Western Theory of
            Development*. London: Oxford University Press.
Noonan, John
1967   Abortion and the Catholic Church. *Natural Law Forum* 12:
            85–131.
1979   *A Private Choice: Abortion in America in the Seventies*.
            New York: Free Press.
O'Connell, M., and D. E. Bloom
1987   Juggling Jobs and Babies: America's Child Care Challenge.
            Population Trends and Public Policy. Population Reference
            Bureau, Paper no. 12. February. Washington, D.C.: Gov-
            ernment Printing Office.
Olivarez, Gracie
1972   Separate Statement. In *Population and the American Fu-
            ture*, by the Commission on Population and the American
            Future, 160–61. Washington, D.C.: Government Print-
            ing Office.

O'Neill, William
1971   *Everyone Was Brave: A History of Feminism in America.* Chicago: Quadrangle.
Oppenheimer, Valerie
1970   *The Female Labor Force in the U.S.* Berkeley: University of California Population Monograph Series, no. 5.
Ortner, Sherry, and Harriet Whitehead
1981   *Sexual Meanings.* New York: Cambridge University Press.
Packer, Herbert, and Ralph Gampell
1959   Therapeutic Abortion: A Problem in Law and Medicine. *Stanford Law Review* 11: 417–55.
Paige, Connie
1983   *The Right-to-Lifers.* New York: Summit Books.
Parsons, Talcott, and Robert Bales
1955   *Family Socialization and Interaction Process.* New York: Free Press.
Pear, Robert
1987   Women Reduce Lag in Earnings but Disparities with Men Remain. *New York Times.* September 9.
Peel, John, and Malcolm Potts
1977   *Textbook of Contraceptive Practice.* New York: Cambridge University Press.
Petchesky, Rosalind
1984   *Abortion and Woman's Choice.* New York: Longman.
1987   Fetal Images: The Power of Visual Culture in the Politics of Reproduction. *Feminist Studies* 13(2): 263–92.
Peterson, Iver
1982   Akron's 1978 Rules Were Enjoined Almost at Start. *New York Times.* December 1.
Phelan, Lana Clark, and Patricia Maginnis
1969   *The Abortion Handbook for Responsible Women.* Canoga Park, Calif.: Weiss, Day and Lord.
Pivar, David
1974   *Purity Crusade: Sexual Morality of Social Control: 1868–1900.* Westport, Conn.: Greenwood Press.
Planned Parenthood, Kansas City, Mo. v. *Ashcroft*
1983   462 U.S. 476.
Planned Parenthood of Central Missouri v. *Danforth*
1976   428 U.S. 52.
Plant, Barbara
1971   A Survey of the U.S. Abortion Literature, 1890–1970. M.A. thesis, University of Windsor, Ontario.

Polgar, Steven
    1972   Population History and Population Policies from an Anthropological Perspective. *Current Anthropology* 13: 205–6.

Price, Laurie
    1977   Anti-Abortion or Pro-Life? Public and Private Culture in an American Protest Program. M.A. thesis, University of North Carolina at Chapel Hill.

Rapp, Rayna
    1978   Family and Class in Contemporary America: Notes toward an Understanding of Ideology. *Science and Society* 42: 278–300.
    n.d.   Translating the Genetic Code: The Discourse of Genetic Counseling. Unpublished paper.

Rapp, Rayna, and Ellen Ross
    1983   It Seems Like We've Stood and Talked Like This Before: Wisdom from the 1920s. *Ms. Magazine*. April: 54–56.

Redfield, Robert
    1953   *The Primitive World and Its Transformations*. Ithaca, N.Y.: Cornell University Press.

Ridgeway, James
    1985   The Pro-Life Juggernaut. *The Village Voice*. July 16: 28–29.

Robinson, Marie
    1959   *The Power of Sexual Surrender*. New York: Free Press.

Roe v. *Wade*
    1973   410 U.S. 113.

Roeser, Theodore
    1983   The Pro-Life Movement's Holy Terror. In *The Chicago Reader* 12(44): 13–20.

Rosaldo, Michelle
    1980   The Use and Abuse of Anthropology: Reflections on Feminism and Cross-Cultural Understanding. *Signs* 5(3): 389–417.

Rose, Thomas
    1969   How Violence Occurs: A Theory and Review of the Literature. In *Violence in America*, ed. T. Rose, 26–51. New York: Vintage Books.

Rosen, Harold
    1954   *Therapeutic Abortion: Medical, Psychiatric, Legal, Anthropological and Religious Considerations*. New York: Julian Rosenberg.

Rossi, Alice S.
    1980   Life-Span Theories and Women's Lives. *Signs* 6(1): 4–32.

Rothman, Barbara Katz
    1986   *The Tentative Pregnancy: Prenatal Diagnosis and the Future of Motherhood*. New York: Viking.

Rothschild, Emma
    1981   Reagan and the Real America. *New York Review of Books*. December 5: 12–18.

Rubin, Eva
    1987   *Abortion, Politics and the Courts*, rev. ed. Westport, Conn.: Greenwood Press.

Rubin, Lillian
    1976   *Worlds of Pain*. New York: Basic Books.

Ryan, Mary
    1979   The Power of Women's Networks: A Case Study of Female Moral Reform in Antebellum America. *Feminist Studies* 5(1): 66–86.
    1983   *Womanhood in America*, 3rd ed. New York: Watts.

Sahlins, Marshall
    1981   *Historical Metaphors and Mythical Realities*. Ann Arbor: University of Michigan Press.
    1985   *Islands of History*. Chicago: University of Chicago Press.

Sarvis, Betty, and Hyman Rodman
    1974   *The Abortion Controversy*, 2nd ed. New York: Columbia University Press.

Scharf, Lois
    1980   *To Work and to Wed: Female Employment, Feminism and the Great Depression*. Westport, Conn.: Greenwood Press.

Scheidler, Joseph
    1985   *Closed: 99 Ways to Stop Abortion*. Westchester, Ill.: Crossway Books.

Schlafly, Phyllis
    1978   *The Power of the Positive Woman*. New York: Jove Publishers.

Schmidt, William
    1982   Conservative North Dakota Stunned by Overnight Boom in Gambling. *New York Times*. March 4.

Scialabba, George
    1985   The Trouble with Roe v. Wade. *The Village Voice*. July 16: 25–26.

Sheils, Merrill
    1983   A Portrait of America (based on 1980 U.S. Census). *Newsweek*. January 17: 20–33.

Shelton, J. D., E. A. Braun, and K. F. Schulz
    1976   Abortion Utilization: Does Travel Distance Matter? *Family Planning Perspectives* 8(2): 258–62.

Shorter, Edward
1977   *The Making of the Modern Family.* New York: Basic Books.
Shostak, Marjorie
1981   *Nisa: The Life and Words of a !Kung Woman.* Cambridge: Harvard University Press.
Shupe, Anson, and David Bromley, eds.
1984   *New Christian Politics.* Macon, Ga.: Mercer University Press.
Silverman, Sydel
1975   The Life Crisis as a Clue to Social Function. In *Toward an Anthropology of Women*, ed. R. Rapp Reiter, 309–21. New York: Monthly Review Press.
Simopoulos v. *Virginia*
1983   462 U.S. 506.
Skerry, Peter
1978   The Class Conflict over Abortion. *The Public Interest* 4: 69–84.
Smith, Daniel Scott
1973   Family Limitation, Sexual Control, and Domestic Feminism in Victorian America. *Feminist Studies* 1(2): 40–57.
Smith-Rosenberg, Carol
1979   Beauty, The Beast and the Militant Woman: A Case Study in Sex Roles and Social Stress in Jacksonian America. Reprinted in *A Heritage of Her Own*, ed. Nancy Cott and Elizabeth Pleck, 197–221. New York: Simon and Schuster.
1980   Politics and Culture in Women's History. *Feminist Studies* 6(1): 55–64.
Stanton, Elizabeth Cady
1868   Infanticide and Prostitution. *Revolution* 1(5): 65.
Stark, Steven
1987   Housekeeping Today: Just a Lick and a Promise. *New York Times.* August 20.
Steiner, Peter
1984   *Russian Formalism.* Ithaca, N.Y.: Cornell University Press.
Steinhoff, Pat, and M. Diamond
1977   *Abortion Politics: The Hawaii Experience.* Honolulu: University of Hawaii Press.
Stone, Lawrence
1977   *The Family, Sex, and Marriage in England: 1500–1800.* New York: Harper and Row.
Storer, Horatio
1866   *Why Not? A Book for Every Woman.* Boston: Lea & Shepard.

1867   *Is It I? A Book for Every Man.* Boston: Lea & Shepard.

Storer, Horatio, and Franklin Fiske Heard

1868 (1974)   *Criminal Abortion: Its Nature, Its Law, Its Evidence.* Cambridge, Mass.: Ayer Company Publications.

Sullerot, Evelynne

1971   *Woman, Society and Change.* New York: McGraw-Hill.

Summerhill, Louise

1968   *The Story of Birthright.* Thaxton, Va.: Sunlife Press.

Tatalovich, Raymond, and Byron W. Daynes

1981   *The Politics of Abortion.* New York: Praeger.

Taussig, Frederick

1936   *Abortion: Spontaneous and Induced.* St. Louis: C. V. Mosby.

Taylor, Howard

1944   *The Abortion Problem.* Baltimore: Williams and Wilkins.

Terdiman, Richard

1985   *Discourse/Counter-Discourse.* Ithaca, N.Y.: Cornell University Press.

Thornburgh v. *American College of Obstetricians and Gynecologists*

1986   106 U.S. 2169.

Tilly, Charles, ed.

1978   *Historical Studies in Changing Fertility.* Princeton, N.J.: Princeton University Press.

Turner, Victor

1974   *Dramas, Fields and Metaphors.* Ithaca, N.Y.: Cornell University Press.

1981   Social Dramas and Stories about Them. In *On Narrative*, ed. W. J. T. Mitchell, 137–65. Chicago: University of Chicago Press.

Tweton, Jerome, and Theodore B. Jelliff

1983   *North Dakota: The Heritage of a People.* Fargo, N.D.: North Dakota Institute for Regional Studies.

Uchitelle, Louis

1987   Making a Living is Now a Family Enterprise. *New York Times.* October 11.

Uhlenberg, Peter

1974   Cohort Variation in Family Life-Cycle of U.S. Females. *Journal of Marriage and the Family* 36: 284–92.

U.S. Department of Commerce, Bureau of the Census

1970   General Social and Economic Characteristics of North Dakota, table 85. Washington, D.C.: Government Printing Office.

1980   Supplementary Report: Advance Estimate of Social, Economic and Housing Characteristics, N.D., table P-3. Washington, D.C.: Government Printing Office.

1986a   Household and Family Characteristics: March 1985. *Current Population Reports* series P-20, no. 411, table 1. Washington, D.C.: Government Printing Office.

1986b   Child Support and Alimony: 1983. *Current Population Reports* series P-23, no. 148. Washington, D.C.: Government Printing Office.

Van de Walle, Etienne

1980   Motivations and Technology and the Decline of French Fertility. In *Family and Sexuality in French History,* ed. R. Wheaton, and Tamara Hareven, 135–38. Philadelphia: University of Pennsylvania Press.

Vanek, Joann

1974   Time Spent in Housework. *Scientific American.* November: 116–21.

Van Gennep, Arnold

1960 (1908)   *Rites of Passage.* Chicago: University of Chicago Press.

Van Velsen, J.

1967   The Extended-Case Method and Situational Analysis. In *The Craft of Social Anthropology,* ed. A. L. Epstein, 129–49. London: Tavistock.

Viguerie, Richard

1980   *The New Right: We're Ready to Lead.* Falls Church, Va.: Viguerie Company.

Wallis, Jim

1980   Coming Together on the Sanctity of Life. *Sojourners* 9(11): 4.

Ware, Susan

1981   *Beyond Suffrage: Women in the New Deal.* Cambridge: Harvard University Press.

Weiner, Annette

1979   Trobriand Kinship from Another View: The Reproductive Power of Women and Men. *Man* 14(2): 328–48.

Weitzman, Lenore

1985   *The Divorce Revolution: The Unexpected Social and Economic Consequences for Women and Children in America.* New York: Free Press.

Wells, Robert V.

1975   Family History and Demographic Transition. *Journal of Social History* 9: 1–19.

Welter, Barbara
   1966   The Cult of True Womanhood, 1820–1860. *American Quarterly* 18: 151–74.
Weyrich, Paul
   1980   The Pro-Family Movement. *Conservative Digest*, 6.
Wiebe, Robert
   1967   *The Search for Order.* New York: Oxford University Press.
Willke, Jack, and Barbara Willke
   1971   *Handbook on Abortion.* Cincinnati: Hayes Publishing Co.
Willard, Frances
   1888   Minutes. 15th Annual Meeting of the Women's Christian Temperance Union.
Willis, Ellen
   1971   *Up from Radicalism.* New York: Vintage.
Wolf, Eric
   1982   *Europe and the People without History.* Berkeley: University of California Press.
Wrigley, E. A.
   1966   Family Limitation in Pre-Industrial England. *Economic History Review* 19: 82–109.
Yasuba, Yasukichi
   1961   *Birth Rates of the White Population in the U.S. 1800–1860: An Economic Study.* Baltimore: Johns Hopkins University Press.
Zaretsky, Eli
   1982   The Place of the Family in the Origins of the Welfare State. In *Rethinking the Family,* ed. B. Thorne and M. Yalom, 188–224. New York: Longman.

Subject Index

Abortion activism: and consciousness, 123–29, 134, 154–55, 159, 163, 188, 195, 218–20; as interpretive frame, 7–19, 48, 83–87, 89, 97–100, 139, 141, 219–20. *See also* Social movements

Abortion activists, 6–7, 37–42; convergence in interests, 69–70, 111–14, 125–26, 195–97, 218–19, 222–26, 278n15, 280n8, 280–81n3; in North Dakota, 6–7, 16–18, 70, 71, 78–92; and professionals, 37–39, 69–70, 74, 139, 154–57, 270n10; and radical feminists, 39–40, 245; and social change, 6–7, 12–13, 129, 134, 195; and violence, 50–52, 115–17, 265nn16–17, 276n8. *See also* Citizens for a Real Choice; Feminism; Feminists for Life; LIFE Coalition; National Right to Life Committee; Right-to-Life; Save-A-Baby; Scheidler, Joseph

Abortion and the courts, 40–42, 260n20; in Fargo, 120; pro-life challenges, 45–46; and Supreme Court appointments, 253n17. *See also* Roe v. Wade; Supreme Court

Abortion and hospitals: committees, 34; in North Dakota, 64; percentage offering abortions, 55, 266n21; policies, 55, 257–58n17

Abortion and underground networks, 37, 56, 258n20; in North Dakota, 64

Abortion clinics, 3, 76–93, 94–110, 111–29, 266–67n22–23; caseloads, 249n1, 249n3; Feminist Women's Health Center, 53; harassment, 50–51, 54–57, 252n15, 265nn16–17, 266n20, 275nn5–6; location, 54–57, 75, 266n23; safety records, 56. *See also* Fargo Women's Health Organization; National Women's Health Organization

Abortion debates: in nineteenth century, 14, 23–33, 254n1; in North Dakota, 61–75, 94–110, 119–29; in twentieth century, 15, 35–42, 254n1, 259n27. *See also* Abortion reform; Abortion repeal; Right-to-Life

Abortion funding policy: for family planning, 252–53n16, 262n7; for government employees, 262n7; overseas, 252–53n16

Abortion imagery: and New Right, 47, 48; in the nineteenth century, 27, 29, 31, 33; in right-to-life movement, 9, 71, 216, 274n6; in the twentieth century, 38, 40–41, 105–10, 259n26. *See also* Assignment Life; Fetus; Media; *Silent Scream, The*

Abortion legislation, 40, 269–70n7; ALI model code, 35; anti-abortion statutes, 25; and Comstock laws, 31–32; and English common law, 24; and fetus, 32; in nineteenth century, 23–26; in North Dakota, 64–70, 119–20, 147–49, 175, 270n8; and parental notification, 261n4; and physicians, 14, 32, 37–41, 65; and restrictions on clinics, 261nn3–4; and twentieth-century challenges, 36–42. *See also* Hyde amendment; Roe v. Wade; Supreme Court

Abortion practice, 269n6, 274n7; in the nineteenth century, 24–28, 30–33,

307

Author Index

Compositor: G & S Typesetters
Text: 11/13 Caledonia
Display: Caledonia
Printer: Maple-Vail Book Mfg. Group
Binder: Maple-Vail Book Mfg. Group